G000275074

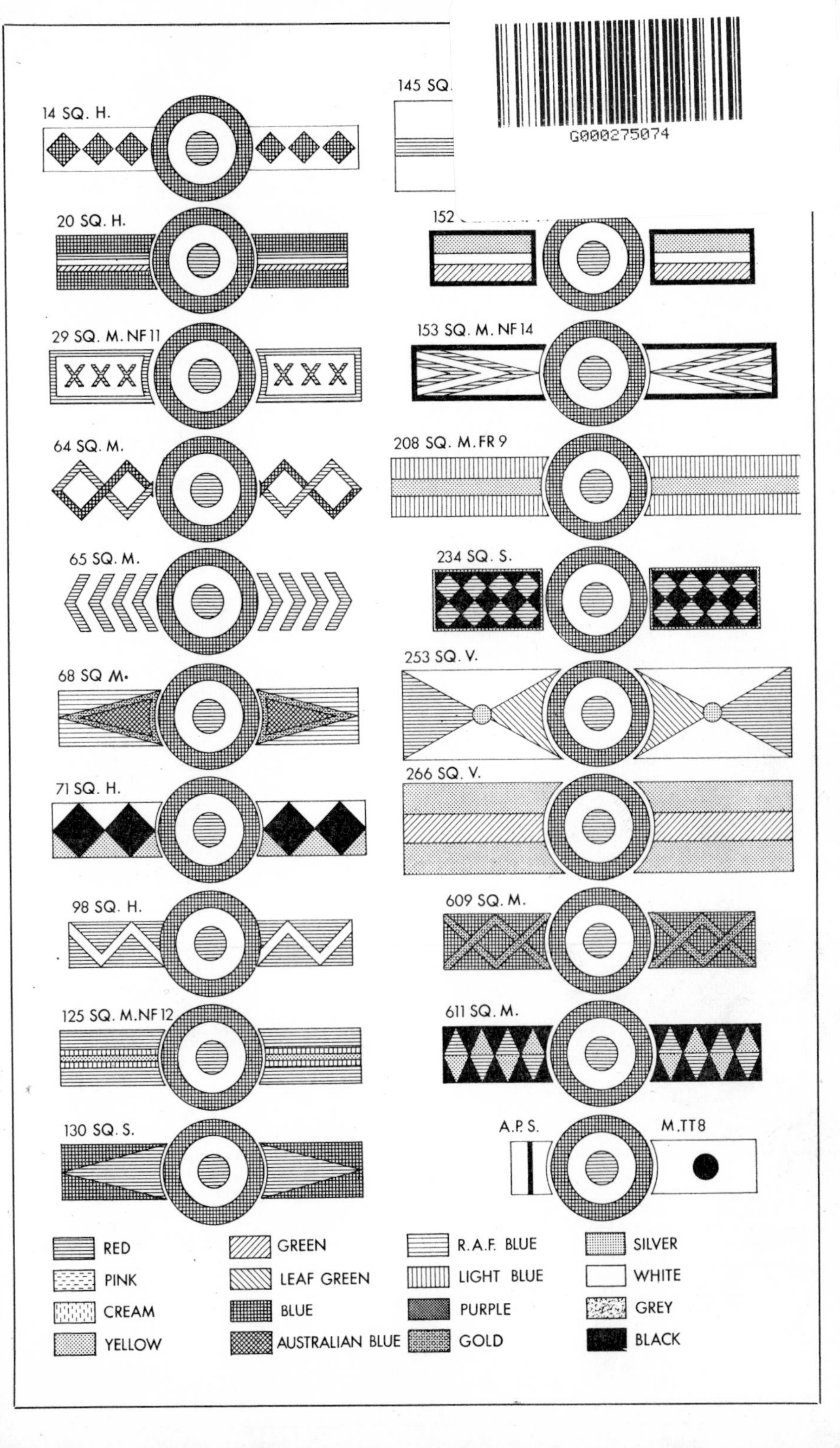

14 SQ. H.
145 SQ.
20 SQ. H.
152
29 SQ. M. NF 11
153 SQ. M. NF 14
64 SQ. M.
208 SQ. M. FR 9
65 SQ. M.
234 SQ. S.
68 SQ M.
253 SQ. V.
71 SQ. H.
266 SQ. V.
98 SQ. H.
609 SQ. M.
125 SQ. M. NF 12
611 SQ. M.
130 SQ. S.
A.P.S.
M.TT8
RED
PINK
CREAM
YELLOW
GREEN
LEAF GREEN
BLUE
AUSTRALIAN BLUE
R.A.F. BLUE
LIGHT BLUE
PURPLE
GOLD
SILVER
WHITE
GREY
BLACK

fighting colours

A

fighting colours

RAF Fighter Camouflage and markings 1937-1969

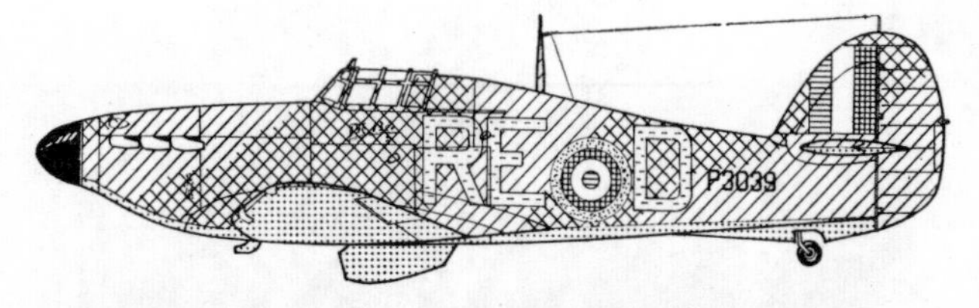

MICHAEL J F BOWYER

Patrick Stephens
London

PSL

© Copyright 1969
MICHAEL J. F. BOWYER AND ALFRED M. ALDERSON

All Rights Reserved. No part of this publication may be reproduced, stored in a retrieval system, or transmitted, in any form or by any means, electronic, mechanical, photocopying, recording or otherwise, without prior permission of Patrick Stephens Limited.

SBN 85059 041 8

First edition—October 1969

Set in 9 on 10pt Times Roman type.
Printed in Great Britain
for Patrick Stephens Ltd, 9 Ely Place, London EC1
by Blackfriars Press Ltd, Leicester and
bound by Hunter & Foulis Ltd, Edinburgh.

foreword

FIGHTING COLOURS first appeared in basic form as a series of articles in *Airfix Magazine,* the intention being to provide a comprehensive review of the development and changes in RAF fighter colours, camouflage and markings over the past 30 or so years. Michael Bowyer's idea, ably assisted by the skilled draughtsmanship of his colleague Alfred Alderson, was to relate the changes to contemporary events rather than just provide a bald survey of the colours themselves. Thus the series also formed a brief chronicle of air fighting and fighter development over the years since 1937.

The success of the series, which appealed equally to those aviation enthusiasts and modellers who remembered the actual aircraft and events and to the new generation to whom even 1950 is 'old time', has led to the publication of this present volume, which collects all the original articles into one handy book. However, *Fighting Colours* is more than just a collection of old articles, for Michael Bowyer has taken the opportunity of adding a long extra section bringing the story from 1950—where the original series ended—up to the present day, at the same time expanding some of the earlier chapters. Gaps in previous code and serial listings have largely been filled, partly from new information which has come to light since the articles were first written, and partly by the kindness of *Airfix Magazine* readers who wrote in with extra information.

Other new material includes appendices giving brief data of RAF fighter types over the period, a listing of RAF fighter paint shades with model paint equivalents, specially to assist modellers, a full listing of World War 2 fighter squadron and unit codes and a full listing of fighter serial allocations. All the original illustrations appear, plus many extra pictures. Finally, we have included numerous extra drawings from the pen of Alfred Alderson showing more aircraft and more markings. We would like to thank the Imperial War Museum and other organisations and individuals credited for the reproduction of photographs.

Now that RAF Fighter Command has 'disappeared' as a separate entity in the Royal Air Force, we hope that this book will provide a useful record of its colours, markings, camouflage, and aircraft throughout its most momentous years.

Chris Ellis, Editor, Airfix Magazine

author's preface

FIGHTING COLOURS covers two topics. One, the part played in World War 2 by fighters of the Royal Air Force and two, the markings and colours of the aircraft used. It is also concerned with the years of re-armament and considers fighter markings in the years of so-called peace since 1945.

Much of the material here is from my own notes, most of them carefully recorded throughout the period under review. Thus it is possible to put a specific date to many items and avoid the more woolly 'month' as is often quoted. It brings to light much hitherto unpublished material since the source for this book is private, based largely on my own observations rather than official records. Thus it may sometimes contradict some ideas held for far too long on the subject of fighter camouflage and markings. It is, however, probably the most detailed and accurate volume yet to appear on this subject.

The drawings are by Alfred Alderson, who, like myself, was throughout the war, and in the years of peace, recording the type of material presented. I would like to thank those enthusiastic *Airfix Magazine* readers who, subsequent to the appearance of the original articles on which this book is based, have supplied information or details to supplement gaps in the story. Others kindly lent photographs.

Cambridge, October 1969 **Michael J. F. Bowyer**

contents

illustrations

Diagrams in Text

Diagrams in Text

Chapter I

1937-39: Into warpaint

FEW TOPICS AROUSE as much interest amongst enthusiasts as aircraft colouring and markings. Answering the needs of model makers and others this book has been compiled. Such a complex topic is best presented in sections controlled by time and place, and for the benefit of the younger enthusiasts, I will be treating the topic in a basic manner in each chapter before presenting items for the more knowledgeable.

Camouflage experiments commenced in 1914, but it was 1916 before means of disguising the presence of aircraft—as much in the air as on the ground—came into general use. Thus the upper surfaces of military aircraft are usually painted in dark shades whilst under surfaces are light in colour. A dark green finish was originally prescribed. In reality, and in answer to local needs, it ranged through tones to a greenish shade of khaki, for application to upper surfaces and sides. Under surfaces were left in the natural fabric 'creamy' colour. For better concealment metal parts were painted black and grey. Some night-fighting machines had an overall green finish. Such colours were general until the end of World War I and well beyond the close of hostilities, on British fighters.

From 1919 a clear varnish finish came into common use, soon to be overtaken by aluminium dope applied to all surfaces over a special dull-red primer. Engines were black, or left in natural finish. Parts of cowlings were often polished bare metal, likewise metal panels close by. The need for camouflage gone, RAF aeroplanes fell in line with public gaiety. In 1923 camouflage returned to the 'silver' bombers but it was the start of 1937 when the RAF decided that future fighters would be camouflaged.

Rapid deterioration in international relations made conflict almost a certainty. When the aircraft ordered under the Expansion Schemes appeared they did so wearing camouflage.

The early Hurricanes

First of the new generation of fighters was the immortal Hawker Hurricane. The first camouflaged production machine L1547, first flown on October 12, 1937, was used as a trials aircraft. L1548 was delivered to the RAF on December 15, 1937, becoming its first camouflaged fighter, and was taken on charge by 111 Sqn with whom it was still serving when the war commenced. L1549-L1552 were at Northolt by the end of the year.

From the start the Hurricanes wore matt dark earth (brown) and dark green paintwork, applied to a specific pattern. Two versions were decided upon, Schemes 'A' and 'B'. The second was the mirror image in pattern of the other, and these were applied alternately to the aircraft, so that L1547 had the 'A' Scheme and L1548 'B', etc. This system was continued well into the war years. Under surfaces, painted silver, were defined as those beneath wings and tail and in the case of the fuselage, that part 'the tangent of which makes an angle of not more than 60 degrees with the horizontal'. Planned patterns were most carefully adhered to, very detailed GA drawings being issued, and patterns were chalked on the aircraft. The wooden propellers were varnished brown.

To render the RAF roundels clearly visible in peace-time a yellow surround was added to the usual Type A (or blue-white-red) roundel. Officially this new type was called Type A.1 (Matt). On the fuselage sides the Hurricanes had 35 inch diameter A.1 (Matt) roundels. Above the wings they were 4 ft 3 in across, and situated in the standard position 1/6 of the wing span inward of each wing tip. The size of roundels was regulated by the instruction that 'they should be as large as possible, of one of the prescribed sizes, and not overlap control surfaces'. Each ring of the roundel equalled in width the diameter of the centre red disc. Tail/rudder national markings were now discarded.

By March, 1938, No 111 Sqn at Northolt had added an 8 inch squadron crest to the Hurricanes' fins. A few aircraft then acquired the light blue number '111' 18 inches high aft of the roundel. Later variations of this included '111' with the top half of the number dark blue or red. Another version, possibly the earliest, was the application of '111' in yellow only.

Above the wings were the 4 ft 3 inch roundels centred 6 ft 8 inches in from the tips. On the under surfaces, Type A roundels were painted quarter of the span from the wing tip and 3 ft 9 inches in diameter. Black serials were 6 inches high on the fuselage and 2 ft 6 inches high under the wings.

With the deletion of squadron markings a need for unit identification was officially recognised. One accepted method was the painting of a white spearhead pointing forward. No 56 Sqn adopted this on its Hurricanes, and painted a white 6 inch individual aircraft letter beneath the exhaust stack. L1593 was 'C' and L1599 'L'.

Camouflage for biplanes

Almost simultaneous with the first Hurricane deliveries was the order to camouflage all older home-based front-line fighters. It took several months to achieve. A motley collection in green-brown-silver finish emerged from the sheds shorn of squadron colours, often with serials over-painted, and retaining Type A roundels. Some squadrons may have applied numbers to their biplanes, but it seems unlikely. What is certain is that it was a lengthy process embracing hosts of anomalies, judging from the aircraft that I observed. The best known of the camouflaged biplanes are probably the Furies of Nos 1 and 43 Squadrons.

In September, 1938, a new camouflage feature appeared, when the decision to paint the under surfaces of fighters black and white was implemented. Although the order specified black under surfaces to port wings and white to starboard there were many variations even to this simple theme, perhaps brought about by supply shortages. Several squadrons for sure painted their aircraft in a manner the reverse of that specified. Picture 7 is an example of this on a Spitfire of 19 Sqn photographed about February, 1939, wearing white (starboard) and silver (port) under surfaces whereon the serial remains and the roundel has been painted out—both typical anomalies of the period. There was confusion, too, as to where the two colours met, sometimes this being on the fuselage centre line, sometimes at a wing root. Usually Hurricanes had all-black or all-white tailplane under surfaces. Many aircraft had their starboard under-wing roundel merely painted out in a dark colour, leaving this and the serial still visible. The removal of serials was usual, and to the outbreak of war many aircraft did not carry them, or, if they did, then it was a small replica on the fin or perhaps the 'last two'—as on Hurricane NQ-G which had '34' about one inch high in white on its fin tips. A feature of factory produced aircraft was the 'silver' panelling beneath the nose on Hurricanes and Spitfires which terminated at the mainplane.

In the winter of 1938-39 outer yellow surrounds to roundels were deleted and the roundels either left without the outer ring, or were enlarged to cover the same area as before—but this was rarely seen.

Changes in March, 1939

Further deterioration in international affairs led, in March, 1939, to the appearance of two major changes in markings. It was decided that red and blue roundels (officially called Type B, in which the centre red disc was 2/5 of the total diameter) should now become standard on fuselages and wings of fighter aircraft. On those in service, the existing roundels were further painted to meet the new requirements, but on aircraft now leaving the factories the roundels were much smaller, usually of 25 or 30 inch total diameter. All traces of under-wing serials and roundels were now removed, and often the aircraft bore no traces of any serial number for security reasons.

The second feature which, at the time, aroused much interest amongst the handful of enthusiasts of those days—and doubtless across the North Sea—was the introduction of squadron 'code letters' or, more officially, unit identification letters, for signalling and in-flight unit identification reasons, which were to remain to the 1960s in one form or another. These letters were applied in a mid-grey paint usually (bearing in mind that the individual's idea of mid-grey can vary a lot, verging on dark grey at Duxford and light grey, very light indeed, at Kenley!). Most, if not all units applied the unit identity letters (two) ahead of the roundel on the port fuselage side and aft on the starboard. The aircraft's identity letter was positioned on the other side. It was not possible to tie up the individual aircraft with squadron codes initially, thus it was not immediately possible to relate the 'codes' to likely owners. But since the squadrons did not move stations at the same time it left little to the imagination to associate unit and coding. In any case, air-to-air identification was the main reason for the lettering.

By the time codes were added the entire fighter force had certainly become camouflaged, albeit in mixed manner, but in the summer of 1939 the dark green and dark earth aircraft were seen to be correctly coloured with black and white under surfaces, the colours meeting along the centre line on more and more aircraft. The alternative scheme for factory built aircraft introduced silver under the nose and, on some, under the rear fuselage.

The odd-man-out always characterises the markings schemes, and it is interesting to muse over the likely reason (an error in signalling, or typing perhaps) that caused some of the Spitfires of No 66 Sqn at Duxford to be coded MB initially instead of RB. This I vividly recall seeing briefly in March, 1939. The squadron 'codes' were selected at random, incidentally, and not duplicated on squadron aircraft in the UK (at least, not intentionally) and were in no sense combinations which could be 'de-coded'. One interesting point to note is that some squadrons carried letters widely differing from those listed in the appropriate Air Ministry Order. The letters used by the pre-war fighters in the period March-September, 1939, and associated squadrons and examples of their aircraft where known, are as follows:

Sqn	*Letters*	*Serial no*	*Aircraft type*	*Notes*
1	WA	L1689	Hurricane I	(Furies camouflaged, uncoded.) Previously had black and white under-wing colours correctly applied.
3	a) uncoded	K6147	Gladiator (camouflaged)	March, 1939
	b) OP:T	L1937	Hurricane I	July, 1939, small roundels
17	UV:B	K5346	Gauntlet	March, 1939
19	WZ:N	K9790	Spitfire I	April, 1939
23	MS:G	K5698	Demon	1939, as illustrated (photo 4)
25	RX:R	L1436	Blenheim If	May, 1939
29	YB:L	L8372	Blenheim If	May, 1939
32	KT:G	L1659	Hurricane I	May, 1939
41	PN	K9843	Spitfire I	May, 1939
43	NQ:D	L1726	Hurricane I	June, 1939. (Furies of the sqn were painted like those of No 1 Sqn, previously uncoded.)
46	RJ	L1853	Hurricane I	June, 1939
54	DL:D	K9901	Spitfire I	May, 1939
56	LR:R	L1987	Hurricane I	July, 1939, small roundels
64	XQ	L1478	Blenheim If	June, 1939
65	FZ:L	K9909	Spitfire I	May, 1939
66	RB:S	K9810	Spitfire I	March, 1939
72	SD	K9924	Spitfire I	June, 1939
73	HV	L1572	Hurricane I	July, 1939
74	JH:B	K9937	Spitfire I	June, 1939
79	AL:D	L1716	Hurricane I	July, 1939, small roundels
85	NO:J	L1833	Hurricane I	May, 1939
87	PD	L1646	Hurricane I	July, 1939
111	TM:V	L1820	Hurricane I	August, 1939
151	GG:K	L1768	Hurricane I	May, 1939
213	AK:F	L1790	Hurricane I	June, 1939. An interesting point here is that the war-time coding of the sqn was AK.

1 *Typifying the finish of RAF fighters o the early 1930s, this is the restored Bristol Bulldog K2227 which delighted enthusiasts at airshows until it crashed a few years ago. It wears the red/white checks of 56 Sqn, also carried on the upper wing from roundel to roundel. Maker's 'Bulldog' emblem on tail was not often seen on service machines* (Bristol Aircraft Ltd).

2 *Gauntlets of No 19 Sqn lined up in 1935. K4095 carries light blue and white checks on fin, fuselage and mainplane.*

3 *A Gladiator of No 3 Squadron wearing green/brown black/white camouflage with grey 'OP' coding. Just visible is the white painted aileron in the lower port wing* (Ron Clarke).

4 *Demon K5698, subiect of the three-view drawing in Figure 1 photographed in 1939 shortly before Blenheim fighters took over completely on the unit. The black cowl is an unusual anomaly.*

5 *A predecessor of the Blenheims, Demon K4504 wears the red (dark area) and yellow triangle squadron markings of the peace-time era. These were the colours of 604 Sqn in 1937.*

6 *Gladiator RR-T of 615 Sqn in the summer of 1939 at Kenley. Serials were over-painted, codes light grey, fuselage roundels bore traces of the white rings and the usual colours had been applied* (Ron Clarke).

7 *Spitfire I K9851 photographed late in February 1939. Fuselage nose and port wing are silver and it carries a blotted out roundel and small black serial. The prop is black and has yellow tips. The starboard underwing is already white. and to add to the assortment of markings a grey letter 'I' is visible. Possibly it was coded WZ too* (Ron Clarke).

8 *Prototypes and a few other fighters remained silver when others were camouflaged. This is the Defiant prototype in 1938. The anti-dazzle panel and spinner are black* (IWM).

9 *A group of Blenheims of No 604 Sqn with NG-O:L4908 nearest at Northolt early in 1940.*

10 *Hurricane L1934:OP-D of No 3 Squadron flying in about July 1939. The single upper wing roundel was featured by quite a number of fighters including Spitfires. Previously Type A.1 roundels had been carried—although this aircraft was not delivered until May 1939.*

11 *Another view of a 604 Sqn Blenheim If at Northolt late in 1939 This time L6798 prior to application of the individual aircraft code letter as shown on other machines in photograph 9 and 12* (IWM).

12 *Blenheim If NG-N of 604 Sqn allegedly photographed on 'Squadron Embodiment' on August 24 1939. If the date is correct then the application of wartime codes was premature. It seems more likely that the picture dates from winter 1939-40.*

13 *Blenheim If ZK-P:L1437 of 25 Sqn wearing January 1940 style markings* (The Aeroplane).

14 *Blenheim If K7090:ZK-V of 25 Sqn with black/white undersurfaces. 'V' appears on nose in white, other letters being grey. K7090 was originally delivered to 144 Sqn as a bomber in October 1937* (The Aeroplane).

15 *YP-Q:L67?? a Blenheim If of 23 Sqn in the snow at Wittering in the winter of 1939-40. Light grey codes and black/white undersurfaces* (MoD).

16 *Blenheim If L1336 of 29 Sqn in green-brown/black-white finish in the winter of 1939-40. Grey codes* (The Aeroplane).

17 *Hastily camouflaged Gladiators of 615 Sqn in France late in 1939 with serials painted out and KW-T, the nearest aircraft, still partly silver (or possibly primer grey* (Leslie Hunt).

18 *Gladiator KW-M was another machine of 615 Sqn photographed at the same time as those in photograph 17. Note the crudely applied codes and the patch (in red dope) obliterating the serial just aft of the M* (Leslie Hunt).

19 *Two Spitfire Is of 609 Sqn taxi out at a Scottish airfield on April 8 1940. Both have black/white/silver undersides and grey codes* (Flight International).

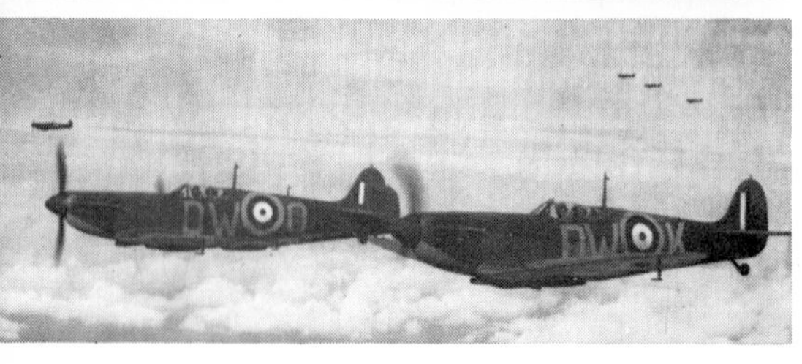

20 *Well-known but interesting view of 610 Sqn Spitfire Is in 1940. Research suggests that DW-K is N3289 which was shot down on May 29. Underside of fuselage is black but rest of underside appears to be a shade of sky. Neither machine has underwing roundels. DW-O has larger roundel and possibly all-sky undersides. Evidence suggests that picture dates from defence of the French ports* (IWM).

Sqn	*Letters*	*Serial no*	*Aircraft type*	*Notes*
501	ZH	L1949	Hurricane I	July, 1939, small roundels
504	AW	L1956	Hurricane I	July, 1939, small roundels
600	MV	L1401	Blenheim If	July, 1939, YF was allocated
601	YW	L1518	Blenheim If	July, 1939, YN possibly used
602	ZT	L1018	Spitfire I	July, 1939
603	RL	K7924	Gladiator II	August, 1939
604	WQ:G	L6615	Blenheim If	July, 1939, WG was allocated
605	HE	N2308	Gladiator II	August, 1939
607	LW	K7995	Gladiator II	August, 1939
609	PL	L1083	Spitfire I	August, 1939
610	JE	K3311?	Tutor	May, 1939
611	GZ	L1080	Spitfire I	August, 1939
615	RR:A	K7854	Gauntlet II	July, 1939
616	QJ	K4085	Gauntlet I	June, 1939

Overseas there was as yet no need for camouflage, so fighters there—Demons, Gladiators and a sprinkling of Blenheim Ifs—were left in aluminium finish, except for the Blenheims which retained their 1937 bomber camouflage similar to that of the first Hurricanes, though they had black under surfaces with white serials. Their Type A.1 (Matt) roundels they kept well into the war years. Some of the silver aircraft nevertheless carried squadron code letters.

Second-line aircraft on front-line squadrons, eg, Magisters, Tiger Moths, etc, had yellow under surfaces which extended well up the fuselage sides. Exceptions were Battles used for pilot conversion to high-powered aircraft, which retained bomber camouflage but acquired Type B roundels.

The first of the few

No consideration of RAF fighter markings can be complete without reference to the greatest fighter of all time, the Spitfire. However much one may rate the Hurricane surely there can be no denying that, in all fairness, the Spitfire had 'the edge'!

K9787, the first production Spitfire wearing 'A' Scheme camouflage, was completed in June, 1938. On July 29, 1938, K9792 was allocated to No 19 Sqn, followed by K9789 on August 4. These two wore 'B' and 'A' camouflage schemes respectively, and arrived at Duxford in green-brown-silver finish. Upper-wing roundels six feet from the wing tip and of Type A.1 (Matt) were of 4 ft 3 inch diameter. Fuselage roundels were 35 inches across and under-wing roundels, Type A, were applied as large as the space at the appropriate centring would allow to avoid overlapping the control surfaces. Alongside came the surprisingly small one-foot under-wing serials in black.

The Spitfires of No 19 Squadron made their public debut at the opening of Cambridge Airport on October 8, 1938—by which time the squadron had applied yellow '19' numbering to the fins of Spitfires, including K9794. During the winter several appeared with red 19s (eg, K9797), but no other colours were applied (as claimed elsewhere) before the Munich crisis altered the whole appearance of the Spitfires at Duxford.

No 19 was now the premier fighter squadron—although if you never served with it you probably don't agree! Whether it was first in another respect, the application of unit codes, is not known. By March 15, 1939, all traces of '19' had gone from the tails of the Spitfires and 'WZ' in a dark shade of grey was being worn by the machines, which now had red-blue roundels and black/white under surfaces. K9805: RB-R of 66 Sqn in use at this time had half black/half white under surfaces with 25 inch diameter fuselage roundels (Type B) on this date, the red being the customary 2/5 of the total diameter. Such changes as were apparent during the summer were few, so that when the fighter squadrons went to war on September 3, 1939, they did so in their drabbest colouring for years.

Figure 1: ***(1) Hawker Demon K1954, one of a batch of six (K1950-1955) 'Hart Fighters' delivered in July 1931 to No 23 Sqn, remained with the squadron until the end of 1936. It wears typical pre-war squadron colours. Cowling panels were of burnished metal. 23 Squadron's eagle emblem was in red on the fin, exhaust pipes were a dull fawn colour. (2) Hawker Turret-Demon K5698 in early 1939 markings which entirely replaced the previous markings of the owner, No 23 Squadron. An unusua ifeature is the black nose panelling. '98' was chalked on the fin of the machine. Gunner's shield had silver segments; cockpit interior was light green and black. (3) Hurricane I L1768 was initially delivered in January 1939 to 151 Squadron in whose markings it is depicted.***

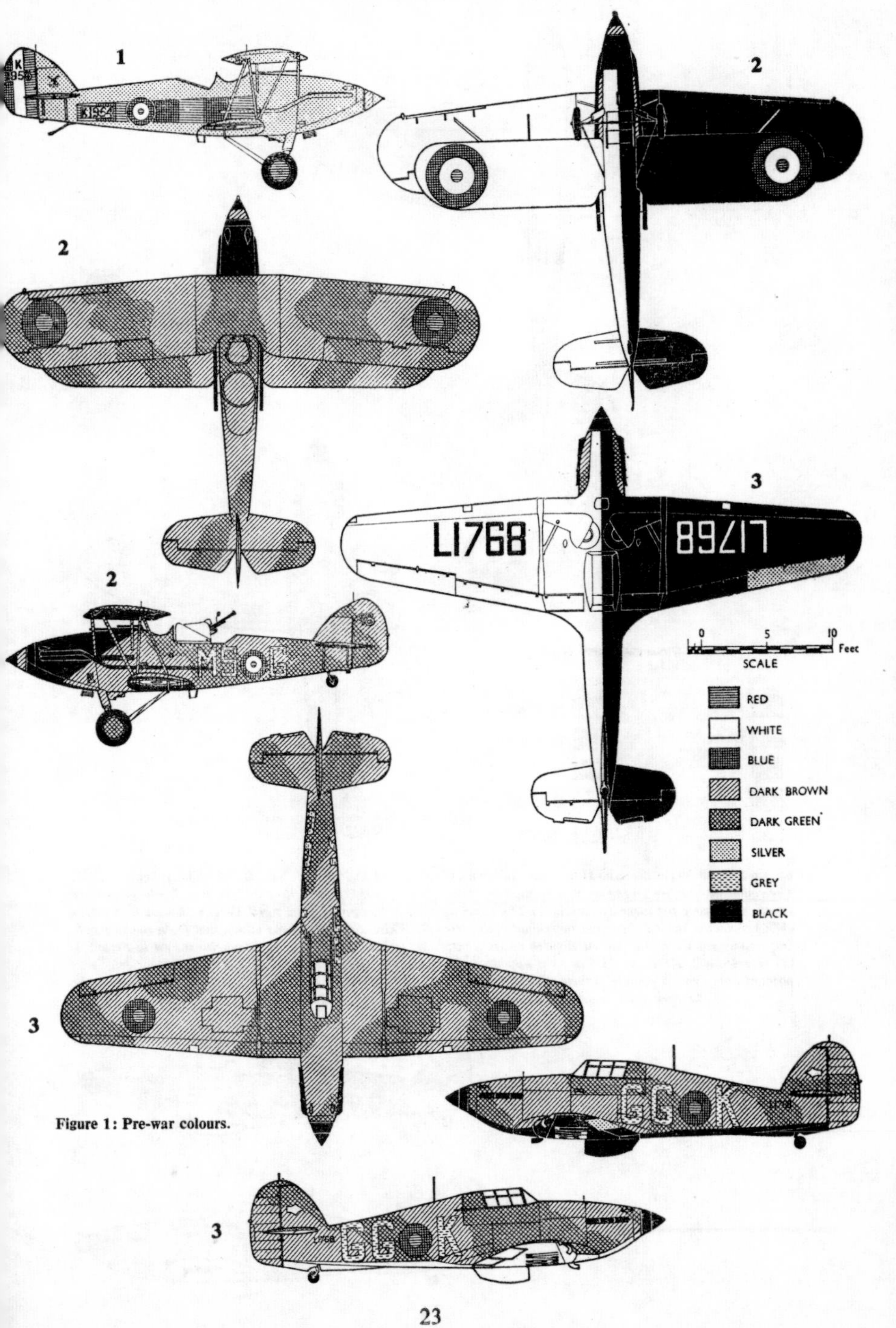

Figure 1: Pre-war colours.

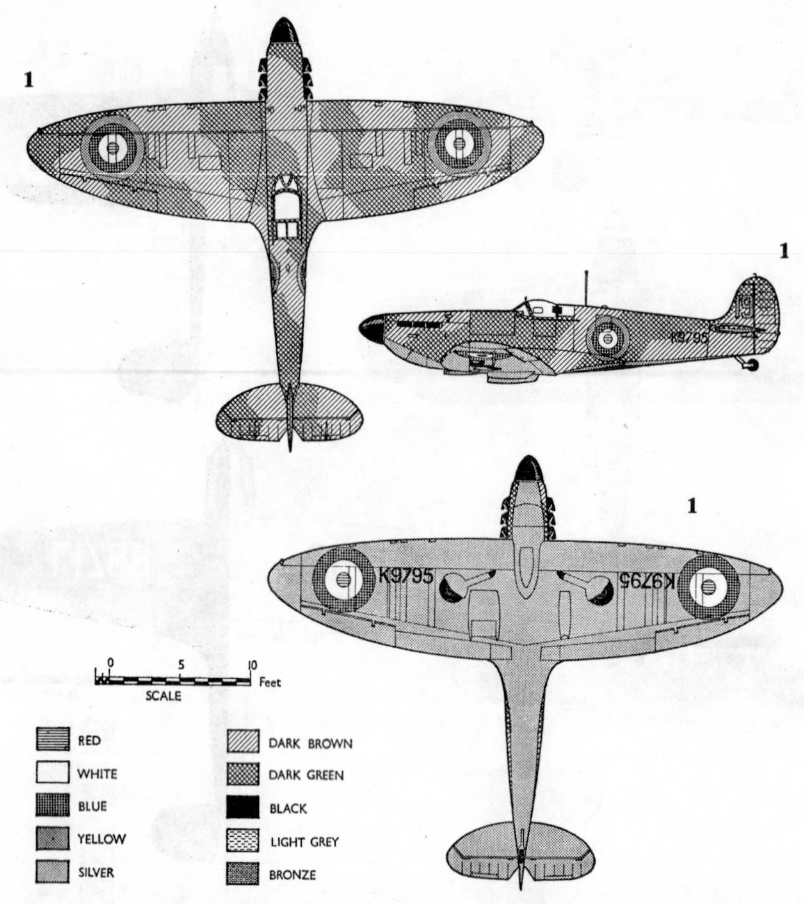

Figure 2: 1938-39 Spitfire and Hurricane markings. (*1*) *Spitfire I K9795 of 19 Sqn, Duxford, in November 1938. The squadron number on the fin was painted in flight colours, in this case yellow ('C' Flight). Undersides were silver, displaying the aircraft serial.* (2) *The same aircraft as it appeared in April 1939 with squadron codes* (*WZ*) *replacing the number, and individual code letter B. White and yellow was eliminated from the roundels and undersides were black/white divided on the centre-line in similar style to the Blenheim shown in Figure 3.* (3) *Hurricane I, FT-K, of 43 Sqn as it appeared in November, 1939, the early period of the war. Serial was painted out. Type A roundel appeared under wings, and the undersides were black/white but the silver of the factory finish remained under the wings. This aircraft had a two-bladed propeller.*

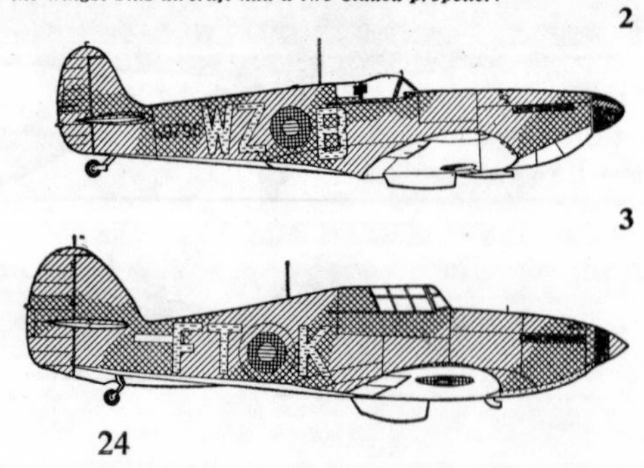

Chapter 2

1939-40: Fighters at war

ALTHOUGH HURRICANES and Spitfires formed the backbone of the fighter force in September, 1939, seven squadrons (Nos 23, 25, 29, 64, 600, 601 and 604) had Blenheim If long-range fighters. Previously Blenheim bombers, they had been modified at Nos 24 and 27 MUs, to carry a four-machine-gun belly pack. Conversion and planning was quite hasty, trial installation being made at RAE on L1424 in November, 1938, and test firings a few days later at Martlesham. In mid-December, 1938, L1433, '36, '37, '39 and '40 reached 25 Squadron as the first examples to enter service. By the end of February, 1939, the seven squadrons had them, and most were almost fully equipped. From their entry to service they had dark green and dark earth upper surfaces with black and white under surfaces as prescribed, the colours meeting half-way beneath the fuselage. A few weeks later they adopted their pre-war squadron identity letters, applied in mid-grey.

When war commenced, RAF squadrons changed their identity letters. The precise date of change seems to have varied, for 604 Squadron altered theirs to NG in late August, 1939. Within days of the outbreak of hostilities the letters had all been changed as follows:

Sqn	*Letters*	*Example*	*Aircraft type*	*Notes*
1	Nil; JX later	N2358:Z	Hurricane I	Marked 'Z' only in March, 1940, in France
3	QO	N2828	Hurricane I	February, 1940
17	YB	N2397	Hurricane I	February, 1940
19	QV	L1031	Spitfire I	February, 1940
23	YP	L8617:X	Blenheim If	March, 1940
25	ZK	L1257:H	Blenheim If	February, 1940
29	RO	L6637:S	Blenheim If	March, 1940
32	GZ	L1970	Hurricane I	October, 1939
41	EB	K9991	Spitfire I	February, 1940
43	FT	L1726:D	Hurricane I	ex-NQ-D. Many squadrons re-allocated the individual letter on recoding; this was an exception
46	PO	N2652	Hurricane I	May, 1940
54	KL	N3124	Spitfire I	February, 1940
56	US	L1983:N	Hurricane I	February, 1940
64	SH	L8371	Blenheim If	February, 1940
65	YT	K9906:T	Spitfire I	February, 1940

Sqn	*Letters*	*Example*	*Aircraft type*	*Notes*
66	LZ	N3033	Spitfire I	February, 1940
72	RN	K9936	Spitfire I	February, 1940
73	Nil; TP later	P2569:D	Hurricane I	Winter, 1940. Later example: TP-D:P2569
74	ZP	K9933:Y	Spitfire I	February, 1940
79	NV	L1698:8R	Hurricane I	October, 1939
87	LK	P2798:A	Hurricane I	May, 1940
85	VY	P3119:X	Hurricane I	March, 1940
111	JU	L1973:L	Hurricane I	October, 1939
151	DZ	N2651	Hurricane I	April, 1940
213	AK	L1882	Hurricane I	October, 1939
501	SD	L1624:R	Hurricane I	December, 1939
504	HX	L1941	Hurricane I	September, 1939
600	BQ	L6639:M	Blenheim If	November, 1939
601	UF	L6603	Blenheim If	September, 1939
602	LO	L1005	Spitfire I	January, 1940
603	XT	L1007:K	Spitfire I	October, 1939
604	NG	L6608:B	Blenheim If	October, 1939; previously WQ-B. Sqn changed unit letters only on aircraft
605	UP	N2349	Hurricane I	April, 1940
607	AF	P2564	Hurricane I	May, 1940. Code open to question
609	PR	P9427:P	Spitfire I	May, 1940
610	DW	N3289:K	Spitfire I	May, 1940
611	FY	K9999:D	Spitfire I	December, 1939
615	KW	K7976:A	Gladiator	January, 1940
616	YQ	L1055	Spitfire I	May, 1940

A second change was evident on fighters when in October, 1939, Type A roundels appeared under the extreme tips of the wings on many machines, this position becoming standard and remaining so today. Fuselage roundels changed to Type A too, by the addition of a white ring or by enlarging existing roundels to resemble those of pre-camouflage vintage with the centre disc in diameter usually the equal of the width of the other rings. Serial numbers by now had largely crept back into place on the rear fuselage of fighters, and were black, eight inches high.

Some of the Blenheims Ifs seemed to lag in these respects, for I saw many as late as March, 1940, without the underwing roundels.

Although there was comparatively little action before the German invasion of Norway the fighters stood at readiness, and were engaging raiders over the North Sea. About 400 enemy sorties were made and 40 bombers destroyed in raids on shipping and naval bases. The first major enemy attack occurred on October 16 when nine bombers of KG30 attacked warships in the Firth of Forth. Spitfires of 602 and 603 (eg, L1048) Squadrons engaged them and two enemy aircraft were destroyed. On October 28 the two squadrons brought down a He 111 of KG26 on the Lammermuir Hills. An interesting feature of the machine was that it had two Balkenkrüz markings above each wing, the smaller being near the tip. Throughout the winter individual engagements were fought, N2340 of 111 Sqn flown by Sqn Ldr H. Broadhurst destroyed a He 111 on November 29, nine days after 74 Sqn had their first success over the Thames Estuary. L1744:FT-A of 43 Sqn destroyed a He 111 at sea on January 30, and L1723:FT-N shared another (off Whitby) with L1722:FT-R on

February 3. Flt Lt Peter Townsend, flying L2116 of 43 Sqn, with L1847: FT-J and another Hurricane, brought down yet another He 111 at Sneaton Castle Farm, near Whitby, the same day; an He 111H Werke Nr 2323 from KG26. The Hurricanes involved wore standard markings with under-wing roundels.

In September, 1939, the AOC-in-C of Fighter Command was pressing for 12 new squadrons, but production was such that there could only be the possibility of forming two equipped with Blenheims. Six extra Hurricane squadrons had been alerted for France, then came the German raids at an opportune moment. On October 17 the CAS had called a meeting to discuss the requirement and it was formally agreed that four 'half squadrons' of Blenheims to be used as nightfighters mainly, two 'half' training squadrons and two whole squadrons (to replace any 'lost' to the French theatre) should now form by the end of October. Then somewhat surprisingly, with a view to the battles to come, it was decided that ten more should form in the next fortnight. In the event it was December before all were going concerns. One feature of interest arose as a result, for there were not enough fighters for the squadrons. Thus, Tutor and Magister trainers joined the units which also received Battles, these latter machines actually wearing fighter camouflage. But in the main they received Blenheims, the fighter versions of which are known to have included these: L1164, '68, '77; L1265, L1397-99; L1401, '2, '4, '6, '8, '9, '19, '23, '24, '33, '36, '37, '39, '40, '47-78; L6600-05, '07-21; L6644-46, '71, '75-89, '91, '99; L6710-12, '19, '21, '23-27, '28-39, '41-50, '52, '60; L6790-6812, L6834-43. An interesting addition to a few of the Blenheim squadrons during the period under review was the Mk IV fighter the first of which, N6233, had gone to 25 Sqn on August 30 — along with N6196. Another, N6193 also with 25 Sqn, was fitted with A.I. Mk III with full external aerial array, and was in the hands of 248 Sqn at Hendon by February, 1940. Three 600 Sqn Mk Is also had A.I. Mk III.

The new squadrons added to the fighter force at this period were as follows:

Sqn	*Letters*	*Example*	*Type*	*Notes*
92	GR	L6776:D	Blenheim If	Formed 10.10.39
141	TW	L6729	Blenheim If	Formed 4.10.39
145	SO	K7159:N	Blenheim If	Formed 10.10.39
152	SN	K7972	Gladiator I	Formed 1.10.39
219	FK	L8685:N	Blenheim If	Formed 4.10.39
222	ZD	K7161	Blenheim If	Formed 5.10.39
229	RE	L6472	Blenheim If	Formed 10.39
229	RE	L1889:E	Hurricane I	April, 1940
234	AZ	L1330	Blenheim If	Formed 30.10.39
235	QY	L5312	Battle	
	QY	L1367	Blenheim If	Formed 30.10.39, passed to Coastal Cmd, 27.2.40
236	ND?	L6801	Blenheim If	Formed 31.10.39, passed to Coastal Cmd, 29.2.40
242	LE	L1521	Blenheim If	Formed 10.39
245	DX	L6796	Blenheim If	Formed 10.39
247	ZY	N5576	Gladiator II	Formed 22.11.39, as 'Fighter Flight, Sumburgh'
248	WR	L1336:E	Blenheim If	Formed 30.10.39, passed to Coastal Cmd, 20.6.40

Sqn	*Letters*	*Example*	*Type*	*Notes*
253	SW	L5110	Battle	Formed 30.10.39
253	SW	L1660:F	Hurricane I	April, 1940
263	HE	N5579	Gladiator II	Formed 2.10.39
264	PS	L6965	Defiant	Formed 3.10.39; pre-war code allocated was KV
266	UO	P5244	Battle	Formed 30.10.39; pre-war code allocated was AO

In their green/brown-black/white colouring the aircraft of the new squadrons took their place in the enlarged defence system.

Fighters in Norway

The German invasion of Norway brought high states of readiness, but the campaign was fought beyond the range of all the fighters except the Blenheims, whose range in any case gave them little time for fighting so far from home. To provide some protection to British troops ashore in Norway it was decided to take No 263 Gladiator squadron aboard HMS *Glorious* on April 22. Two days later its aircraft including N5579, '5633, '5909 and '5915 were ashore, and operating from the frozen Lake Lesja-skog. By noon next day ten of the 18 aircraft had been put out of action, after very gallant action. The remnants eventually withdrew to Setnesmoen where only one was left and there was no petrol, when the remaining crews withdrew on April 27 to sail home on a cargo ship.

On May 14 a reformed 263 Squadron again set off for Norway and on May 22 began installing its aircraft at Bardufoss. Again the story was the same—valiant and intense action, and crippling losses which culminated in the loss of almost the entire squadron aboard HMS *Glorious* on June 8, along with No 46 Squadron and its Hurricanes (eg, L1793, 1814, 1980, N2543, P2652). As is so often the case, whilst the serial numbers of the aircraft involved in this tragic episode are known their individual aircraft letters seem unrecorded which, for model makers, is most unfortunate. Three other Gladiators used at an earlier date by 263 Sqn at Filton and, like those used in Norway, painted in the standard mid-winter scheme were K7942; HE-H, K7944; HE-Q and K7946; HE-R.

Fighters in France

A few days after war began, four squadrons of Hurricanes moved to France, where they could be seen exhibiting unusual features. Nos 1 and 73 Squadrons joined the AASF at Vassincourt. They soon abandoned their squadron letters, leaving only one grey letter in the aft positioning. Their black/white under surfaces with wing tip roundels remained, but their rudders carried red-white-blue stripes, covering the entire surface, red forward, as an added international identity marking. Spinners were black. L1842, a No 1 Sqn machine, shot down a Do 17 near Toul on October 30 and on November 23 it claimed an He 111 near Saarbrucken in two well-recorded combats.

Nos 85(VY) and 87(LK) Squadrons joined the Air Component in September, 1939, and retained squadron letters. Typifying the usual anomalies, 85 Sqn opted for three-foot code letters and both usually had two-foot diameter red/white/blue Type A fuselage roundels. 85's aircraft carried a white hexagon on the fins of its machines, measuring 18 inches across. This was a curious feature for it revealed the unit, being 85's well known motif. On the three-bladed airscrew Hurricanes, received early in 1940, larger roundels were observed. The blue and white rings were 5 inches wide and the red 4 inches across on some, whereas others, rather surprisingly, had their fuselage roundels with each band of different width, namely 7 inch blue, 8 inch white and 6 inch red. When 87 Sqn received the later Hurricanes it applied two-foot code letters, but 87 maintained the larger type. 87's Hurricanes had on their fins a white arrowhead like the fighters had carried before the war, on which was painted their badge.

Two Gladiator squadrons reinforced the Hurricanes in France, No 615 (KW) and No 607 (AF?). The latter had flown defensive sorties from the UK and on October 17 three Gladiators had forced a Do 18 into the sea. 615 took over 605's Gladiators at Croydon in October, 1939, and both squadrons flew to Merville in November. They made patrols but had no engagements before the *blitzkreig* of May. There had, incidentally, been five biplane squadrons active on September 3, 1939, the others being Nos 603, which flew Gladiators on a few patrols, and No 616 which still had Gauntlets but never flew operational missions.

On November 18 the air war took on a new phase when He 115s of Kustenfliergerstaffel 3/906 made the Luftwaffe's first (unsuccessful) attempt to lay magnetic mines off the East Coast. Two nights later they dropped mines off Harwich and in two positions in the Thames Estuary. Heinkels of 3/106 joined in on November 22, and this brought forth a response from 12 Blenheim fighters of Nos 25 and 601 Squadrons firing their guns in anger for first time during a daylight beat-up of the seaplane base at Borkum on November 25 (when 25 Sqn's complement included L1437, L1440 and L6676), an action repeated on November 28.

Judged against the later stages of the war this period has always been considered dull. From an interested observer's point of view it was far from that, for there was so much to see that was strangely unfamiliar—new squadrons, modified Hurricanes and Spitfires, Battle fighters, the large day bomber formations, much practice flying, and of course those fascinating Wellingtons of the GRU's with their anti-mine hoops—but that is another story, and so is the opening of the onslaught against France and the Low Countries in which once more the Blenheims were to play an early pathetic part.

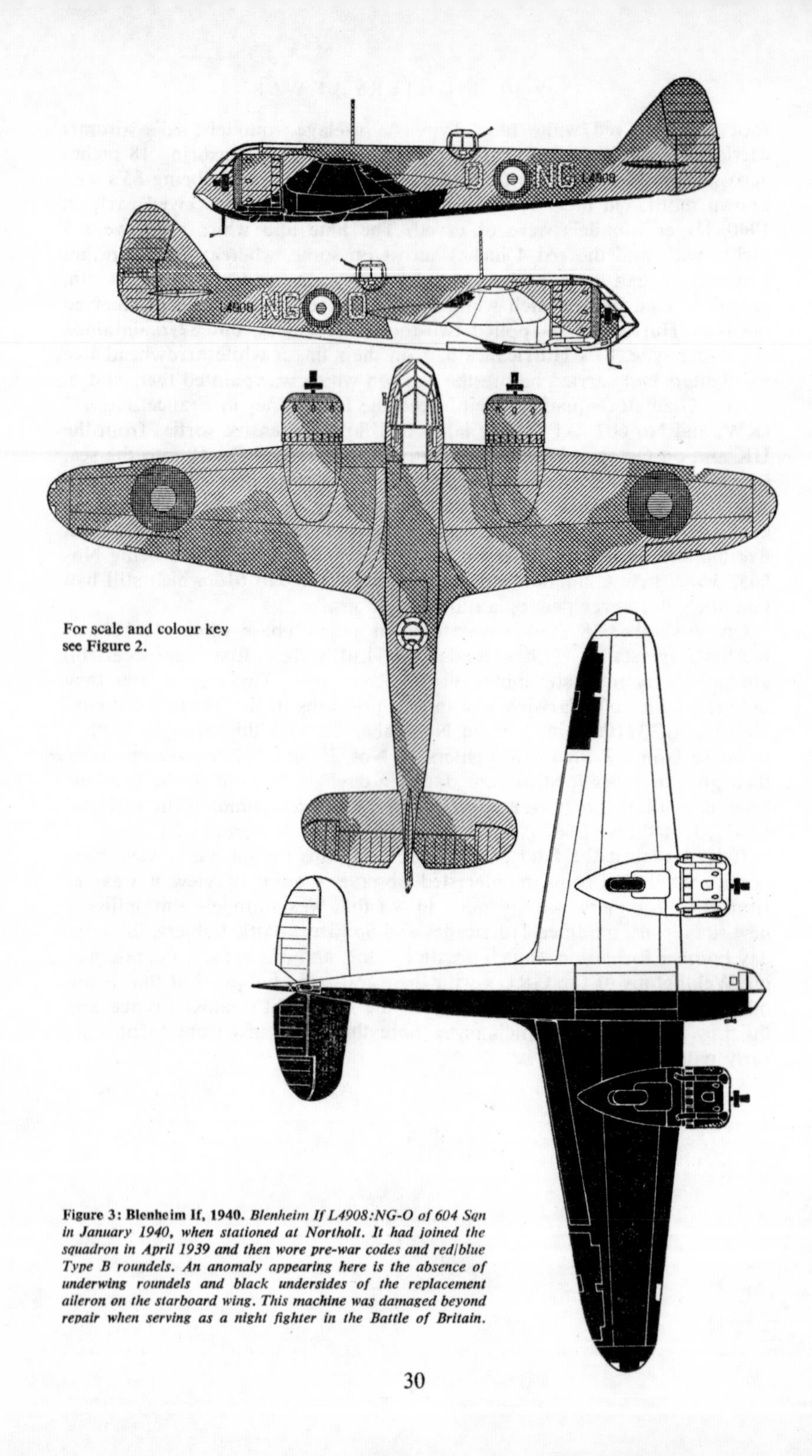

Figure 3: Blenheim If, 1940. *Blenheim If L4908:NG-O of 604 Sqn in January 1940, when stationed at Northolt. It had joined the squadron in April 1939 and then wore pre-war codes and red/blue Type B roundels. An anomaly appearing here is the absence of underwing roundels and black undersides of the replacement aileron on the starboard wing. This machine was damaged beyond repair when serving as a night fighter in the Battle of Britain.*

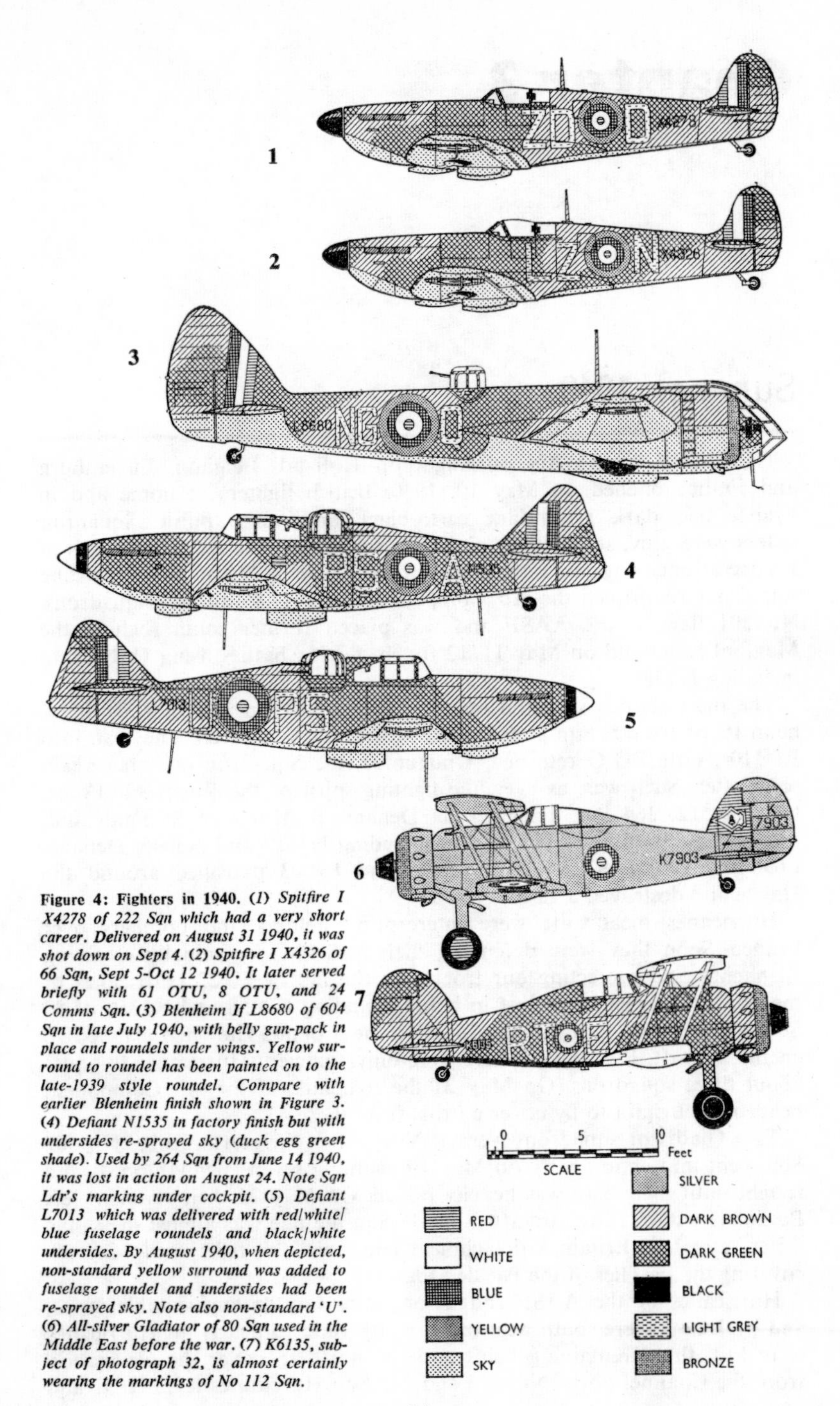

Figure 4: Fighters in 1940. *(1) Spitfire I X4278 of 222 Sqn which had a very short career. Delivered on August 31 1940, it was shot down on Sept 4. (2) Spitfire I X4326 of 66 Sqn, Sept 5-Oct 12 1940. It later served briefly with 61 OTU, 8 OTU, and 24 Comms Sqn. (3) Blenheim If L8680 of 604 Sqn in late July 1940, with belly gun-pack in place and roundels under wings. Yellow surround to roundel has been painted on to the late-1939 style roundel. Compare with earlier Blenheim finish shown in Figure 3. (4) Defiant N1535 in factory finish but with undersides re-sprayed sky (duck egg green shade). Used by 264 Sqn from June 14 1940, it was lost in action on August 24. Note Sqn Ldr's marking under cockpit. (5) Defiant L7013 which was delivered with red/white/blue fuselage roundels and black/white undersides. By August 1940, when depicted, non-standard yellow surround was added to fuselage roundel and undersides had been re-sprayed sky. Note also non-standard 'U'. (6) All-silver Gladiator of 80 Sqn used in the Middle East before the war. (7) K6135, subject of photograph 32, is almost certainly wearing the markings of No 112 Sqn.*

Chapter 3

Summer, 1940

WHEN THE GERMAN onslaught on Holland, Belgium, Luxemburg and France opened on May 10, 1940, British fighters at home and in France had dark green-dark earth/black and white finish. Squadron letters were grey, serials and spinners black. Thus adorned, Hurricanes in France at once engaged huge enemy forces. Nos. 3, 79 and 504 Hurricane squadrons reinforced the Air Component's Nos 1, 85 and 87 Squadrons. No 501 flew to the AASF and was placed further south (behind the Maginot Line) and on May 11/12 fought terrific battles using Hurricanes including N2586.

The most serious situation on May 10 was that in Holland. Six Blenheim Ifs of No 600 Sqn attacked the airfield at Waalhaven. They ran into Bf 110s; only BQ-O returned. Undaunted, the Squadron operated again soon after. Such was, as ever, the fighting spirit of the Royal Air Force. On May 12, 264 Sqn detached six Defiants to Horsham St Faith and, escorted by Spitfires of No 66 Sqn including N3027 and N3043, Defiants L6964, L6970, L6972, L6973, L6975 and L7003 patrolled around the Hague and destroyed a Ju 88.

Hurricanes meanwhile were intercepting fighters and bombers over France. Soon they were defending their airfields, occasionally escorting Blenheims and protecting our troops. In the first week 22 Hurricanes of the Air Component were lost in battle including N2353 and N2360 of 87 Sqn. Fifteen were seriously damaged on the ground. They had claimed 70 enemy aircraft. By May 17 there were only sufficient Hurricanes to equal about three squadrons. On May 21 the remnants of the Air Component headed for Britain to fly cover patrols from there.

Two Gladiator squadrons were at Vitry when the storm broke. No 607 Sqn went into action early on May 10 claiming seven enemy aircraft and fought until their base was heavily raided. On May 21 their remnant left Boulogne without any aircraft. For 615 Sqn the tale was almost the same. After retreat to Britain a detachment continued the fight until May 30, covering the beaches of the Pas de Calais.

Hurricanes of the AASF fought on, retreating to any suitable strips, and by June 3 were south-west of Paris. By June 15 nearly all Hurricanes were lost, those remaining being ordered north to cover the evacuation from the Channel ports. Now 17 and 242 Sqn Hurricanes (eg, N2651 and

N2345 of 242 Sqn) flew to France, Nos 1, 73 and 242 being deployed to defend the ports of Brest, Nantes and St Nazaire, Eventually Nos 17 (whose machines included P2557, P2558 and P2559) and 501 Squadrons fell back to Dinard, then the Channel Islands to defend St Malo and Cherbourg. On June 18 the AASF Hurricanes were ordered home. Of 261 Hurricanes which had served the Air Component 75 were destroyed by enemy action, 120 by other causes. Only 66 made the journey to Britain. Another 44 of the AASF were lost.

Spitfires had mainly been held in reserve for home defence. However, they were alerted for defensive patrols on May 10, and made some offensive patrols. The temptation to send them to France was resisted, although four from 92 Sqn escorted Churchill's Flamingo to Paris on May 16. Blenheim fighters, easy prey by day, now stood by for night patrols, although as yet there was no special allocation of squadrons specifically for this purpose. Thus it was that Spitfires of 19 Sqn were scrambled on the night of June 18/19 to investigate a raid on Mildenhall. L1032 caught up with an He 111 and engaged it near Bury—just as searchlights lit the fighter. The bomber fired back and soon the Spitfire was afire. The bomber was, however, doomed. It fell in flames near Fulbourn village. At the same time K9807 was chasing a Heinkel which it destroyed near Southend. But only if the searchlights were effective could the Spitfires expect success. As yet A.I. radar was not a standard fitting in the Blenheims, seven of which from 23 Squadron had scrambled like the Spitfires. YP-X shot down a Heinkel near Newmarket before crashing itself, and YP-S was shot down by a German bomber. It was an expensive night, and memorable for the author as the bombs from another Heinkel whistled overhead in the most serious attack yet on any British town.

Yet the fight over Britain had not yet really begun. It was the battle to defend the evacuation of the BEF that Fighter Command was now savagely waging. The first major dog-fight involving Spitfires came on May 23 when 74 Sqn engaged Bf 109s. Soon 54 and 92 were busy, and the Spitfires were now embroiled. The decision to withdraw from Dunkirk really brought the home-based fighters into action and, often unseen by the troops below, they unceasingly patrolled the beaches and areas surrounding, heading off hordes of German aircraft. At night the Blenheims of 604 Sqn played their part. As soon as the BEF was home a sort of respite in the fighting came, before the greatest battle in Britain's history was forced upon her.

Many squadrons were engaged in the tough action over the Channel ports, and aircraft known to have been involved include Hurricanes P2557 (17 Sqn), N2655 (32 Sqn), N2584 (43 Sqn), P2721 (213 Sqn), P2876 (229 Sqn), N2559 (245 Sqn), and P3393 (601 Sqn). Spitfires involved included N3237 (19 Sqn), N3272 (64 Sqn), N3232 (222 Sqn) and N3289 (610 Sqn). Regrettably their 'individual letters' seem never to have been noted . . . there were problems, even for the handful of unauthorised spotters.

Colour changes, 1940

In Autumn, 1939, some Blenheim day-bombers had their under surfaces sprayed light grey-blue. This was a more suitable hue than the matt black with which they began their war. Black/white fighter finish was satisfactory for a fighter expected to do battle in cloudy conditions by day and night, but fighting would now clearly be in blue skies—and between milling hordes. Better, surer, means of identity were also required.

From evidence available it seems likely that Fairey Battles of the AASF were first to have broad red-white-blue fin striping, applied before the May campaign. Some certainly had a yellow surround added to fuselage roundels too, ensuring Allied fighters could (and would) recognise them. Fin striping was an additional aid, particularly for the French whose aircraft carried rudder stripes in paler tones. Quickly the addition of a yellow surround to fuselage roundels spread in May and June, 1940, and to all RAF aircraft. Both fin stripes and yellow surrounds varied enormously, and from aircraft to aircraft on the squadrons, but not in basic positioning, etc. An outer ring was frequently added to the under-wing roundel on the black wing, in yellow or in white or grey—depending upon dope availability. It seems doubtful whether many of the Hurricanes in France survived long enough to have the additions, but home-based fighters quickly adopted them for the fight over the beaches of France.

By the end of May home-based fighters were beginning to wear new under surface colours. At first under surfaces were silver, a colour evident on some Spitfires—at least in June, 1940. In July this was superseded by pale 'blue' shades which, on some of the Hurricanes I saw at Debden and Duxford, were almost as dark as the azure blue of later years. For the most part this Sky tint meant to be blue was more accurately a pale shade of green sometimes having intoned a blue tint commonly and fairly accurately called duck egg green. Most fighters eventually settled for this, and by the end of August it was the most common shade. In later years the officially designated Sky Type 'S' ('S' denotes smooth) was a much lighter tone than that of 1940.

The confusion of those hectic days was bound to bring anomalies. Before the battle-damaged fighters went in for repair some were in use that summer with black/white, black/Sky, or black/white/silver under surfaces. It is difficult to generalise about any aircraft markings, but squadron letters were usually applied ahead of the roundel on the fuselage port side, aft on the starboard. Letter size varied considerably, some fighters having two sizes of codes, others opting for huge lettering. Of the many aircraft I saw in 1940 none had other than mid-grey to rather darker grey letters. Spinners remained black. Hurricanes appeared to have 'standard sized' under-wing roundels, but many Spitfires—especially in the later stages of the Battle of Britain—had very large underwing roundels.

It was the end of July, 1940, when I first recorded a 264 Sqn Defiant with duck egg green under surfaces. Others adopted these soon after and still had them at the start of their night-fighting attempts. Like the Blenheims, the Defiants did not usually have underwing roundels it would seem. The twin-engined fighters were painted similarly to others, and this extended to the Blenheim fighters of Coastal Command.

With the return of winter, under surfaces of the port wing were again painted matt black, the roundel officially having a yellow outline usually half the width of the other rings. The fighters had then come into line with the few Whirlwinds in service in the summer which retained this scheme as a special identity feature.

Fighters of the few

It would be pleasing to describe marking of aircraft flown by well-known Battle of Britain pilots, for over the years the idea has grown that each had a particular mount. In reality this was rarely the case. Occasionally a pilot did keep the same machine for a short period, but battle damage, unserviceability, modification programmes, major overhauls, etc, meant that one aeroplane could be available for only a short period. All that can really be said is that such-and-such an aeroplane was a mount on certain occasions. 'Sailor' Malan flew with No 74 Sqn where aircraft he used included K9953, R6773 (June 31, 1940) and P9306 (July 13), Sqn Ldr Douglas Bader flew Hurricane P3061 on September 7 (his usual mount of the period) but on September 15 he was using V7467 also of 242 Sqn.

During May, 1940, the first production Spitfire II flew. It differed from the Mk I in having a Merlin XII, Coffman cartridge starter, and curved canopy as a standard fitting along with other less obvious small modifications. P7280, the first Mk II, was delivered to Boscombe on June 27. No 152 Sqn received P7286 on July 17, but it was 611 Sqn which was the first to fully equip with and operate the new version. Delivery was largely made in the third week of August, aircraft involved including P7291, '92 and 7300. No 266 Sqn received Mk IIs (eg, P7296, '97) in the first week of September, then 74 Sqn had them by mid-September (eg, P7306). No 19 Sqn next equipped, then 603 Sqn. Production of the new version at Castle Bromwich gathered tremendous momentum. About 150 Mk IIs were delivered by the end of October.

The finest hour

On May 22 No 32 Sqn mixed with Bf 109s and N2406, N2459, N2641, N2527, N2582, P2755 were each credited with an enemy fighter. P3671 of 111 Sqn rammed a Do 215 on July 10, the first day of the Battle. August 11 was one of the most hectic days—R6614 was a Spitfire then used by 152 Sqn, R6630 by 610 Sqn. Aircraft used on August 15 included P3047 (1 Sqn), R4193 (111 Sqn), L6985 (264 Sqn), R6988 (234 Sqn), R7015 (54 Sqn). Amongst the aircraft flown into battle on September 15 were P2725 (504 Sqn), which rammed a Do 17 over Victoria Station, R6699 (609 Sqn) which shot down a Do 215 near Portsmouth, R4089: NN-R of 310 Sqn, X4179 of 19 Sqn which claimed two Bf 109s and X4351, also of 19 Sqn, which destroyed a Do 17. Others used on this day included P9324 (41 Sqn), R7019 (603 Sqn), V6888 (607 Sqn) and P2760 (501 Sqn).

Hurricanes with duck egg under surfaces seen at Croydon in June, 1940, included V7128:DT-D, V7167:DT-H. A silver undersided Spitfire in use at this time was N3267:XT-S. Blenheim L8068:NG-E was then in use (Sky under side) without underwing roundels. Croydon's residents in July included YO-L:313 and YO-N:319 of No 1 RCAF Sqn. TM-V: P3774 and VK-A:P2946 were then wearing standard sized and proportioned roundels. PR-D:R6769 in use in August still did not have a yellow surround to its fuselage roundels, and L1059:OU-B still had silver under surfaces. L7013:PS-U with mid-grey codes had Sky under surfaces. P3055:US-P with large scale code letters was in use in September, and had Sky under surfaces.

At the end of the Battle of Britain the Italian Air Force made a brief appearance over Britain. Amongst the intercepting fighters were Hurricanes V6680 and V7607 of No 257 Sqn.

Fighters available for the summer battles

Hurricanes available for action were drawn from the following batches delivered to the end of October, 1940, approximately: L1547-2146 (delivered 12.37-6.10.39); N2318-2367, N2380-2409, N2422-2441, N2453-2502, N2520-2559, N2582-2631, N2645-2674, N2700-2729 (delivered 29.9.39-1.5.40); P2535-2584, P2614-2653, P2672-2701, P2713-2732, P2751-2770, P2792-2836, P2854-2888, P2900-2924, P2946-2995, P3020-3069, P3080-3124, P3140-3179, P3200-3234, P3250-3264 (delivered 10.39 to 7.40); P3265-3279, P3300-3324, P3345-3364, P3380-3399, P3400-3419, P3420-3429, P3448-3487, P3488-3492, P3515-3554, P3574-3578, P3579-3623, P3640-3684, P3700-3739, P3755-3789, P3802-3836, P3854-3903, P3920-3944. P3960-3984 (delivered 21.2.40-20.7.40); R4074-4123, R4171-4200, R4213-4232, R2680-2689, T9519-9538, W6667-6670, V7200-7209, V7221-7260, V7276-7318, V7337-7386, V7400-7446, V7461-7510 (delivered 2.7.40 to 10.40). Deliveries of the batches V6533-6582, V6600-6649, V6665-6704, V6722-6761, V6776-6825, V6840-6889, V6913-6962, V6979-7028, V7042-7081, V7099-7138 and V7156-7195 had also been made.

Spitfires delivered by the end of October, 1940 were Mk 1: K9787-L1096 (delivered 27.7.38-9.39); N3032-3072, N3091-3130, N3160-3203, N3221-3250, N3264-3299 (delivered 9.39-1.40); P9305-9339, P9360-9399, P9420-9469, P9490-9519, P9540-9584 (delivered 20.1.40-4.40); R6595-6644, R6683-6722, R6751-6780, R6799-6818, R6829-6840, R6879-6928, F6957-6996, R7015-7023 (delivered April-July, 1940); X4009-4038, X4051-4070, X4101-4110, X4159-4188, X4231-4280, X4317-4356, X4381-4390 (delivered from 19.8.40 to October, 1940). From these aircraft it must be remembered that there were various conversions to other marks, and for PR purposes. Spitfire Mk II delivered by 10.40 were approximately P7280-7329, P7350-7389, P7420-7449, P7490-7509. Defiants delivered by October 1940 were L6950-7036, N1535-1582, N1610-1653, N1671-1706, N1725-1773, N1788-1812.

The squadrons and their aircraft

Principal fighter squadrons engaged in the summer of 1940 and examples of aircraft used during the fighting follow. All too often it will be seen that whereas unit identification letters are known (although Hurricanes were seen in squadron use coded JB and ML which remain as unidentified unit letters) and confusion occurs over the use of HE and HP, perhaps duplicated at some period, only the serial number of an aircraft actually used can often be set alongside without its individual letter.

21 *Hurricanes of 73 Sqn on patrol in France, winter 1939-40, with red/white/blue stripes on the rudder to conform with French practice. Undersides are black/white with silver under the nose. J is P2575, D is P2569, and TP-E is N2517* (IWM).

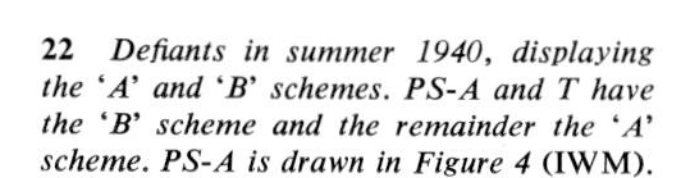

22 *Defiants in summer 1940, displaying the 'A' and 'B' schemes. PS-A and T have the 'B' scheme and the remainder the 'A' scheme. PS-A is drawn in Figure 4* (IWM).

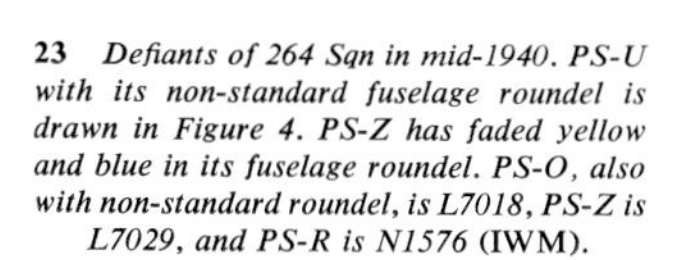

23 *Defiants of 264 Sqn in mid-1940. PS-U with its non-standard fuselage roundel is drawn in Figure 4. PS-Z has faded yellow and blue in its fuselage roundel. PS-O, also with non-standard roundel, is L7018, PS-Z is L7029, and PS-R is N1576* (IWM).

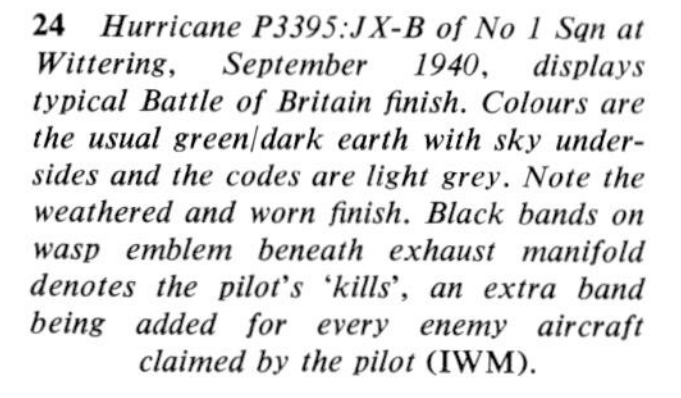

24 *Hurricane P3395:JX-B of No 1 Sqn at Wittering, September 1940, displays typical Battle of Britain finish. Colours are the usual green/dark earth with sky undersides and the codes are light grey. Note the weathered and worn finish. Black bands on wasp emblem beneath exhaust manifold denotes the pilot's 'kills', an extra band being added for every enemy aircraft claimed by the pilot* (IWM).

25 *Late Battle of Britain finish is typified by these 85 Sqn Hurricanes. V6611:VY-U, P3854:VY-Q and VY-M* (IWM).

26 *Spitfire I X4474:QV-I of 19 Sqn, Duxford, in the last week of September 1940 showing typical Spitfire style of marking for the late Battle of Britain period* (IWM).

27 *R2052, the first prototype Beaufighter with black/white under surfaces. Photographed during the change of national markings, the fin stripe is just being applied* (IWM).

28 *R2054 the third Beaufighter prototype in green-brown/black-white finish, possibly photographed as late as June 1940* (IWM).

29 *A Blenheim If night-fighter, K71?? of No 54 OTU used for training purposes, wearing overall black finish. YX-N has been applied in a light grey, likewise the tiny serial* (IWM).

30 *R2198 was delivered to No 252 Sqn early in January 1941. This was a Coastal Command long-range fighter squadron, but the machine here typifies the markings applied to over 100 of the first Beaufighters. Its upper surfaces are brown and green, the remainder duck egg green. Code letters were pale grey* (IWM).

31 *A Gladiator in the Western Desert in the summer of 1940. Note the black port wing under surfaces. The under belly is all white, and the fuselage roundel appears to be Type B. Observe the chock stowed temporarily in the interplane rigging wires* (Warbirds).

32 *Gladiator K6135:RT-E photographed in the summer of 1940 in the Middle East This aircraft is drawn in Figure 4.* (Warbirds)

33 *Defiant PS-P:N3313 of 264 Sqn in early night-fighter finish of RDM2. Codes and serials are light grey and the fuselage roundel has been lightly picked out yellow with the white band overpainted in red. A drawing of this aircraft appears in Figure 5* (IWM).

34 *Hurricane Mk Is of No 257 Sqn taking off late in 1940, with black under-wings and yellow outline to the roundels. DT-A with the blunt spinner is V6962, DT-O is V6873 and DT-G is V7137. The sky bands and spinners date the photograph as probably late December or January 1941* (IWM).

35 *Hurricane P2627 in mid-1941 with tropical filter and dark green/dark earth upper surfaces. The under surfaces can be seen in black and probably a shade like duck egg green. Under wing roundel outlined in yellow to port but obliterated under starboard wing* (IWM).

36 *A most interesting line-up of Hurricanes of No 56 Sqn almost certainly photographed during the change-over to grey-green paintwork, perhaps during an advanced stage of trials. 'K' nearest (possibly Z3352?) can be seen to have a very narrow code letter. The next machine appears to have a wider sky band than usual—and it has a very narrow yellow surround to its fuselage roundel. The Z3 . . . serial has been overpainted* (IWM).

37 *Spitfire IIa P7665(?):YT-L of No 65 Sqn photographed early in 1941 with duck egg green under surfaces and sky adornments. Codes were mid-grey. Note the unusual tail fin striping. 'East India Squadron' presentation panel is painted beneath cockpit* (IWM).

38 *Spitfire IIa P7895:RN-N with green-brown-duck egg green finish and grey codes. Note that this machine has the standard shorter fin stripe. April 1941* (IWM).

39 *A Spitfire Vb W3373, with grey-green finish. The apparent black outline to the roundel is caused by the use of ortho film. This picture was taken prior to the aircraft's delivery to a squadron, hence the absence of code letters* (IWM).

Sqn	*Letters*	*Example*	*Aircraft type*	*Notes/date recorded*
1	JX	P3395:B	Hurricane	October 1940
1	YO	P3080:C	Hurricane	September 1940
3	QO	P3318	Hurricane	July 1940
17	YB	P2874	Hurricane	July 1940
19	QV	P9386:K	Spitfire	September 1940
	QV	P7319	Spitfire II	September 1940
	QV	R6776	Spitfire IB	August 1940
23	YP	L6841	Blenheim If	August 1940
25	ZK	L1512	Blenheim If	July 1940
	?	P6966	Whirlwind	June 1940
29	RO	L6637:S	Blenheim If	August 1940
	RO	R2072	Beaufighter If	September 1940
32	GZ	P3144:B	Hurricane	September 1940
41	EB	X4173:K	Spitfire	September 1940
43	FT	P3665:X	Hurricane	September 1940
46	PO	P3052	Hurricane	August 1940
54	KL	L1093	Spitfire	July 1940
56	US	P3055:P	Hurricane	September 1940
64	SH	P9563	Spitfire	September 1940
65	YT	K9906:T	Spitfire	May 1940
66	LZ	N3043:K	Spitfire	September 1940
72	RN	K9942	Spitfire	May 1940
73	TP	P2559:D	Hurricane	July 1940
74	ZP	L1089	Spitfire	August 1940
79	NV	P3050	Hurricane	August 1940
85	VY	P3119:X	Hurricane	August 1940
87	LK	P2829:G	Hurricane	July 1940
92	GR	N3194:Z	Spitfire	May 1940
111	JU	L1822:K	Hurricane	June 1940
141	TW	L7014	Defiant	July 1940
145	SO	P3567:K	Hurricane	June 1940
151	DZ	P3065:G	Hurricane	August 1940
152	SN	P7286	Spitfire II	July 1940
213	AK	P3174	Hurricane	September 1940
219	FK	L8685:N	Blenheim If	July 1940
222	ZD	X4278:D	Spitfire	
229	RE	P3265	Hurricane	July 1940
232	EF	P3411	Hurricane	July 1940
234	AZ	N3239	Hurricane	August 1940
236	ND	L1334	Blenheim If	July 1940
238	VK	P2946:A	Hurricane	August 1940
242	LE	N2714:G	Hurricane	July 1940. V7467 often flown by Douglas Bader
245	DX	P3762:E	Hurricane	August 1940
247	HP	K8049	Gladiator	July 1940
248	WR	P6952	Blenheim IVf	July 1940. To Ftr Cmd 20.6.40, returned to C Cmd soon after
249	GN	V6610	Hurricane	September 1940. Flown by Flt-Lt J. B. Nicholson, VC
253	SW	L2026:A	Hurricane	May 1940
257	DT	V6722:P	Hurricane	October 1940
263	HE?	P3145	Hurricane	August 1940. 1940 sqn code is still open to question since HE may have been used by 605 sqn
	HE	P6968	Whirlwind	July 1940
264	PS	L7026:V	Defiant	August 1940
266	UO	P7309	Spitfire II	September 1940
302	WX	P3085	Hurricane	September 1940
303	RF	N2460:D	Hurricane	August 1940
310	NN	P3148:N	Hurricane	August 1940

Sqn	*Letters*	*Example*	*Aircraft type*	*Notes/date recorded*
312	DU	V6885:V	Hurricane	October 1940
501	SD	P3397:H	Hurricane	September 1940
504	TM	P3774:V	Hurricane	September 1940
600	BQ	L6626	Blenheim If	July 1940
601	UF	P2673:N	Hurricane	August 1940
602	LO	N3221	Spitfire I	August 1940
603	XT	X4277:M	Spitfire I	September 1940. Flg-Off Richard Hilary ditched this aircraft 3.9.40
604	NG	L6610:E	Blenheim If	August 1940
605	HE?	N2349:V	Hurricane	May 1940. This aircraft coded HE when used by 605 Sqn. Possibly sqn sometime recorded ML or NR? N2349 was not used by 263 Sqn
607	AF	P2874:F	Hurricane	September 1940
609	PR	R6769:D	Spitfire	August 1940
610	DW	L1062:K	Spitfire	May 1940
611	FY	P7300	Spitfire II	September 1940
615	KW	R4194:P	Hurricane	July 1940
616	YQ?	N3269	Spitfire	July 1940
FIU	ZQ	L6837	Blenheim If	July 1940

Chapter 4

1940-41: Fighters overseas

WHILST THE BATTLE OF BRITAIN raged, opening shots in the Middle East campaign were being exchanged. There the RAF had been engaged in policing operations against rebels in the manner of the 1966 Aden operations. The war in Abyssinia caused home-based squadrons to be despatched as a warning to Mussolini: mainly they were bomber squadrons. These units returned, some leaving their aircraft behind. Instead of the handful of fighters being left behind it was decided better to despatch Gladiators available when re-equipment of home-based squadrons with Hurricanes was well under way. No 80 Squadron based at Debden was chosen and in May, 1938, its silver painted Gladiators including K7901, K7904, K7905 reached Abu Sueir. Here they retained the white arrowhead on the fin bearing the squadron motif. Each Flight Leader had the fin of his machine in Flight colour, 'A' red, 'B' yellow, 'C' green, applied respectively to K7903, K7902 and K8011.

The first Gladiators despatched to Egypt arrived in February, 1938, and equipped No 33 Sqn providing defence for Cairo, Jerusalem and the Canal Zone. Its all-silver Gladiators included K8054, L7608, L7613. The first fighter squadron to appear in Egypt was No 112. It arrived at Alexandria late May, 1939, its Gladiators including K6134, '35, '36. These and a handful of Gauntlets of 6 Sqn including K7792, K7863 and K7881 based at Ramleh, and Blenheim Ifs of 30 Sqn (L8541, L8542 possibly included) constituted the fighter force when the war began.

There was no urgent need for camouflage, although the Blenheims retained green-brown/black-white finish applied before delivery from the UK. Codes allocated to the squadrons, but possibly not all applied, were: 6(XE), 30(DP), 33(TN), 80(GK) and 112(XO). When the war commenced these were ordered to be changed to 6(JV), 30(RS), 33(NW; possibly used NY, 80(EY?) and 112(GA), the letters being allocated initially not duplicating those of home-based squadrons. In later years codes allotted for use in that theatre sometimes duplicated those used in the European region.

Need to build up the home fighter force still precluded reinforcement in an area removed from operations so that, when the Italians declared war on June 10, 1940, the fighter force facing them remained as in 1939.

Following the declaration of war, Gladiators of 33 Sqn began patrols over the Libyan border. On June 14 the first major skirmish took place between Gladiators including N5761, N5774 and N5783 and an escorted Caproni 310. Patrols and brief engagements followed between Gladiators (now camouflaged) and Italian forces. There was also one Hurricane now available for action. This and the Gladiators wore brown-green/black-white camouflage like home-based fighters in early 1940. They had grey codes and seem in many cases to have had white serials.

In July, No 112 Sqn joined the battle and soon No 80 was in action, too. All were using mainly Gladiator Is, 80 Sqn's including N5583 (Mk II) and Mk Is K7901-7905 and No 112's including K7969, L7612. In September, 1940, No 33 Sqn passed its Gladiators to No 3 Sqn, RAAF, and 112 Sqn was operating a detachment in East Africa.

Defending Malta

Malta was a well-established naval base, and therefore an attractive target to the Italians. It was destined to bear a fearful onslaught, only to be cruelly treated politically 25 years later. In 1939 crated Royal Navy Sea Gladiators arrived at Kalafrana, there to remain until needed. Some served aboard the carriers *Glorious, Furious* and *Formidable.* When the German attack in May, 1940 opened, there were still about a dozen Gladiators in the crates. Defence of the island now lay in the hands of a few outdated naval fighters, for the RAF had none to spare.

A few weeks previously, obvious dangers in the situation were apparent and a handful of RAF officers were posted into Malta. Four Sea Gladiators (N5519, '20, '24, '31) were erected at Hal Far to equip its Fighter Flight. Being naval aircraft they wore medium grey and greyish green upper surfaces with Sky fuselage sides and under surfaces. Roundels were as applied to RAF fighters in June, 1940, at home. Roundels appeared beneath the lower plane tips, and tall fin stripes were carried. Serials and individual letters (painted aft) were black. N5523 and '29 were erected in June as reserves. They were soon backed by a few Hurricanes which probably had green-brown/blue-black camouflage.

The day after Italy entered the war, Italian bombers began attacks on the island. The Gladiators could do little against them, except upset their aim and boost the defenders' morale. Throughout June and July the Sea Gladiators fought until gradually written off in action or by less spectacular attrition. The few survivors of the epic stand were taken over by 261 Squadron formed at the start of August and equipped with Hurricanes.

Aden and East Africa

Aden occupied a strategic position on the Far East route in a way after that of Malta, facing Italian forces in Ethiopia and Eritrea. Its defence was in the hands of the brown-green/black-white painted Gladiators of No 94 Sqn coded GO. On March 26, 1939, the squadron had formed and during April took on charge Gladiators N2278-80 and N2283-95 which were available in 1940.

First attempt to bomb Aden was made on June 13, when the Gladiators mercilessly cut more outdated aircraft down. 94 Sqn soon assumed an offensive ground-strafing role supporting our troops in East Africa. Early in 1941 it supported the British advance which ended the Italian occupation in East Africa. Then No 94 moved to Egypt and rearmed with Hurricanes wearing the same colour scheme as those used in the last weeks of the Battle of Britain.

Greece and Crete

Spasmodic desert fighting took place as the Italians craftily massed in the Balkans then attacked Greece from Albania. Britain gave support to Greece in the form of three Blenheim squadrons and Nos 80 and 112 Squadrons using Gladiators which took a satisfying toll of the *Regia Aeronautica.* The Gladiators were now in brown-green/Sky finish with grey codes and black serials. No 33 Sqn took its similarly painted aircraft to Greece in early 1941, Hurricanes the like of which would soon equip other squadrons. 80 Squadron's Gladiators included K7892 and K8017.

Few fighters survived the campaign, but seven Gladiators, six Hurricanes and a few Blenheim fighters were available along with three Fulmars to put up a pathetic defence of Crete against a huge German armada.

All of the fighters still had brown and green upper surface camouflage. Type A roundels on the fuselage sides in the Middle East area had a yellow ring added in June, 1940, and Type B roundels were placed above the wings when camouflage was applied. Type A roundels beneath the wing tips were usual. During the campaign in Greece some Hurricanes were seen with half black under surfaces and some certainly had the remainder of their under surfaces light blue, although 'all-Sky' (duck egg green shade) was usual.

Chapter 5

1940-41: Fighters at night

THE BATTLE OF BRITAIN had been won by October, 1940. Poorer weather and the long nights provided the Luftwaffe with ideal conditions with which to continue operations, spasmodically and with reduced forces by day and with ever-increasing forces by night.

Against the night-bomber the RAF was still ill-prepared. Emphasis had long fallen on expanding the day fighter force. In September,1940, when Phase I of the night offensive opened, there were only eight night-fighter squadrons. Six had Blenheim Ifs (Nos 23, eg, L6841, 25, eg, L6741, 29, eg, L1463, 219, eg, L8685:FK-N, 600, eg, P4829 (Mk IV), 604, eg, L4908: NG-O) and two Defiants (Nos 141, eg, N1552, 264, eg, L7013:PS-U). In addition, 'B' Flight of 87 Sqn at Bibury was flying Hurricanes for night-fighter work. Many other SEF (single-engine-fighter) squadrons had sections available whose chances of successful interceptions seemed slight.

The main trouble was that no really suitable aircraft was available for night fighting in any numbers, but the first examples of the Bristol Beaufighter were trickling into several squadrons. The short nosed all-silver Beaufighter prototype, R2052, had first flown on July 17, 1939. The aircraft had been completed in the amazingly short time of six months after the initial layout was drawn. When the war began 300 Beaufighters (R2052-2101, R2120-59, R2180-2209, R2240-84, R2300-49, R2370-2404, R2430-79) were on order, and soon after the prototype lost its silver finish, Type A roundels on the fuselage and above and below wings and its under-wing black serials. In their places came the brown-green/white-black standard fighter finish with Type A fuselage roundels, and Type B roundels above the wing tips. In May, 1940, a yellow ring was added and fin striping when the machine was at A & E E. R2052, incidentally, had Hercules I SM engines (similar to the Mk III) with small oil coolers beneath its cowlings and exhaust stacks along the side of the cowlings. Later, the intakes were re-positioned on wing leading edges. R2053 had Hercules I M (similar to the Mk II), and then came R2054 the third prototype with Hercules IIIs used for official acceptance trials. On July 27, 1940, the first Beaufighter If was delivered to an MU for operational fittings. It had brown-green/silver finish like other 'Beaus', although it was not long before Sky under surfaces became general. Code letters were light grey. RO-H still had silver under surfaces on March 24, 1941, ZK-H was still wearing ostensibly 'day fighter' colours (sky under surfaces) on March 25, 1941 and ZK-M as late as January 2, 1942.

Aerodynamic refinements, engine modifications, changes to the undercarriage and cannon installation took place in the year before delivery. Then, on September 2, 1940, Beaufighters began to join squadrons when R2056 was delivered to No 25 Sqn, R2072 to No 29 Sqn at Digby, No 219 Sqn at Catterick received R2070 and 604 Sqn took R2073 on charge at Middle Wallop. Within a week 600 Sqn had five Beaufighters including R2071 and R2076, and 23 Sqn had one for trials, R2077.

In comparison with the Blenheim the Beaufighter was a heavy powerful aeroplane with an unpleasant take-off swing and pronounced longitudinal instability. Added to these were cannon troubles, and the collection of snags rendered these aeroplanes of limited operational value for many months. But, they had tremendous hitting power, were fast and large enough to carry airborne interception radar (Mk IV at first) for which nose and wing 'bow and arrow' aerials were soon fitted. When an aircraft was serviceable its equipment was not. Even when the radar and aircraft worked in unison there was a major snag — the A.I radar had limited range and not until interceptions were ground controlled (the fighter being guided towards the foe upon which it then closed on its A.I) did the success of the Beaufighter begin to reveal itself.

An expansion of the night-fighter force came when No 73 Sqn (replaced in December by No 87), No 85 and No 151 Hurricane squadrons joined the third Defiant squadron, No 307. By early November the Beaufighters were mingling during the night with the Blenheims on operations.

Phase II of the night-offensive opened with the Coventry raid of November 14/15. Thereafter attacks were switched to the Midlands, Merseyside, Scotland, Plymouth and Belfast—as well as continuing against London. For defence in the Coventry raid, Blenheims flew 35 sorties, Beaufighters flew 12, Defiants 30, Hurricanes 43, and Gladiators of No 247 Sqn five from Roborough. 449/509 bombers claimed to attack, yet only one was destroyed—and this by gunfire near Loughborough. On November 19 a 604 Squadron Beaufighter flown by that most famous of all night-fighter pilots, John Cunningham, destroyed an enemy bomber engaged over Oxfordshire probably the first to fall to an A.I equipped night-fighter in squadron hands. There was no more success, though, for many months and until ground-controlled interceptions began.

By November 25 six twin-engined squadrons earmarked for Blenheims were to have Beaufighters. There were now eleven night-fighter squadrons on operations, five with Defiants, three with Hurricanes, the FIU at Tangmere, No 420 Flight experimenting with aerial mine-laying, No 422 Flight studying the use of single-seat night-fighters. A second OTU was to form, No 60 at Leconfield flying Defiants. The other, No 54 at Church Fenton, trained crews for Blenheims. Early Douglas Boston bombers unsuited to their intended role were being considered with interest for night-fighter conversion; but the delivery rate was disappointing. Such was the state of the build-up of the force that on February, 1941, the seven twin-engined squadrons had only 87 pilots. These, of course, were matters of importance to the policy makers.

Externally there was one blatantly obvious change in the force. In

December night-fighters began appearing in an overall soot-black finish. Its selection was an obvious one—black provided camouflage for a dark night. This was a special finish, its super-matt quality giving it the texture of suede. Officially it was called RDM2. But there were snags. Camouflage effect was spoilt by two factors. Squadron letters usually sited as on day-fighters were painted in a very pale shade of grey, also serial numbers. Risk of enemy attack on airfields was considered slight, winter shadows in any case helping to hide the fighters whose finish soon was grimy. Where the colours really failed was on a moonlight night, and at high altitudes, when the fighters stood out as strong silhouettes which enemy aircraft saw and avoided. Nevertheless these markings were retained, although the diameter of the fuselage roundels was reduced late in 1941. Some aircraft had the white ring and area on the fin overpainted in red, or black or blue. During autumn, 1941, squadron letters and serials changed to dull-red, otherwise the finish was little changed until autumn, 1942, on night-fighters.

Interesting tactics devised to combat the night bombers included the 'Fighter Night'. Hurricanes and other SEFs patrolled high above the target area, whilst guns below were temporarily silenced or fired at a much lower ceiling trapping the enemy for interception. On moonlight nights the Luftwaffe crews could, however, see the fighters silhouetted and very few successful interceptions were made. In December guns claimed 10 bombers, fighters four.

Another idea was the trailing of mines from barrage balloons. When the bomber hit a cable a mine was whipped up to the aircraft to explode on impact. More mines exploded on the ground after the balloons had drifted on the prevailing wind! Only limited success attended the plan to sow mines or trail them first from converted Harrow bombers including K6993 and K7020 operating from Middle Wallop in concert with the radar station at Worth Matravers. At least one He 111 was claimed, over Dorset on December 22, but there were considerable problems and several premature mine bursts in the aircraft. Havoc IIIs (eg, AX913 in use May, 1941) later trailed the 'Long Aerial Mine' over the south and around Norwich, the weapons often landing and exploding.

On December 21, 1940, there began a campaign which was to be waged until the end of the war, increasingly effective and of ever greater intensity and variety. This was Operation *Intruder,* and six Blenheim Ifs of 23 Sqn opened it, flying to airfields in Normandy and around Artois. They saw four enemy bombers, but were unable to engage them: instead they bombed their bases. These Blenheims were all black.

Overall success of the black fighter was probably higher than results suggested, for the enemy loss rate due to combat, weather, untrained crews, etc, was surprisingly high. 'Fighter Night' claims were only three enemy aircraft in the first three months of 1941. 'Twins' detected 194 enemy aircraft, and engaged 31 with little success over the same period. Anti-aircraft guns claimed 37, and in February-March, balloons seven. In April, 'twins' had 55 engagements and SEFs 39. During the last raid on London in May 1941, sixty Hurricanes and Defiants patrolled over London whilst 20 more were over Beachy Head. Between them they claimed

19 victories. Four more were claimed by 'twins' around the capital and four by gunners. In reality only eight enemy aircraft had been destroyed.

Lighter nights and the need to amass forces for 'Barbarossa', the attack on Russia, brought a withdrawal of much of the German bomber force. For the Luftwaffe this was fortuitous, for it came at a time when A.I. radar was just beginning to be effectively used in increasing numbers of Beaufighters. Odds against the night bomber were closing fast—and the Mosquito was taking shape at Hatfield.

Home-based night-fighter squadrons, and examples of the aircraft they used, over the period September, 1940 to May, 1941 were:

Sqn	*Letters*	*Serial*	*Aircraft type*	*Notes*
23	YP	L1438	Blenheim If	Night-fighter
23	YP	L6837	Blenheim If	Intruder, January, 1941
23	YP	R2077	Beaufighter If	Night-fighter trials. October 1940
23	YP	BB900:G	Havoc I	Solid nose aircraft. April 1941
23	YP	BD124:D	Havoc I	'Boston' nose; 1940 - June 1941
25	ZK	R2058	Beaufighter If	October 1940
29	RO	L1375:J	Blenheim If	December 1940
29	RO	R2138:L	Beaufighter If	November-May 1941
68	WN	L6839	Blenheim If	February 1941
68	WN	R2264	Beaufighter If	May 1941
85	VY	V7074:K	Hurricane I	December 1940
85	VY	N3327	Defiant I	February 1941
85	VY	BJ461	Havoc I	March 1941
87	LK	W9154:D	Hurricane I	May 1941
93	HN	BD117	Havoc I	January 1941
96	ZJ	V7752	Hurricane I	May 1941
96	ZJ	N1083	Defiant I	May 1941
141	TW	T3926	Defiant I	May 1941
151	DZ	V7286:U	Hurricane I	January 1941
151	DZ	N1790:P	Defiant I	May 1941
219	FK	L1403	Blenheim If	December 1940
255	YD	N3335	Defiant I	January 1941
255	YD	V7304	Hurricane I	May 1941
256	JT	N3450:N	Defiant I	May 1941
256	JT	V3995:Y	Hurricane I	May 1941
264	PS	N3368	Defiant I	May 1941
307	EW	N3315	Defiant I	April 1941
600	BQ	L6879:D	Blenheim If	December 1940
600	BQ	R2256:F	Beaufighter If	May 1941
604	NG	L8680:Q	Blenheim If	January 1941
604	NG	R2098:H	Beaufighter If	April 1941, R2101 usually flown by Wg Cdr John Cunningham
FIU	ZQ	R2125:V	Beaufighter If	February 1941, 'Day' colours

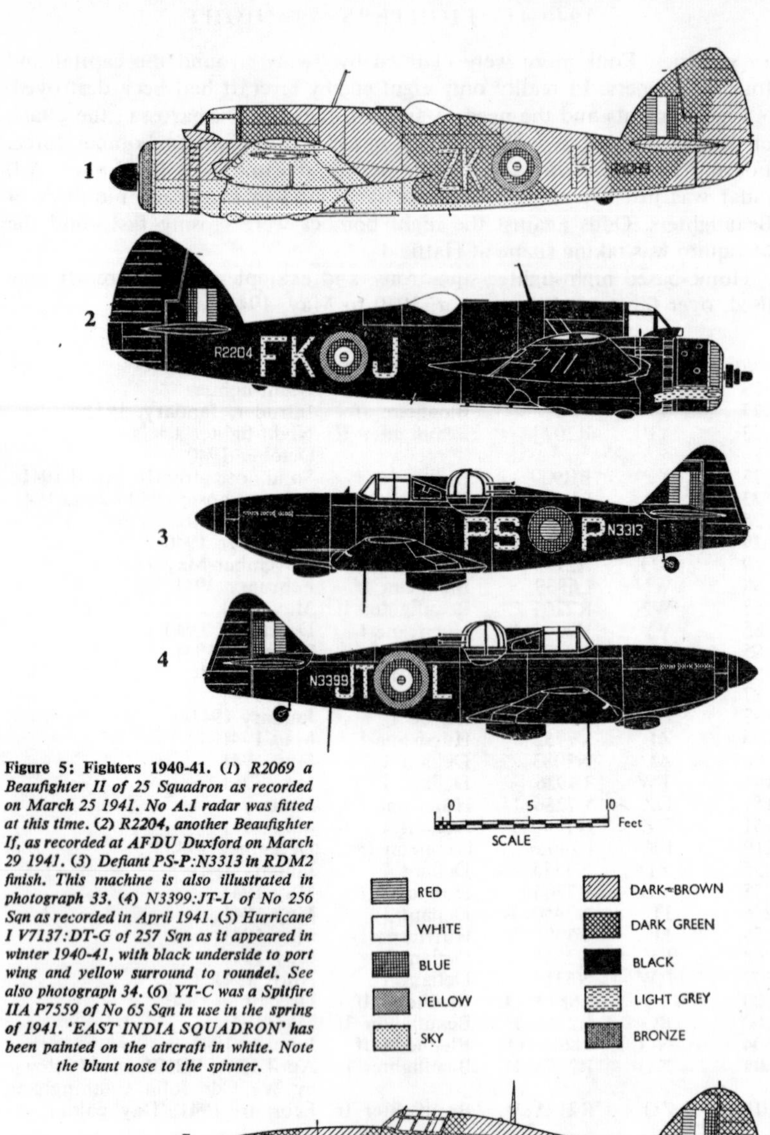

Figure 5: Fighters 1940-41. *(1) R2069 a Beaufighter II of 25 Squadron as recorded on March 25 1941. No A.1 radar was fitted at this time. (2) R2204, another Beaufighter If, as recorded at AFDU Duxford on March 29 1941. (3) Defiant PS-P:N3313 in RDM2 finish. This machine is also illustrated in photograph 33. (4) N3399:JT-L of No 256 Sqn as recorded in April 1941. (5) Hurricane I V7137:DT-G of 257 Sqn as it appeared in winter 1940-41, with black underside to port wing and yellow surround to roundel. See also photograph 34. (6) YT-C was a Spitfire IIA P7559 of No 65 Sqn in use in the spring of 1941. 'EAST INDIA SQUADRON' has been painted on the aircraft in white. Note the blunt nose to the spinner.*

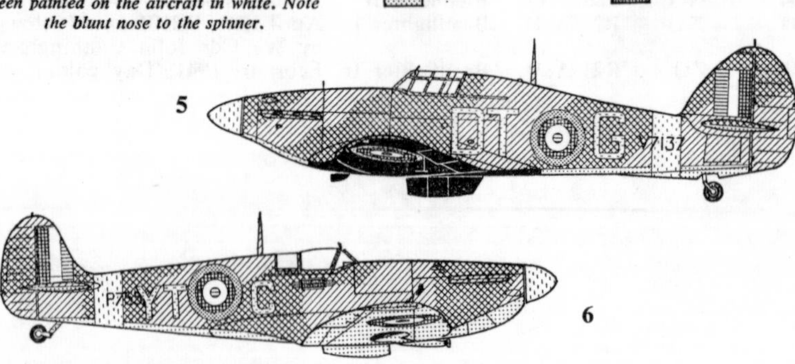

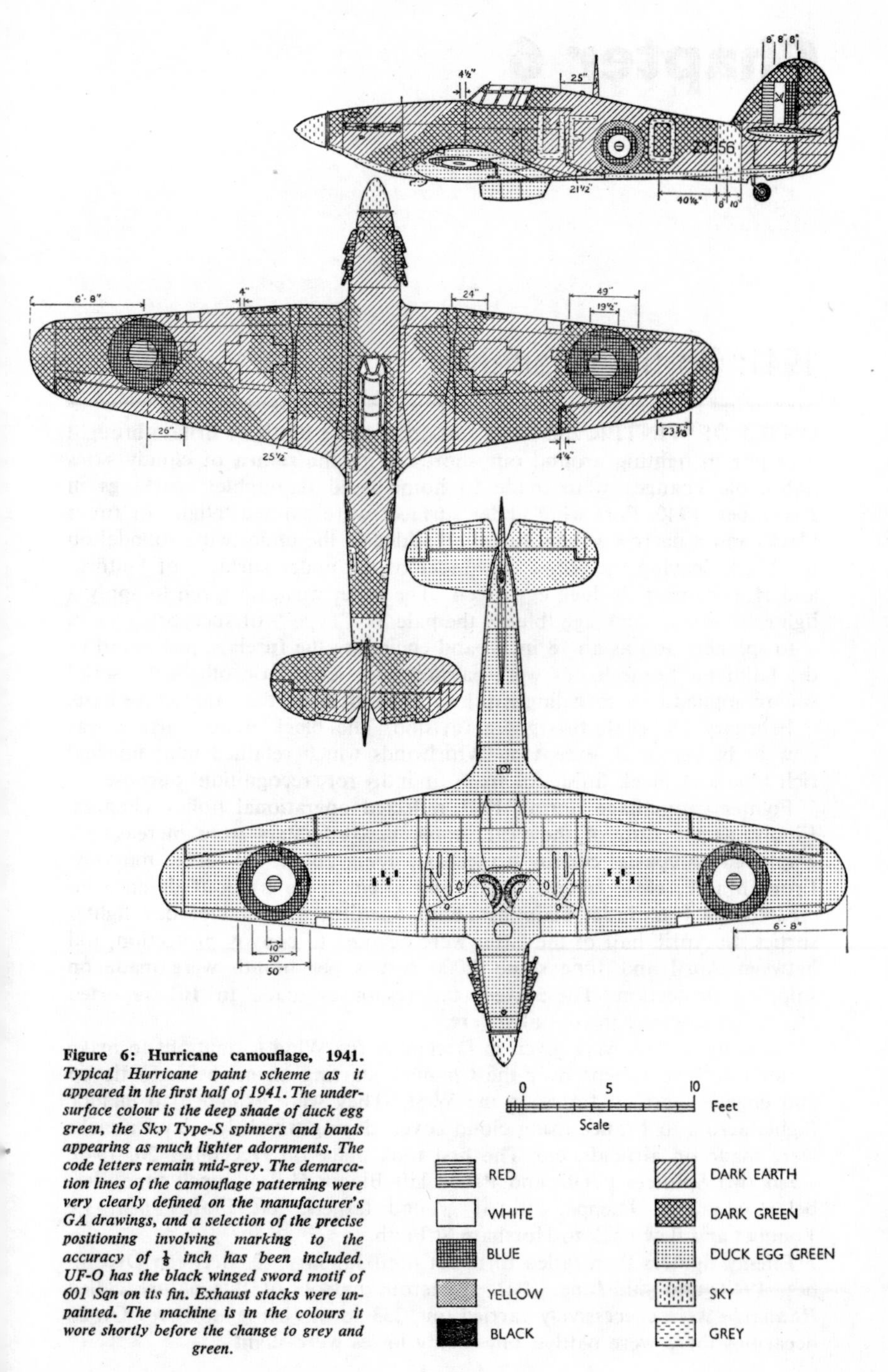

Figure 6: Hurricane camouflage, 1941. *Typical Hurricane paint scheme as it appeared in the first half of 1941. The undersurface colour is the deep shade of duck egg green, the Sky Type-S spinners and bands appearing as much lighter adornments. The code letters remain mid-grey. The demarcation lines of the camouflage patterning were very clearly defined on the manufacturer's GA drawings, and a selection of the precise positioning involving marking to the accuracy of ⅛ inch has been included. UF-O has the black winged sword motif of 601 Sqn on its fin. Exhaust stacks were unpainted. The machine is in the colours it wore shortly before the change to grey and green.*

Chapter 6

1941: On the offensive

ONSET OF WINTER and losses sustained in the Battle of Britain brought a respite in fighting around our shores. With the return of cloudy skies noticeable changes were made to home-based day-fighter markings in December, 1940. Port wing under surfaces were painted 'Night' or (matt black) and a narrow yellow surround added to the under-wing roundel on the black, leaving the entire remainder of the under surfaces of Spitfires and Hurricanes rich duck egg green. The order was also given to apply a lighter shade of duck egg 'blue'—the pale Sky Type S of succeeding years—to spinners and as an 18 inch band encircling the fuselage just ahead of the tailplane. Some bands were painted over serials; on others the serial was re-applied or a revealing gap left the number on the camouflage base.

February 18, 1941, brought a revision. The black under surface was now to be removed, except on Whirlwinds which retained their unusual rich blue and black finish for many months for 'recognition' purposes.

Fighter camouflage during 1941 reflected operational policy changes. Firstly, at the turn of the year, home based fighters were increasingly employed on coastal convoy protection, flying about 400 sorties monthly. From March, closer escort began and attention to harbour defence increased the two duties claiming about one-fifth the total of day fighter sorties. In April, half of the latter were devoted to convoy protection, and between April and June some 7,000 sorties per month were made on shipping protection. These were the responses made to 161 reported attacks on shipping in coastal waters.

Secondly, orders were given in December for Wing formations to make sector offensive sweeps over the Channel, starting an offensive to tie up and engage German forces in the West. They were extended to include flights across to France using cloud cover, during which low level attacks were made on airfields, etc. The first took place on December 20, 1940, when two Spitfires P7602 and P7669 left Biggin Hill at lunch time, flew below cloud to Dieppe, strafed ground targets, left France near Le Touquet and flew back to Horsham St Faith.

Enemy fighters then failed to re-act until January 12. Between December, 1940, and mid-June, 1941, numerous patrols of this nature called *Rhubarbs* were successively carried out, 233 sorties being effective. On 26 occasions there were battles, but enemy losses were slight.

Thirdly, there came larger 'sweeps' by Wings and sometimes larger formations tempting German fighters into action. Feelings were mixed over this policy, for the RAF was now fighting over enemy territory and pilots lost could not be retrieved. The first Wing Sweep took place on January 9 when two formations totalling five squadrons were employed. By mid-June, 85 such *Rodeos* had been flown ranging in strength from 14 aircraft to 20 squadrons. Fifty-one RAF pilots were lost. Enemy returns showed a total loss of 40 fighters, 18 shot down in combat. Despite losses —including experienced pilots—these operations were wonderful for morale, providing Fighter Command with a daylight offensive role.

Fourthly, there came the scheme whereby small forces of strongly escorted bombers covered and escorted by fighters acted as bait for the Luftwaffe and bombed targets in Northern France. This stage of the offensive opened on January 10, when six Blenheims of 114 Squadron escorted by six fighter squadrons bombed the Fôret de Guines. Three other squadrons swept the Dungeness-Gris Nez-Dunkirk area. There were ten more of these *Circus* operations in the next five months, added to which were 14 escorted attacks on shipping and two on docks, protected in all by 2,700 fighter sorties.

It was evident by June, 1941, when 60 day-fighter squadrons (84 fighter squadrons in all) were available for operations, that German forces were moving East with Russia as the obvious target. Therefore, on June 17 it was decided to open larger scale operations including bombing attacks on areas around Lille, Lens, in the Ruhr, on shipping and enemy land communications, and also to employ bigger bait including Stirlings and Hampdens. By December 31, 90 more escorted raids were made and over 100 attacks on shipping. There had then been hundreds of sweeps and fighter strike sorties. Losses were not light and claims much inflated, but the important thing was that clearly the RAF was building up its day offensive.

Despite these dashing operations, protection of coastal shipping remained Fighter Command's most important task. The only enemy attacks on shore were made by Bf 109 fighter-bombers operating over the south coast from February to July. Thereafter the Luftwaffe continued cloud cover raids by small forces, or individual aircraft, made weather reconnaissance flights and continued attacking shipping. In the second six months of 1941, 28,000 defensive fighter sorties were flown to protect shipping—7/10 of the entire effort. Clearly the Command was fighting largely over the grey sea around our shores.

Important colour changes

On May 26, 1941, three Hurricane IIs of No 56 Squadron, North Weald, flew to Duxford for three-day experiments with camouflage for over-water purposes. On the second day, perchance, I saw to my surprise two of them, US-P:Z2586 and US-W:Z2767. Standing by the green-brown-Sky machines of 310 Sqn they looked most strange. Their upper surfaces were a very dark shade of grey where once they were green, the brown had been replaced by a rather dark grey and the under surfaces, too, were dark grey. Whether these colours equated any of future months it is not possible to say. Squadron codes were still light grey.

Back at North Weald the squadron apparently continued tests, for by mid-June all its machines were being experimentally and similarly painted. No 56 Squadron moved to Duxford on June 26, and when I next visited the airfield (on July 13) I counted nine Hurricanes with 'US' coding in Sky Type S and the colours described, although at least one certainly had dark green in place of the darkest grey. During July the squadron operated on sweeps, and it seems likely that these were the first fighters to go into action wearing the new paint scheme. At the time we called them 'sweep Hurricanes'. They had no Sky adornments, incidentally—at least not at any time when I saw them.

At Hawkers a change of camouflage had also been under review. On July 24, 1941, drawings produced showed the hitherto brown camouflage areas replaced by a shade called 'ocean grey', but possibly what became known as dark sea grey for the true Ocean Grey in use later had a very bluish tone. Dark green was retained, but duck egg green under surfaces changed to medium sea grey. Within the next four weeks the colour changes were again reviewed, and finalised in the case of the Hurricane on August 26, 1941. Fighter Command notified units that the change was to be made on August 21. Hurricanes were now to have an 18 inch wide Sky Type S rear fuselage band and Sky spinner. Squadron codes were also to change to Sky Type S (the true, light shade, that is), and serial numbers still eight inches high and five inches wide were to be applied so that their tops were in line with the tailplane centre-line. The serial was painted over the Sky band. The fuselage roundel was applied with the foremost part in line with the position of the radio mast. Upper wing 'B' roundels, centred 80 inches from the extreme tip of the wing, had an outer diameter of 49 inches, the red disc being 19½ inches across. The size and proportions of these roundels was in accord with Air Diagram 2001. A new feature now introduced was a yellow stripe extending 96¼ inches outboard of the wing leading-edge landing light, along the wing leading edge to a depth of three inches on top and beneath the wing, and extending two feet around the wing tip from the navigation light, and from there tapering to a stripe two inches wide on the wing tip surface—one inch above and one below. This was to aid identification from ahead. Gone, now, were the colours of the countryside, and in their place came sea greys and green which were to remain on European-based day-fighters during the war.

Fighters in service, 1941

At the start of 1941, home-based fighter squadrons were largely equipped with Hurricane Is and Spitfire Is and IIs, machine-gun fitted fighters. Soon new versions entered front line squadrons.

Basically a refined version of the Mk I, the Hurricane II was powered by a Merlin XX the prototype of which flew as P3269 on June 11, 1940. Production of the first version, the Mk IIA Series 1, commenced in August, 1940, at Langley. Z2308, first of these eight-gun fighters, was delivered to 'Treble-One' Squadron on September 2, 1940, along with

Z2309, Z2318 and Z2319. After a few days and the loss of one they were withdrawn for modifications. No 605 Sqn received a few before the year ended, including Z2323. The first batch of Mk IIA Series 1 comprised Z2308-2357, Z2382-426, Z2446-65, Z2479-528 and Z2560-94, delivered August 22, 1940, to January 12, 1941. During the early months of 1941 they were delivered to Nos 1, 17, 32, 56, 242, 249, 302 and 310 Squadrons.

An extra fuselage bay seven inches wide was added to the forward fuselage of the Mk IIA in October, lengthening the nose and producing the Mk IIA Series II upon which later versions of the Mk II were based. It had provision for the fitment of wings with heavier armament and attachment points for long-range tanks and various stores. The first machines were earlier IIAs modified, Z2344-47, Z2357, Z2382-85, Z2426, Z2446-47.

At the start of 1940 a 12-gun version of the Hurricane was proposed, but the shortage of Browning guns delayed introduction of this until after the Battle of Britain; thus the IIA appeared as an interim version. Production of the 12-gun version began in late November, 1940, and squadrons started to receive these in April, 1941, as Mk IIBs. Recipients were at first Nos 1, 3, 43, 71, 242, 249, 256, 302, 402, 601 and 615 Squadrons, for by then six factories were delivering, between them, about a dozen Hurricanes a day.

Delays in the delivery of cannon, and gun feed problems, delayed the cannon-armed Hurricane. Thirty sets of damaged wings were fitted with cannon, and the first (with drum feed) was flown on V7360 on December 5, 1940. On February 6, V2461, the first with the Chatellerault feed system, brought from France in 1940, was flown. By this time 100 'cannon wings' had been ordered from Hawkers. Production of the cannon armed version, the Mk IIC, then began and squadron deliveries started in June, 1941. Throughout that year Mks IIA/B/C were in large scale production, and in small batches of each to no particular pattern and within almost each serial block. BN370 had been reached approximately by the end of the year.

One other Hurricane variant deserves mention, the fighter-bomber. P2989 served as the trial installation machine during April, 1941, and in May, Z2326 went to Boscombe Down for type trials. 2 x 250 lb bombs were carried—later 2 x 500 lb bombs—on under-wing racks. The so-called 'Hurribomber' first went into action with No 607 Sqn on an anti-shipping attack with 607 Sqn on October 30, 1941.

As with the Hurricane, so with the Spitfire. An engine change led to a new range of Spitfires basically similar. The Merlin XLV was easily fitted to the Spitfire II airframe which was provided with strengthened longerons to carry the more powerful engine. Twenty-three re-engined Mk I and II Spitfires were produced by Rolls-Royce by February, 1941. Next month engine production permitted the Castle Bromwich factory to begin building some Spitfire Vs with the new engine. By June, all leaving the works were Mk Vs. At first these were Mk VAs with eight guns, as before. The next stage was the fitting of a special new wing accommodating two 20 mm cannon and four machine-guns, and later there was to come a further new wing able to mount two or four cannon and four .303

inch guns. Possible retrospective fitting of guns and engines soon made the Spitfire modification states too complicated to record fully here. Another field of research investigated was the addition of long-range tanks. First externally carried took the form of large slippers fitted to the outboard section of the port wing. Nos 66, 118 and 152 Squadrons used Spitfires thus modified for patrols of south-west England, and they were useful for convoy escort work. No 66 Squadron's aircraft at the end of 1941, Mk IIAs with these tanks, included P7607, P7999, P8072 and P8430.

To ensure that squadrons in the front line had the latest equipment, the newer Spitfires were based at the southern stations, so that when squadrons moved south they exchanged their old for the new, and left them behind when taking rest periods.

Some of the first cannon-armed Mk Vs were the old Mk IBs used unsuccessfully during the Battle of Britain by No 19 Sqn. They included R6809, R6833, R6923 and X4272, all of which served with No 91 Squadron at Manston in the early months of 1941. One of these, X4272, is believed to have been the first Mk VB to destroy enemy aircraft, a He 111 shot down off Southend on February 3, 1941.

Many of the earliest conversions to Mk V standard were of Mk Is or IIs re-engined but not re-armed and re-named Mk VA. These included N3044 (to 145 Sqn early 1941), P7447 (to 66 Sqn), P8236 (to 266 Sqn) and P8563 (315 Sqn). The first main batch of Mk Vs came in the 'W' serial range, of which W3109-14, '18, '19, '21, '23, '30, '36, '38, '69, '84, '85, 3213, '16, 3379 were Mk VAs and the remainder VBs. Delivery began on April 30, 1941, and by the end of the year Spitfires in the AA, AB, AD, AR and BL series (to about BL600) had been delivered.

Squadrons and their aircraft

The following listing is of home-based day-fighter aircraft and squadrons during 1941. Examples dated pre-August can be safely assumed to have brown-green-duck egg green finish. Those post-September can be accepted as having the ocean camouflage scheme. Usually unit letters were painted forward on the port and aft on the starboard side on the fuselage, but there were frequent exceptions even on individual squadrons.

Sqn	*Letters*	*Example*	*Aircraft type*	*Notes/dates, etc.*
1	JX	Z2810	Hurricane IIB	March 1941
1	JX	Z23778:Y	Hurricane IIC	December 1941
3	QO	Z2885:F	Hurricane IIB	May 1941
3	QO	Z3068:C	Hurricane IIC	October 1941
17	YB	Z2497	Hurricane IIA	March 1941
19	QV	P7995	Spit IIA/LR	Wing slipper tanks, August 1941
19	QV	AD332	Spitfire VB	November 1941
32	GZ	V7425	Hurricane IIA	January 1941 (half black wing)
41	EB	P7618:Z	Spitfire IIA	Early 1941
43	FT	Z3134	Hurricane IIB	April 1941
46	PO	V7443	Hurricane IIA	February 1941 (to Middle East July 1941)
54	KL	P7618:Z	Spitfire IIA	Mid 1941
56	US	Z2664:O	Hurricane IIA	March 1941
64	SH	W3248	Spitfire VB	December 1941

40 *One of the new types which came into its own in 1941 was the Westland Whirlwind. P6984:HE-H of 263 Sqn shown here wears the unusual paint scheme applied to the Whirlwinds. Unlike other fighters they had pale blue (not duck egg green) and black under surfaces. One Whirlwind was recorded so painted as late as June 22 1941, P6997 being the machine. HE-H wears black under surfaces to the port wing, and has sky spinners and fuselage band. This aircraft is drawn in Figure 24* (IWM).

41 *One of the American types, Mohawk IV AR645 wearing grey-green fighter colours with sky trim which included the small 'spinner'.*

42 *AS430, one of the few Buffalo fighters flown in Britain. This has green-brown-duck egg green finish and a black spinner* (IWM).

43 *Curtiss Tomahawk AH769 photographed about January 1941, with her port wing (only) painted black and the roundel thereon outlined in yellow. Other under surfaces duck egg green: sky bands and trim. Note the unusual styling of the serial digits and letter A.*

44 *Havoc II AH522 in the very matt RDM2 black finish. This machine was pictured before delivery to a squadron. Serials are in light grey and the ortho film used at this time makes the yellow surround to the roundel appear darker than the blue* (IWM).

45 *This close view of Havoc II AH522 shows very well the velvet-like matt black texture of RDM2 night-fighter finish. Note also the A.I radar aerials* (IWM)

46 *A line-up of 601 Squadron Airacobras with AH585:UF-O nearest and AH602:UF-W next* (The Aeroplane).

47 *Airacobra I AH601 being serviced at Duxford. This aircraft and UF-O, above, are drawn in Figure 8* (The Aeroplane).

48 *Without doubt the Mustang I was one of the most aesthetically appealing American aircraft of World War 2. AG348 seen here was the fourth machine. Green-brown-duck egg green finish with spinner probably brown, too, at this stage.*

49 *P5212 the first Typhoon in its original glossy grey finish, worn for only a short time before camouflage superseded it. Under surfaces are black and white* (IWM).

50 *Hurricane IIBs of No 174 Sqn at Manston in the early spring of 1942. XP-Y is BE684, XP-G is BE421. 'G' has exhaust guard for night flying* (IWM).

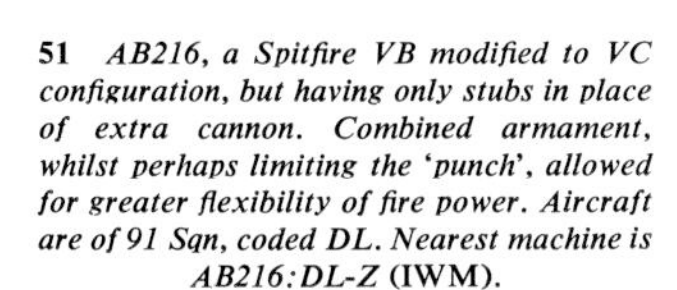

51 *AB216, a Spitfire VB modified to VC configuration, but having only stubs in place of extra cannon. Combined armament, whilst perhaps limiting the 'punch', allowed for greater flexibility of fire power. Aircraft are of 91 Sqn, coded DL. Nearest machine is AB216:DL-Z* (IWM).

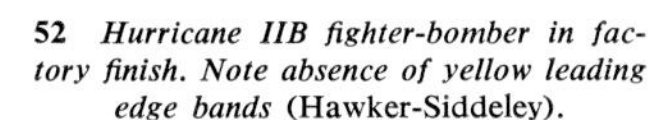

52 *Hurricane IIB fighter-bomber in factory finish. Note absence of yellow leading edge bands* (Hawker-Siddeley).

53 *A famous Hurricane 'night-intruder' was Kuttelwascher's 'Night Reaper', LK-R (a Mk IIC) of 87 Sqn in special night finish, grey-green-black with what appears to be a shade of grey coding. Pictured when freshly painted, the serials are obliterated* (IWM).

54 *Tomahawk IIB AK184 in green-brown-duck egg green scheme. Note the not unusual absence of the sky band. Spinner is also sky. Roundels are Type C. and the aircraft was thus adorned in October 1942.*

55 *R7847, an early Typhoon IB with clear view canopy. Deep exhaust stack fitted, but no underwing stripes or yellow leading edge band yet applied. At Duxford, prior to delivery to 266 Sqn* (IWM)

56 *A formation of 56 Sqn Typhoons with black and white bands and spinners with the black band added. Yellow stripes extend across the upper wing surfaces. US-Y: R8825 is nearest. US-C is DN317* (Flight International).

57 *EK183 in the early months of 1943 showing the ultimate in Typhoon markings of the period. The black band on the spinner was intentionally marked to aid head-on recognition and retained during 1943* (Flight International).

58 *Close-up of the nose installation of centimetric radar on a Beaufighter Mk I.*

59 *Beaufighter VIF V8619 with A.I aerials, grey-green finish, and dihedral tail-plane* (IWM).

60 *Another view of a Beaufighter VIF, V8442, shows clearly the sea grey medium used for lower and upper surfaces alike with dark green providing the disruption for upper surface camouflage. There are no underwing roundels* (IWM).

Sqn	*Letters*	*Example*	*Aircraft type*	*Notes/dates, etc.*
65	YT	P8147:W	Spitfire IIA	March 1941
66	LZ	X4331	Spitfire I	March 1941
71	XR	V6919:T	Hurricane I	April 1941
71	XR	BL382:J	Spitfire VB	December 1941
72	RN	X4486:C	Spitfire I	February 1941 (half black wing)
72	RN	P8517:N	Spitfire IIA	May 1941
72	RN	W3437:A	Spitfire VB	September 1941
73	TP	Z4697:G	Hurricane I	June 1941
74	JH	W3210	Spitfire VB	May 1941
79	NV	Z3156:F	Hurricane IIA	June 1941
91	DL	P7735	Spitfire IIA	February 1941 (half black wing)
91	DL	W3126	Spitfire VB	May 1941
92	QJ	R6923:S	Spitfire VB	June 1941
111	JU	P8191	Spitfire IIA	July 1941
118	NK	P7913:K	Spitfire IIA	Dec 1941 (Sqn reformed Feb 1941)
122	MT	AA930	Spitfire VB	Dec 1941 (Sqn reformed May 1941)
123	XE	BL373	Spitfire VB	Dec 1941 (Sqn reformed May 1941)
124	ON	R7074	Spitfire IIA	May 1941 (Sqn reformed May 1941)
129	DV	W3824	Spitfire VB	Sept 1941 (Sqn reformed June 1941)
130	PJ	BL712:X	Spitfire VB	Early 1942? (Sqn reformed June 1941)
131	NX	AD411:B	Spitfire VB	Dec 1941 (reformed June 1941)
132	FF	P8257	Spitfire IIB	Dec 1941 (reformed July 1941)
133	MD	P7994	Spitfire IIA	Sept 1941 (reformed August 1941)
137	SF	P6972	Whirlwind I	November 1941
145	SO	X4854:A	Spitfire VB	May 1941
152	SN	P7844	Spitfire IIA	March 1941
154	?	P7983	Spitfire IIA	November 1941 (Sqn formed November 1941)
222	ZD	AB140:F	Spitfire VB	December 1941
232	?	P3422	Hurricane I	February 1941
234	AZ	W3936:W	Spitfire VB	October 1941
234	AZ	P7925:W	Spitfire IIA	May 1941
242	LE	Z2513	Hurricane II	April 1941
245	DX	Z3237	Hurricane IIB	October 1941
247	ZY	Z2572	Hurricane IIA	July 1941
249	GN	Z2522	Hurricane IIA	March 1941 (Sqn to Malta 1941)
253	SW	V7619	Hurricane I	February 1941
257	DT	V6873:O	Hurricane I	December 1940 (half black wing)
263	HE	P6969:V	Whirlwind I	July 1941
266	UO	W3828	Spitfire VB	December 1941
302	WX	Z3023	Hurricane IIB	May 1941
303	RF	V6637	Hurricane I	January 1941
303	RF	P7962	Spitfire IIA	April 1941
306	UZ	Z3065	Hurricane IIB	May 1941
308	ZF	W3825	Spitfire VB	September 1941
310	NN	P3148:N	Hurricane I	March 1941
312	DU	V6885:V	Hurricane I	January 1941 (half black wing)
313	RY	R7117	Spitfire IIA	May 1941
315	SZ	W3761	Spitfire VB	September 1941 (formed January 1941)
316	PK	AA928	Spitfire VB	November 1941 (formed February 1941)

Sqn	*Letters*	*Example*	*Aircraft type*	*Notes/date recorded*
317	JH	AD367	Spitfire VB	December 1941 (formed February 1941)
331	FN	Z3987	Hurricane I	September 1941
340	GW	P7915:J	Spitfire IIA	December 1941
350	MN	P8146	Spitfire IIA	December 1941
401	YO	AA973	Spitfire VB	December 1941
402	AE	BE492:E	Hurricane IIB	November 1941
411	DB	AD356	Spitfire VB	November 1941
412	VZ	AD318	Spitfire VB	October 1941
416	DN	AB370	Spitfire VB	December 1941
452	UD	AB792	Spitfire VB	September 1941
457	BP	X4023	Spitfire I	September 1941
485	OU	AD355	Spitfire VB	October 1941
501	SD	X4854:G	Spitfire IIA	May 1941
501	SD	AB279:G	Spitfire VB	December 1941
601	UF	V7104:B	Hurricane I	January 1941 (half black wing)
601	UF	BD712:Y	Hurricane IIB	September 1941
602	LO	AA942	Spitfire VB	December 1941
603	XT	AB134	Spitfire VB	December 1941
605	UP	Z4969:O	Hurricane IIA	March 1941
607	?	Z3082	Hurricane IIB	September 1941
609	PR	W3238:B	Spitfire VB	June 1941
609	PR	W3117	Spitfire VA	April 1941
610	DW	AA975	Spitfire VB	December 1941
611	FY	W3816	Spitfire VB	September 1941
615	KW	Z3028	Hurricane IIB	August 1941
616	YQ	W3560	Spitfire VB	September 1941

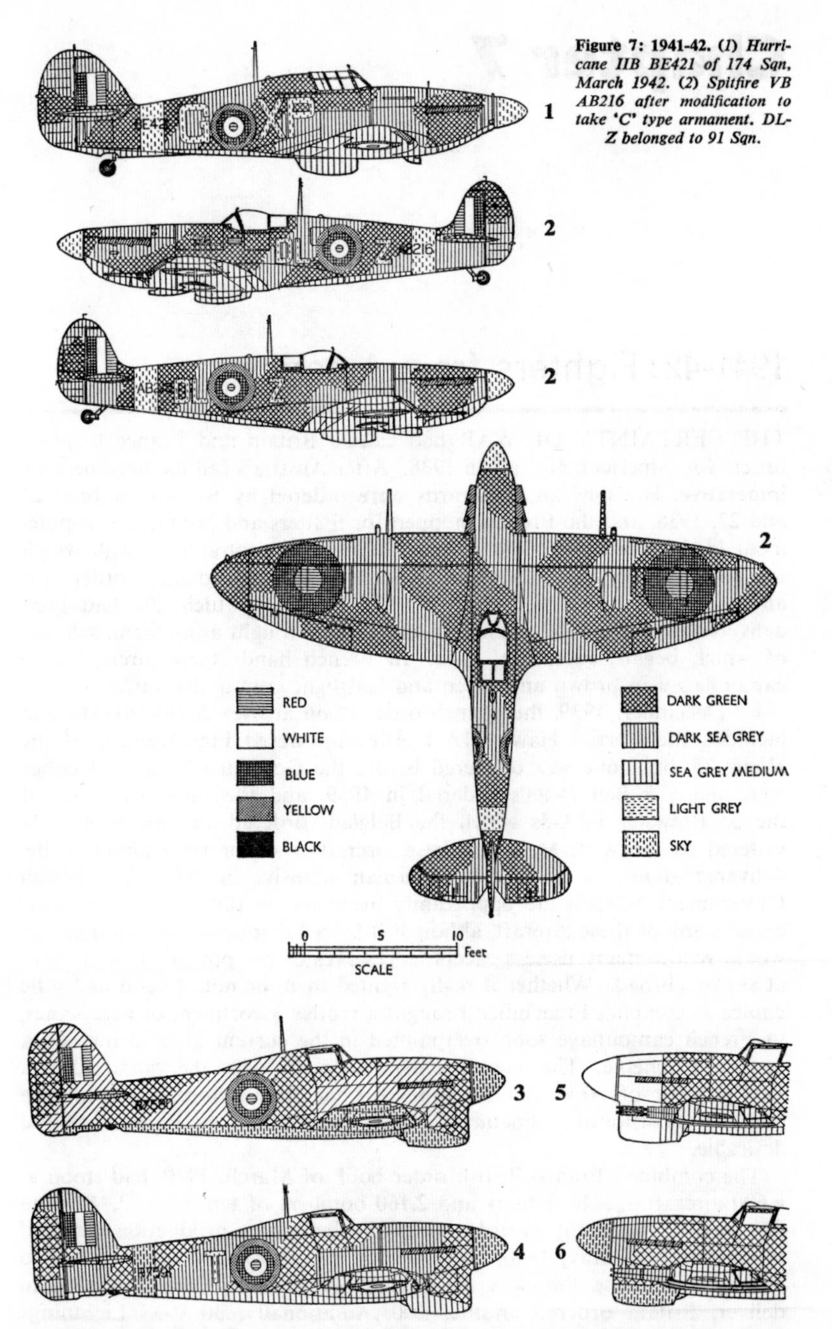

Figure 7: 1941-42. (*1*) *Hurricane IIB BE421 of 174 Sqn, March 1942.* (*2*) *Spitfire VB AB216 after modification to take 'C' type armament. DL-Z belonged to 91 Sqn.*

(3) Typhoon I R7580 depicted as seen at the start of September 1941, at Duxford. (4) Typhoon I R7591 as 'T', one of 56 Squadron's early aircraft as on December 22 1941, coded R at one time, too. (5) Nose with white finish (interim) applied to 56 Sqn aircraft on December 11 1942. (6) Nose with the scheme carried by 181 Sqn aircraft

Chapter 7

1941-42: Fighters from America

THE CERTAINTY OF WAR had caused Britain and France to place orders for American aircraft in 1938. After Austria's fall the need became imperative. Hudsons and Harvards were ordered by Britain on June 22 and 23, 1938, and the French shopped for fighters and bombers to supplement likely production, and replace the archaic contraptions with which they mainly hoped to defend themselves. France placed large orders for an assortment of Curtiss Hawk 75A fighters, of which 291 had been delivered by June, 1940. Many air battles were fought using them, delivery of which began December, 1938. In French hands these aircraft were camouflaged in brown and green and had light grey under surfaces.

By December, 1939, the French order stood at over 2,000 aircraft, and included the Curtiss Hawk 81A-1 Allison-powered improvement of the Hawk 75, but none was delivered before the German take-over. Neither were the 675 Bell P-400s ordered in 1939, and the same was true of the 35 Brewster F2A-3s which the Belgians ordered and the Hawk 75s ordered by Norway. Many of these aircraft were, or were about to be, delivered about the time of the German offensive in 1940. The British Government grasped the opportunity presented to obtain by direct purchase many of these aircraft, although it feared that poor fighting qualities would render many useless except as reserves or for possible employment at sea or abroad. Whether it really wanted them or not, it soon had little choice as escaping Frenchmen brought a motley assortment of aeroplanes, in French camouflage soon overpainted in the current green-brown-duck egg green scheme. The machines Britain bought were the vanguard of a vast number of American machines for the British forces, which were later to incorporate refinements which the conflict in Europe showed desirable.

The combined Franco-British order book of March, 1940, had stood at 4,600 aircraft—2,440 fighters and 2,160 bombers of ten types. 2,440 were for Britain, which cut its order to 2,003 when home production gathered momentum. In May, 1940, an order for 300 Hawk 81s was switched to Britain and, since this was the best fighter that America was able to deliver, Britain ordered another 200. Additionally, 30 P-38 Lightnings were ordered, and 40 of the new Bell P-39s.

On June 8, six Brewster fighters named Buffalo were obtained from the carrier *Berne,* and instead of going to Belgium were shipped to Britain. 'Shipped' immediately became an important word since every aeroplane would have to be crated, be subject to torpedo attack en route and to bombing on arrival. Surprisingly few airframes were lost in either manner, and the big headache which these early American machines gave the British was to prove long lasting.

Sometimes the aircraft arrived in natural aluminium finish with special protective skinning. When the Americans applied camouflage they often applied the wrong shades, and usually curious schemes making the under surface colours creep up the fuselage sides. For months many of the early aircraft hung around erection centres and MUs, and it was late 1940 before they were flying in any numbers.

Five Hawk 75As arrived in July, 1940, and a dozen Buffaloes, vanguard of 180 ordered by Britain as F2A-2s in 1939 embracing W8131-8250 and AN168-217, most of which were diverted to the Far East. They were proved outclassed during the Japanese attacks of December, 1941. Most of the 35 Belgian-ordered Buffaloes (AS410-437 included) came to Burtonwood for preparation in the summer of 1940. Many were transferred to the Royal Navy wearing green-brown/duck egg green camouflage as applied to RAF fighters. A rather unkind notion existed to equip No 71 Squadron, the first American-manned Eagle Squadron, with Buffaloes. Indeed, three were issued to the unit at Church Fenton, but one was soon written off and Hurricanes from 85 Sqn replaced the Buffaloes. Overall performance of the machine was poor. Its .50 inch guns were changed to .303s to reduce weight, and the ammunition load was cut, also the fuel load. Apart from some trial examples at Heathrow, Buffaloes were rare oddities in Britain.

In 1939, a Curtiss Hawk 75A (No 188) was tested in Britain. It had poor fire-power and was too slow for European combat British style, but it was a very manoeuvrable aeroplane. Further extensive tests at Boscombe Down were flown by AR644 and AR645, for the Hawk 75As arrived in Britain in embarrassingly high numbers in the summer of 1940. The trickle from France included Hawk 75A-1s with only two fuselage-mounted guns, 75A-2s with an extra two wing guns, and the 75A-3 with four wing guns. Britain also received 75As ordered by Norway and these. with some of the earliest French machines, were designated Mohawk I.

Possibly the 75A-2s were called Mohawk IIs and the A-3s Mk IIIs, although it seems likely that these early marks covered various anomalies All were powered by a Pratt & Whitney Twin Wasp. Britain ordered Hawk 75A-4 to -8 variants powered by the Wright Cyclone, and designated them Mohawk IVs. Over 100 of the latter came to Britain in 1940, but none flew operationally although they acquired standard fighter colours. For the most part a mere handful became noisy shapes at Farnborough, Boscombe and Duxford. AX886, BS789 and BL220, amongst others, served at Odiham as advanced trainers. Several that I saw flying from Duxford had silver under surfaces. One, BS744, that I recorded firing its guns at AFDU Duxford on July 13, 1941, had duck egg green under surfaces and the usual 18 inch rear fuselage band. By September it had grey-green-grey camouflage.

A few Mohawks lingered almost to the end of the war on communications duties, wearing current fighter paint schemes. They included AR630 and AR633 used by 24 Sqn and later by 510 Sqn at Hendon. Mostly the Mohawks were disposed of to Portugal, South Africa, the Middle East and in particular to the Far East, where they gave very good service.

The first Hawk 81A-1 Tomahawk arrived in England in September, 1940. It was one from 140 which the RAF took over from the French order. Early machines had only two fuselage guns, but successive improvements led to the Tomahawk IA and IB with heavier wing armament. Again, the story was the same. Here was an aeroplane that would be no match for the Luftwaffe, yet had some points to commend it . . . except, of course, its liking for ground loops. Tomahawks were arriving in large numbers towards the end of 1940. Whilst many were being erected, trials were flown and possible employment considered. Boscombe tested AX900 and at Duxford I found AH863 still on trials and firing her guns at the butts on April 5, 1941. AH861 was there, too, and the markings on these two typified those of Tomahawks. Both were camouflaged dark green and dark earth, and had duck egg green under surfaces. Sky spinners and rear fuselage 18 inch bands were worn. During the winter weeks, incidentally, the Tomahawks had acquired black under surfaces to their port wings, the underside roundels of which had yellow outlines.

Tactical trials showed that the aircraft performed quite well at low levels. It was decided, therefore, to issue Tomahawks to army co-operation squadrons, mainly replacing Lysanders, a process begun in April, 1941. These machines were coloured like those aforementioned, and typified by AH848 coded SP-Y (medium grey codes, unit letters forward) which I recorded thus marked on August 18, 1941. Brown-green finish was retained on the army co-operation recce-fighters until July-August, 1942, when the change to grey-green was made an Official general requirement, as opposed to a Fighter Command order.

Later the Tomahawk IIA and IIB, Hawk 81-A2 and -A3 respectively, appeared with four wing guns and two fuselage guns. The first version had British equipment and the second American. Late in 1942, Tomahawks retained their browns and greens, and on September 6, AH947 and AK137 at Bottisham in the hands of 241 Sqn, but uncoded, still wore these colours, though soon after they conformed to the usual grey-green finish with Sky codes and trim and yellow wing leading edges. The Tomahawk squadrons and examples of their machines used in Britain were:

Sqn	*Unit Code*	*Serial*	*Date/notes*
2	XV:S	AH942	In use 8.41; earlier aircraft were coded KO
4	?	AH791	Possibly never carried any squadron code; 4.42
26	RM:Y	AH896	6.41. Used for offensive ops, late in 1941
168	EK	AH861	7.42. Sqn formed summer 1942; green-brown acft
171	?	AK137	7.42. Possibly never had squadron code
231	MV?	AH947	5.42. Possibly never had squadron code
239	HB	AH880	7.41

Sqn	*Unit Code*	*Serial*	*Date/notes*
241	RZ	AK137	9.41. 241 Sqn aircraft had grey codes
268	OE:B	AH896	23.8.42; OE forward on both sides; grey-green camouflage. NM code probably carried earlier, but certainly coded OE from 8.42
400	SP:Z	AH756	In use 5.41
403	KH:H	AH896	In use 4.41; grey codes, Sky band, spinner
414	RU:Z	AH935	In use 9.41
613	SY	AH905	In use 8.41

Tomahawks flew low-level offensive strikes, usually in pairs, on fringe continental targets in 1941-42.

The Douglas DB-7 became available to Britain as a result of broken French contracts and a few escapees. This aircraft was in no sense a fighter in its early form, and the first machines were designated Boston I or II bombers depending upon engine type. There seemed initially no apparent use for the machines except as trainers, but deliveries built up as the German night blitz was reaching its climax. It was therefore decided to issue the DB-7 as the Havoc I night-intruder, deliveries probably beginning with AX849 and AX850 to No 23 Squadron in October, 1940. Still in green-brown-duck egg green finish (quite unsuited to night operations), these machines carried four guns in the base of the nose which retained its transparency. In December, before operations commenced, they acquired RDM2 black finish and almost white code letters. During 1941, 23 Sqn completely equipped with Havoc intruders.

A second use to which the Havoc was put was as an all-black night-fighter, with white code letters which changed to red about September, 1941. An extra four .303 inch guns were fitted in the 'solid' nose and full 'bow and arrow' aerials on the nose and wings for A.I Mk VI, readily carried in the plentiful space available. A handful of Havoc Is were modified to carry the Long Aerial Mine as Havoc IIIs, later known as Havoc I (Pandora). Over 30 Mk Is had a Helmore searchlight fitted in their shorn noses. Batteries in the bomb bay gave it power. Unarmed, these aircraft patrolled using A.I radar to guide them to their quarry, which they then illuminated for Hurricanes on either beam to destroy. Development was lengthy and the techniques took long to perfect. By 1942, when it came into use in ten units it was already being outmoded by the success of A.I equipped night-fighters, although it was 1943 before the Turbinlite squadrons disbanded.

Britain also took over the French order for Douglas DB-7As with their longer nacelles and vertical tail surfaces of greater area. They were powered by Double Cyclones. Martin Baker designed a new nose for some of these aeroplanes, carrying 12 × .303 inch machine-guns and nearly 100 were thus modified as fighters.

Space permits only a very brief survey of the Havocs and their squadrons, for this was a most involved story. Main units and representative machines were:

Sqn	*Unit code*	*Example*	*Notes*
Havoc I			
23	YP:G	BB900	Intruder; 'Solid' nose. Mid '41
85	VY:R	BJ472	'Solid' fighter nose. Mid '41
93	HN:G	BB893	L.A.M. machine. Mid '41
605	UP	BB895	Intruder; transparent nose. Mid '42
1422 Flt	?	BJ497	Turbinlite trials machine. Oct '41
Havoc II			
85	VY:A	AH500	In use in the summer of 1942
1422 Flt	?	AH483	Night-fighter trials unit

In addition, Nos 1451-1460 Flights (later 530-539 Squadrons) used a very large number of Havocs, some with Turbinlites and some with 'solid' fighter noses. Typical examples included BD110 (534 Sqn), BJ470 (1456 Flt) and BJ467 (532 Sqn). Probably all of these units carried squadron codes and 1457 Flt may have carried the letters JO. Unit codes on the Havocs were invariably carried immediately aft of the mainplane. Many of the Turbinlite machines were really Boston IIIs converted to carry searchlights, and not Havocs, and included W8257 and W8303 of 531 Sqn based at West Malling and W8398 of 1451 Flt and later used by 530 Sqn whose unit codes are known for sure to have been NH, from late 1942 until it disbanded in January, 1943.

About 80 of the 675 Bell Airacobras eventually ordered for the RAF were accepted for service. Poor performance and low engine-altitude rating made them useful only for ground strafing, but already Tomahawks were well established and proving less troublesome, and the Mustang was not far behind. The first Airacobras for trials arrived at AAEE and AFDU in July, 1941, DS174 was one which I recorded as Duxford on July 13, wearing dark green, dark earth and duck egg, green with Sky spinner and band. A few weeks later, pilots came from 601 Sqn to Duxford to begin working up on the new type. Delivery of Airacobras with dark sea grey-dark green/medium sea grey colouring with Sky band and spinner began at Matlask in August. During October, the squadron, now at Duxford, busily trained. Placing of squadron codes was unusual, for the letters UF appeared ahead of the roundels on both sides of the fuselage and the individual letter far forward, as on UF-J:AH593, UF-O:AH585, UF-W:AH602 and UF-N:AH582. All the Airacobras I saw in 601's hands had the winged sword motif of the squadron painted in black on the white stripe of the fin. An interesting feature of this latter was that on some machines it sloped slightly aft, and did so on UF-W and AH601 the squadron commander's aircraft. On October 9, a handful of Airacobras detached to Manston made the type's debut over France, shooting up coastal targets. But the operational phase totalled only eight sorties and an accumulation of snags led to the aircraft being withdrawn in March. The squadron was then at Acaster Malbis, and the Airacobras left for Colerne and soon joined the large number sent to Rusia.

Another American type which deserves mention is the Lockheed P-38 Lightning, for its unorthodox shape always captured interest. In April, 1940, the RAF ordered 150. Later the order was vastly increased for what seemed like a businesslike machine. Yet again performance was poor, and

For scale and colour key, see Figure 8.

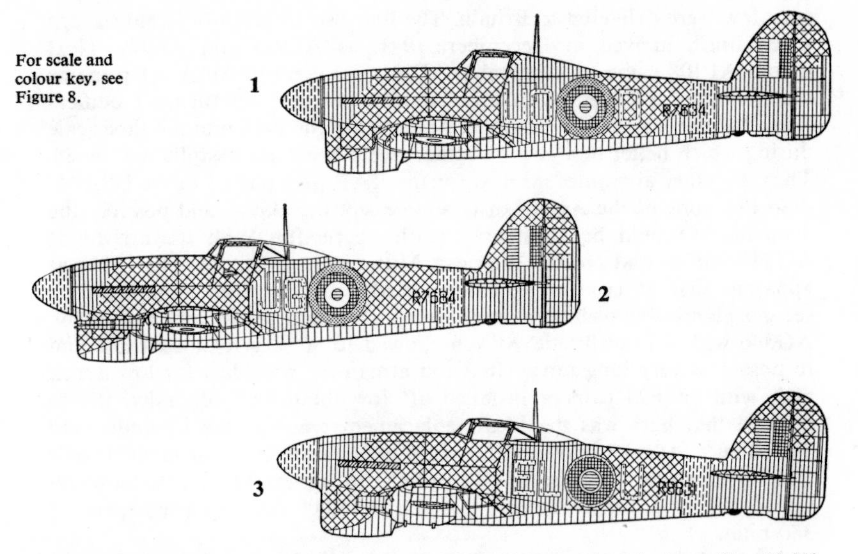

Figure 8: Early Typhoon and Airacobra markings. *(1) R7634:UO-D, an early production machine with 266 Sqn in February-March 1942. (2) R7684:JG, the Duxford Wing Leader's aircraft in the summer of 1942, with fairings in the cannon. (3) R8831:EL-U, one of the first Typhoon fighter-bombers, late 1942, prior to the introduction of special markings. Note minor modifications to the hoods on some aircraft.*

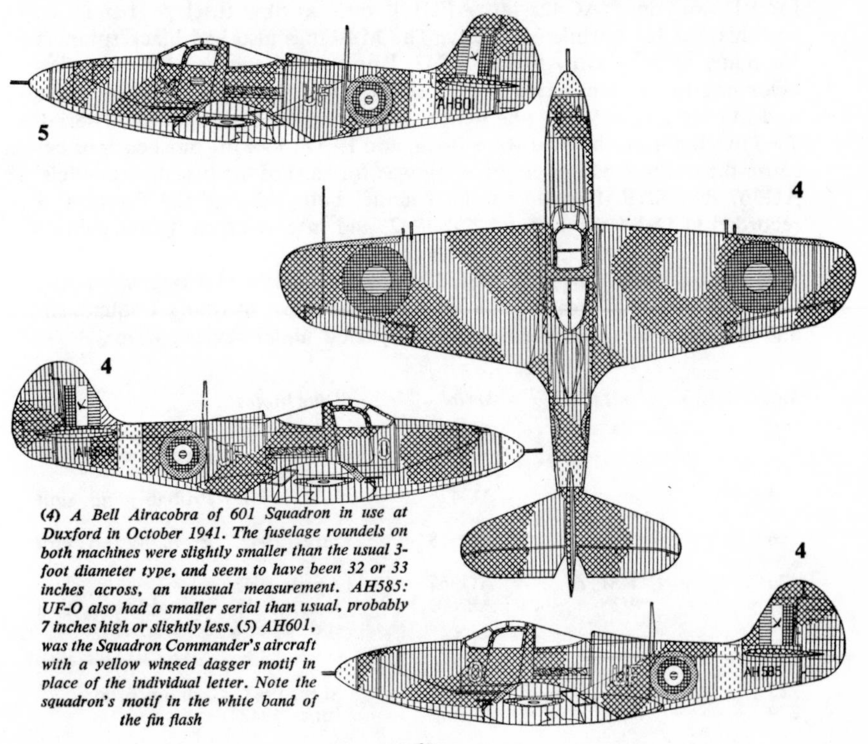

(4) A Bell Airacobra of 601 Squadron in use at Duxford in October 1941. The fuselage roundels on both machines were slightly smaller than the usual 3-foot diameter type, and seem to have been 32 or 33 inches across, an unusual measurement. AH585: UF-O also had a smaller serial than usual, probably 7 inches high or slightly less. (5) AH601, was the Squadron Commander's aircraft with a yellow winged dagger motif in place of the individual letter. Note the squadron's motif in the white band of the fin flash

very few were delivered to Britain. The first two in green-brown-duck egg green finish arrived in December, 1941, as AE978 and AE979. Next month AF108 came to Boscombe. AF106 was there in April, after engine modifications at Coventry. In July, AF105 came with still further modifications, but the lengthy development period took the P-38 into the time scale during which better new British fighters were being successfully developed. Thus the other airframes marked for the RAF were passed to the USAAC

So far, none of the American types—except the Havoc and possibly the Tomahawk—could be considered really successful. With the arrival of AG346, the second North American Mustang I, in October, 1941, it was apparent that at last the Americans had produced something worth a second glance—as well as a machine which might prove very successful. AG346 with a low-altitude Allison showed itself very manoeuvrable and to possess a very long range. Its good armament was ideal for low attack and, with an F24 camera installed aft for oblique photography, it was decided that here was the ideal replacement type for the Lysander and Tomahawk. AG365 arrived at Duxford in January, 1942 for tactical trials and comparison with the Bf 109 which, to an extent, it externally resembled. Low down it was very fast and at 15,000 feet had a top speed of 380 mph.

Again, these fighters delivered in quantity in the first three months of 1942, had dark green-dark earth-duck egg green finish. Although I saw quite a large number of them, it was May 25, 1942 before I saw one (AG422 at AFDU) with a Sky fuselage band . . . and this was for a while an oddity. The Mustangs also had black spinners for many months. On April 26, 1942, I first noted some coded examples, belonging to 241 Sqn based at Bottisham where they had begun to arrive mid-March. AG-405 was one which, like others, had a hyphenated serial. Two machines on the field were B-RZ and E-RZ, looking most curious because the entire medium grey coding was forward of the fuselage roundels. AG367:RM-Z (RM ahead of the roundel both sides of the fuselage) I recorded at Debden on March 17, 1942, and in grey-green fighter colours with usual Sky trim and yellow leading edge stripe.

Mustangs began low-level paired strikes on Continental targets on July 27, 1942, probably wearing the grey-green scheme. Mustang I squadrons and examples of their machines in the period under review, were:

Sqn	*Unit Code*	*Serial*	*Date/notes*
2	XV:V	AM112	July, 1942. Grey-green, C1 roundels; earlier coding UG was used
4	—	AG426	July, 1942. Probably no unit code
16	—	AG573	July, 1942. Probably no unit code
26	RM:Z	AG367	April, 1942
169	VI	AL988	June, 1942. Probably no unit code after a few weeks?
170	—	AL970	June, 1942. Probably no unit code
225	WU?	AG414	May, 1942. Code uncertain
239	HB	AG472	June, 1942

Sqn	*Unit Code*	*Serial*	*Date/notes*
241	RZ:W	AG645	June, 1942; conventional code placing now. AG512:RZ-A green/grey finish. September, 1942
268	NM?	AG413	June, 1942. Probably no unit code
400	SP:P	AG521	November, 1942. Grey/green finish
414	RU	AG420	June, 1942
613	SY:I	AG495	April, 1942

Summary of fighter aircraft acquired from the USA 1940-42, excluding those supplied under Lend-Lease

Bell P-39 Airacobra I: AH570-739 (about 80 of these reached the RAF) AP264-384 (mainly to USAAF in UK; others to USSR), BW100-183 and BX135-434 (mainly to USAAF in UK and to USSR), DS173-175 bought for evaluation and received in Britain July, 1941.

Brewster 339 Buffalo: W8131-8250 mainly shipped direct to Singapore also AN168-217. AS410-437 mainly to Royal Navy. BB450 passed to Royal Navy 9.40, ex-Belgian contract. AX811-820 mainly to Royal Navy.

Curtiss Hawk 75A/P-36/Mohawk Mks I to IV: AR630-694 mixed III/IV, AX880-898 (ex-French order; shipped overseas), BB918-937 and BB974-979 (shipped abroad), BJ531-550 (Mk IV; mainly shipped abroad), Mk IVs known to have BJ serials: BJ574, 575, 577, 581, 582, 583, 587, 588; BK569-588 (Mk III, ex-French; shipped overseas), BK876-879, BL220-223, BS730-738 (Mk IV), BS744-747 (Mk IV), BS784-798 (Mk IV), BT470-472 (Mk IV) all these in the BS series being mainly disposed of overseas. LA157-158 and LA163-165 known to have been airframes assembled in India.

Curtiss Hawk 81/Tomahawk: AH741-880 (Mk I), AH881-990 (Mk IIA), AH991-999 (Mk IIB of which 24 went to USSR), AK100-570 (Mk IIB—some to AVG others lost at sea or to Eygptian Air Force), AM370-519 (Mk IIB mainly to AVG in China), AN218-517 (Mk IIB—many to USSR and Middle East), BK852-853 (Mk I).

Douglas DB-7 Boston/Havoc I: AE457-472 (AE458-463, AE465-469, 471 known to have been converted to Havoc I but mainly left with clear nose—some used as trainers for bomber crews after conversion); AW392-393, AW400, AW401, AW404, AW406—all Havoc I, ex-Boston II; AW411, 412 both Havoc I (Turbinlite); AX848, AX851 (Boston Is converted to Havoc I); AX910-918 (Boston I converted to Havoc I); AX921, AX923, AX924, AX930, AX936, AX974, AX975 (Boston I converted into Havoc I); AX924 and AX930 converted to Havoc I (Turbinlite); BB891-895, BB896-904, BB907-909, BB911-912 (converted to Havoc I ex-Boston I); BB897, 899, 907-909 to Havoc I (Turbinlite): BD110-127 (Boston Is converted to Havoc I); BD110, 111, 120, to Havoc I (Turbinlite); BJ458-477, BJ485-501 (French Boston order; converted to Havoc I: BJ460, 461, 467, 469, 470 to Havoc I (Turbinlite), BK882 Havoc I (Turbinlite), BK883 (Havoc I Intruder and LAM), BL227-228 Havoc I, BT460-465 Havoc I, BV203 Havoc I, DG554-555 Havoc I.

Douglas DB-7 Havoc II: W8274, W8277, W8317, W8328, W8341, W8352, W8366, W8369, W8393, W8396, AH431, AH432, AH434, AH437, AH445, AH446, AH447, AH450-53, AH455, AH458, AH460, AH462, AH470-73, AH478-79, AH481, AH483, AH487, AH490, AH491, AH497, AH500, AH502-3, AH505, AH509-10, AH512, AH518, AH520, AH523-25, A528-29, AH431, AH432, AH434, AH436, AH444-47, AH450-51, AH453, AH460, AH468, AH470, AH472-73, AH478-79, AH483-84, AH491, AH497, AH503, AL750, AL774, AL778, AL780, all Turbinlite equipped Mk IIs.

Also operated in a fighter role were these Boston II Intruders: W8256, W8262. W8264, W8266, W8268, W8278, W8281, W8283, W8284, W8290, W8292. Some Turbinlite equipped Boston IIIs in the W series were W8257, W8265, W8275, W8276 and W8300. In addition the following were Boston IIIs converted into 'solid nosed' night-fighters; W8274, W8277, W8317, W8328, W8341, W8352, W8366, W8369, W8393 and W8396.

North American Mustang I: AG345-664, AL958-AM257, AP164-263.

Lockheed Lightning: 143 Mk I ordered as AE978-AF220 and 524 Mk IIs as AF221-744. Of these very few reached Britain, although many flew with British serials and quite a number in RAF camouflage. AE978, AE979, AF105, AF106 and AF108 certainly reached Britain for trial purposes.

Figure 9: Havoc night-fighters. *(1) Havoc II AH500:VY-A of No 85 Sqn in summer 1942 with red codes and serials. (2) Havoc I (Turbinlite) AW400:ZQ-A of the Fighter Interception Unit, early 1942, with very light grey codes and red serials. (3) Havoc I (Intruder) BD112:YP-T of No 23 Sqn used as a night intruder in 1941 with very light grey codes and serials. Fuselage roundels on Havocs were basically 48 inches in diameter but alterations could be seen to white and yellow areas on some machines. Fin flashes were 24 inches wide and 27 inches high. Serials, 8 inches high, sometimes looked unusual due to spacing of digits, etc, on imported machines. They sometimes has a 'dot' between prefix letters and digits.*

For scale and colour key, see Figure 14.

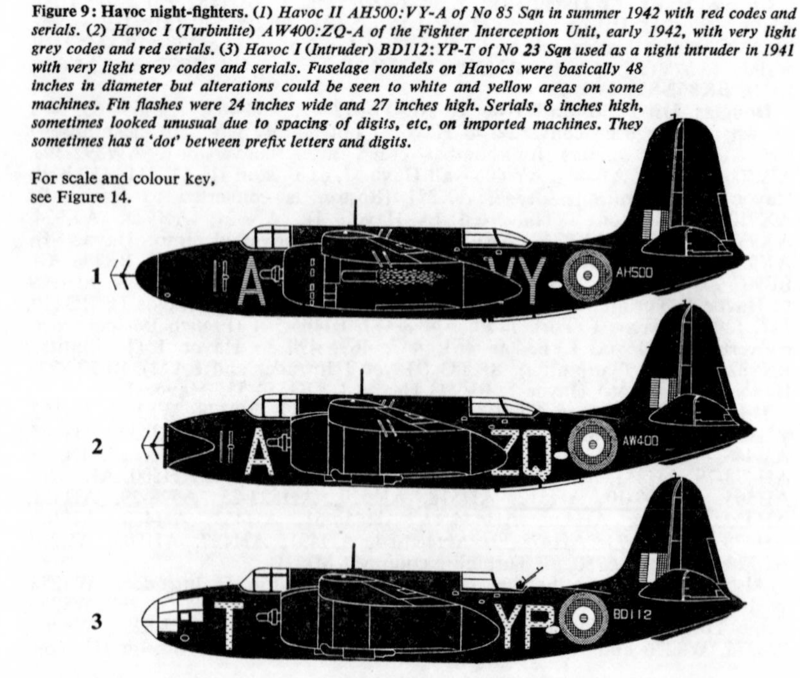

Chapter 8

1942: Offensive over Europe

WHETHER TO PILOT, engineer or keen observer, initial confrontation by a Typhoon was memorable. This, the first 'second generation fighter' to enter RAF service in World War 2, had a long and unhappy development stage. It was the subject of alarming stories—mostly true ones. As the first Hurricanes left Hawkers, attention was already directed towards replacement for the 1940s. This was to be a larger, faster interceptor, packing a 12-gun punch. Events soon frustrated these enthusiastic plans. Two possible engines had been selected. One was the Rolls-Royce Vulture, which proved too troublesome. The other was the very powerful Napier Sabre. Its makers had to their credit the famous Lion engine, and more recently the unusual 'Dagger' which found little service use. In developing the Sabre, Napier took a huge bite at a complex engine and digesting the affair took many years. It was February 24, 1940, when P5212, the first Sabre-engined example of the machine named the Hawker 'Typhoon', first flew. Soon it encountered disastrous structural failure of the fuselage aft of the wing. Early test flights showed the rudder area insufficient for control with a motor which was already giving trouble.

Hardly had the prototype flown when production was concentrated on six major types already in service. CRD contracts were nearly all halted, and the Typhoon fell to one of those axes politicians delight in wielding with all too often disastrous consequences. For six months the Typhoon programme was in abeyance, but in October, 1940, came reinstatement. To cure the mounting snags there was still only one Typhoon flying, until May 3, 1941, when the second P5216 flew. Many months before the first contracts for production Typhoons had been placed, and Gloster went ahead with their order for 250.

Despite the problems far from worked out on the prototypes R7576, the first brown-green-duck egg green production machine with a black spinner, made its first flight on May 27, 1941 . . . three weeks after the second prototype! In some respects this proved fortunate for it seems possible that the Typhoon—which in the later stages of the war proved of great value—might otherwise been cancelled. With production machines at hand there was soon a pool of Typhoons.

Officially the RAF received its first Typhoon on August 27, 1941, when R7579 was posted to the Central Flying School for handling trials. The next machine wearing similar finish was delivered to AFDU Duxford on August 31, 1941. By September 7, dark sea grey had replaced the brown on the aircraft which already had a Sky Type S tail band and spinner, September 7 was also the day that R7581 reached AFDU, the same day that I had made a visit there.

As I arrived the well-known He 111 AW177 was on circuits with Ju 88 EE205. Soon Bf 109E AE479 was airborne, a Fulmar made a pass and the first Whirlwind prototype did a memorable 'beat-up'. None of these machines wore typical fighting colours—but this was not true of some amazing new shapes surprisingly lurking here and there on the field.

A puff of smoke, a new sound . . . no mistaking it; this was a Sabre engine, the sound of which had become familiar over recent months as those bulky Folland test-beds and the Sabre Battle did the rounds from Luton. There was little doubt—these aircraft were Typhoons and not Tornados! Along Duxford's western boundary were the grey-green 'sweep Hurricanes' of 56 Squadron. It needed little imagination to conclude that this distinguished unit had been chosen to pioneer the new seven-ton monster. Monster indeed—a close-up of R7591 proved this. It was in the latest green and dark sea grey paint scheme with yellow outer wing stripe. It had the 'solid' combing aft of the cockpit which much restricted the view, and the unusual car-door-like means of entry, the former featured probably by about the first 50 or so Typhoons and the latter by many more. Sky bands and spinner with 'R' aft of the roundels completed the colour scheme. Meanwhile, the working article was to be seen, for R7580 was taxying out. As it rolled it was clear that the run was going to be long, and there was a pronounced swing. Once airborne the aircraft made a long rather flat climb. But my goodness, what a powerful roar it made, a sound that was to be the Typhoon's trade mark. Then came a very thrilling run across the field, the fastest I had then ever seen. Behind the scenes, however, feeling towards the Typhoon was more mixed and less enthusiastic!

Engine troubles soon became legion at Duxford, and there were some unpleasant fires. Rear view was poor, and during factory trials a second structural weakness, this time immediately ahead of the tail unit, manifested itself. It was cured by a special array of 'fishplates' around the fuselage. Carbon monoxide seepage from the massive engine brought some nasty incidents, cured by pilots wearing their oxygen masks, from engine start to the finish of the flight, and also by extending the exhaust stubs each to four inches long.

Delivery of cannon feed gear was erratic, thus the first Typhoons were fitted with six machine-guns in each wing as originally planned and not the four-cannon now really required. P5216, soon after its maiden flight, had been fitted with four cannon; but it is likely that R7646, which first flew November, 1941, was the first production machine with cannon. The aircraft was also the first to have a completely transparent cockpit hood and combing whilst retaining the car-door-like entry.

One thing became quickly obvious—the Typhoon was quite unsuitable as a high-level interceptor. But at low levels its tremendous power conferred upon it a speed around 400 mph, and it also proved to be a very stable weapons platform and clearly could take hefty punishment.

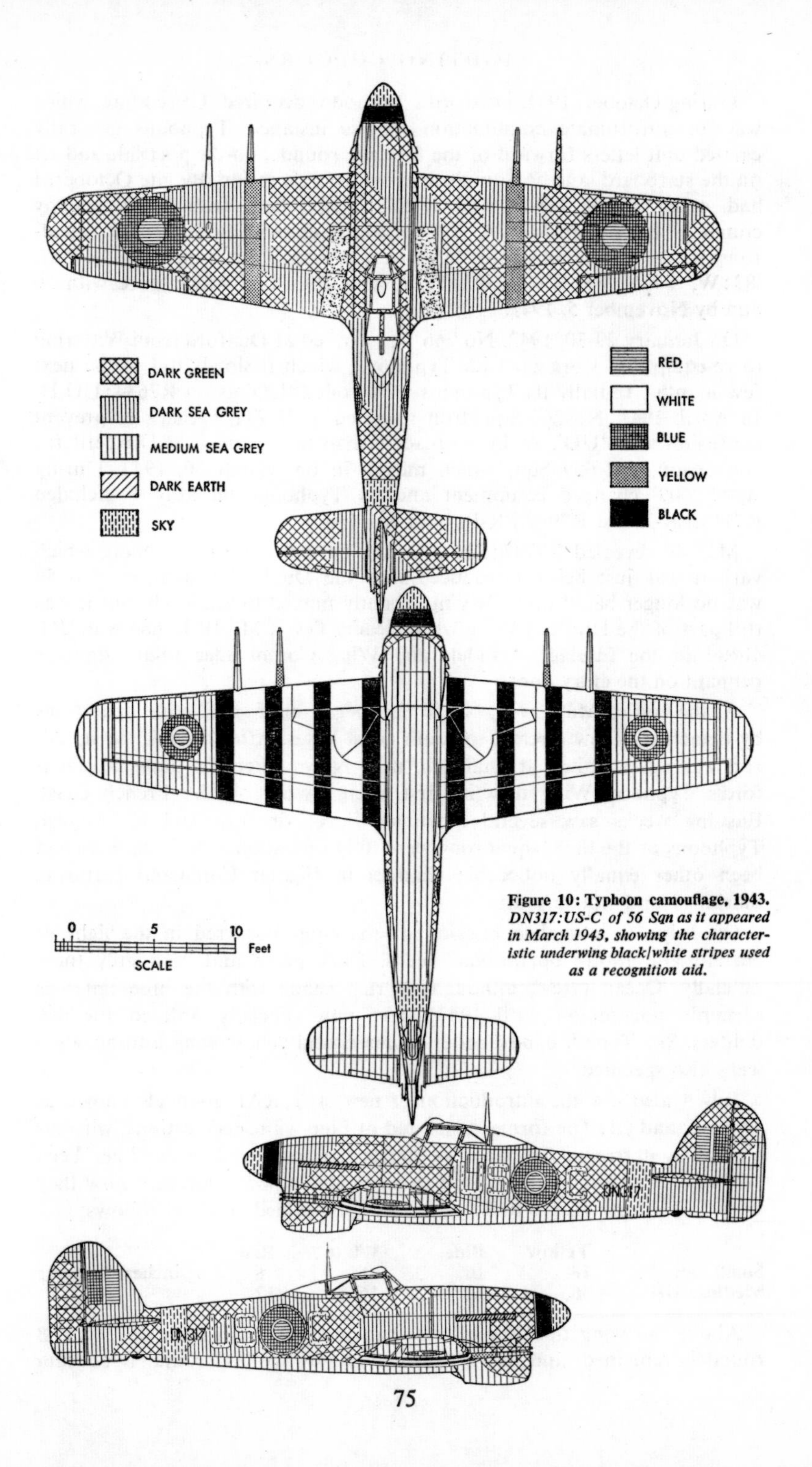

Figure 10: Typhoon camouflage, 1943. *DN317:US-C of 56 Sqn as it appeared in March 1943, showing the characteristic underwing black/white stripes used as a recognition aid.*

During October, 1941, Duxford's Typhoons acquired 'US' coding, which was an unfortunate combination in this instance. Typhoons generally carried unit letters forward of the fuselage roundel on the port side and aft on the starboard, and 56 Squadron proved no exception. By late October, I had noted R7596:US-M and R7588:US-N, both with 'solid' canopy combing. Both were Mk IA, the version equipping 56 and other squadrons for many months. No 56's aircraft that I noted included R7581, '83:W, '84:S, '85, '89:U, '91:T, '92 and '95 all of which were with 56 Sqn by November 5, 1941.

On January 29-30, 1942, No 266 Sqn arrived at Duxford from Wittering to re-equip and work up with Typhoons, which it slowly did in the next few months. Initially its Typhoons were coded 'UO' as on R7634:UO-D. In April, 1942, No 266 Squadron re-coded itself ZH, perhaps to prevent confusion with 'UD'. A third squadron had now arrived at Duxford for conversion, No 609 Sqn, which moved in on March 30, 1942. During April '609' changed equipment and its Typhoons on May 5 included R7713:PR-Z and R7999:PR-P, both Mk IAs.

May 10 revealed R7787:ZH-C, a Mk IB with unfaired cannon, which variant was just being introduced into the Duxford squadrons. No 56 was no longer based there, having recently moved to Snailwell, but it was still part of the Duxford Wing whose leader flew a Mk IB R7684 with 'JG' ahead of the fuselage roundels and Wing Commander John Grandy's pennant on the entry door.

At the end of May, 1942, No 56 Sqn began brief small-scale operations by detaching a few aircraft to south coast bases. After a week the squadron was again united at Snailwell, near Newmarket. On June 20, Duxford's Typhoon Wing flew its first Wing Sweep off the French coast. Ensuing weeks saw several more low level ventures and by August, Typhoons of the three squadrons were fully operational. By then there had been other equally noticeable changes in Fighter Command featuring markings and not aircraft.

On July 1 a complete revision of markings occurred in the light of current and future operational needs. Dark green and dark grey (now officially 'Ocean Grey', although its rich shade with the blue tint was certainly uncommon until 1943) were now officially ordered for day fighters. Sky Type S bands, codes, spinners and yellow wing leading edges were also specified.

July 1 also saw the introduction of new style RAF roundels known as Types C and C1. The former consisted of blue-white-red sections, whereas C1 had a narrow outer ring. Roundels had previously sometimes been applied in sizes sometimes suited to particular types of aircraft, now they were to conform (for a while anyway!) to specified sizes, as follows:

	Yellow	Blue	White	Red	
Small size	18	16	8	6	inches/diameter
Medium size	36	32	16	12	

Above the wing tips 1/6 of the span inwards from each tip, Type B roundels remained, and day-fighters invariably wore C roundels beneath

61 *Beaufighter VIF V8565:ZQ-F of the Fighter Interception Unit with thimble nose.* (IWM).

62 *R2270, the first production Beaufighter II with early roundels and no codes. Extensive weathering leaves some bare metal showing and a panel in the windscreen is painted over. There is a yellow gas detector patch just forward of the tail, a feature of many ex-works aircraft (usually removed) in 1940-42* (IWM).

63 *Mosquito NFII DD609 in all-black 1942 finish. It served with 151 Sqn from April 1942, until January 1944* (IWM).

64 *Mosquito Mk XIII in the winter of 1944-45. It has the 'Universal Nose' characteristic of most of the scanner-type radars fitted to Mosquito night-fighters. Note once again the sea grey medium finish with dark green disruption on upper surfaces* (IWM).

65 *A line-up of Kittyhawk IIIs (P-40M) of 260 Sqn. FR12?:HS-V has blue under surfaces but FL90?:HS-C (the next aircraft along) has sky undersides. Aircraft with azure blue undersurfaces had a yellow outline to the underwing roundels* (IWM).

66 *Mosquito II HJ911 shown on delivery in September 1942 in all black finish with red serials. A drawing of this same machine in the 1943 night-fighter scheme is given in Figure 25.*

67 *Hurricane II HV498:G in earth/mid-stone finish with C type roundels on the fuselage in late 1942. This is a machine of a SAAF squadron in East Africa. G is in light grey* (C. D. Larkins).

68 *Early Hurricanes to arrive in the Western Desert in 1941 still retained the green/dark earth/sky 'temperate' finish as seen on this weather worn machine with long range tanks. Note the fabric patches over the machine gun ports: these were shot away when the aircraft went into action* (R. Wood).

69 *Hurricane IID, HV667, in well worn desert earth/midstone finish showing the 40 mm cannon under the wings and the tropical filter.*

70 *AK772:GA-Y, of 112 Sqn seen in North Africa in the Spring of 1942. Note the serial on the dark green rectangular background and the overpainted yellow surround on the roundel, a legacy of re-painting from 'temperate' finish* (IWM).

71 *A Kittyhawk III with the revised fin fillet. Note once again the yellow surround to the underwing roundel and the partially overpainted serial on a green background* (IWM).

72 *FR817 of No 5 Sqn, SAAF, in Italy. Note the stork with bomb emblem and white tip to tail. Name is 'Lady Godiva'* (IWM).

73 *Hurricane IIc of 237 (Rhodesia) Sqn in earth/midstone/light blue desert finish early in 1943. Note the typical exhaust stains and the smoke marks behind the shell ejector ports under the wings. Personal emblem on nose consists of black/white Matabele shield and crossed spears in brown with silver tips. Beneath badge is painted 'Bulala' (Kill) in white* (I. A. E. Dixon).

74 *An interesting line-up of Spitfire Vc fighters destined for the Middle East. EP201 nearest carries 'temperate' camouflage, like the others, and has sky spinner and rear fuselage band.*

75 *Spitfire Vc JK322:FL-4 damaged after an attack by Ju 88s on Linitini, Sicily in August 1943. Just visible is name 'JO Y' painted in white forward of cockpit. Drawing of this aircraft appears in Figure 12* (Frank Smith).

76 *Spitfire VIII JF814:WFD carries the rank badge and initials of Air Vice-Marshal W. F. Dickson, CB, OBE, DSO, who years later became Chief of the Air Staff. This aircraft is drawn in Figure 13* (IWM).

77 *Another view of Spitfire VIII JF814: WFD, personal aircraft of Air Marshal Dickson* (Stan Staples).

78 *An interesting line-up of Spitfires in USAAF hands in the Middle East. ER219 is clearly shown with AB44? behind. Note the red 'K' on the aircraft fins. All are Mk Vs. American insignia has a yellow outline* (B. C. Morrison).

79 *MK118:FT-F, an LF Mk IXc in use May 1944. The aircraft crashed at Calvi on August 6 1944. Unlike many of the Spitfires in use this one has normal 'home-based' colour scheme of two greys and dark green. Red codes are outlined white. By the later months of 1944 many Spitfires were in the grey-green scheme in Italy* (IWM).

80 *MA454, a Spitfire IXc in desert camouflage on 152 Sqn's dispersal near Naples. Code letters are black in this case. Machine is drawn in Figure 13* (IWM).

their wings. In the case of the Hurricane, these and the above roundels were set 80 inches in from the wing tip and the outer ring of the underwing roundel had a diameter of 32 inches. The fuselage roundel was three feet across, whereas previously the factory-painted roundel had been 42 inches in diameter. The new roundel was centred on side former No 5 on the fifth stringer from the bottom.

On their fins all fighters carried flashes 24 x 24 inches including a white centre stripe two inches wide. Previously the Hurricanes had worn fin flashes 26 inches high by 24 inches wide, each stripe being 8 inches wide. Throughout July and August these markings were applied to a large number of aircraft, those in the front line rapidly acquiring them.

Some Defiants employed upon Air-Sea Rescue Service duty now bore a black stripe one foot wide beneath the nose tapering towards the tail. They began to have their brown upper paintwork changed to dark sea grey, too, but their under surfaces remained Sky to the end of their service.

There are other special markings worthy of mention. They include the CAM Hurricanes which were catapulted from merchant ships. These machines were ordered to be camouflaged dark slate grey and extra dark sea grey, with their under surfaces azure. Roundels were as elsewhere specified for the Hurricane.

An innovation was a yellow chordwise band one foot wide painted around each wing on Mustang I fighters. The outer edge of the stripe coincided with the outer edge of the wing flap. This was to prevent confusion with the Bf 109, and it remained standard practice on the Mustang until December 2 when orders directed removal. The aircraft were too conspicuous on their low-level *Rhubarbs* over enemy territory.

Spitfires shot down two Typhoons of 56 Sqn in error on June 1, 1942. They had mistaken them for Fw 190s—and this was not the first such incident, although the most distressing. There *was* a likeness, so some means of giving the Typhoons special identity was pondered over. In July the painting of a one-foot wide yellow band across the wing from the inner cannon was ordered. Several Typhoons that I saw at Duxford in August had two such bands, running aft from each cannon, but the single band became general and remained in force during 1943.

In November, 1942, 56 Squadron's Typhoons appeared with their noses forward of the mainplane all white, and other squadrons adopted such markings. An exception was No 181 whose fighter-bomber Typhoons had the lower areas of the nose in line with the wing centre line painted Sky Type S. Later that month, 56's aircraft could be seen wearing four one-foot wide black stripes two feet apart below each wing inner section. An order of December 5 instructed that white bands two feet wide were to separate the four black stripes. Although I saw many Typhoons flying at this period, it was February before I recorded one with white bands included. The all-white noses had proven most unpopular with pilots. They were keen to be indentified . . . but not quite so readily.

Squadrons which used the Typhoon in 1942 were:

Mk IA: Principal squadrons only are listed: several others (eg 3 Sqn) used them as conversion trainers at a later date.

Sqn	*Unit Code*	*Example*	*Dates/notes*
56	US:L	R7621	August, 1942
181	EL	R7627	October, 1942; based at Snailwell.
182	XM:L	R7677	December, 1942; formed Martlesham, September, '42
197	OV	R7681	In use when formed Duxford, November, '42
198	TP	R7624	In use when formed in Dec, '42
266	UO	R7619	Rec'd just before 266 arrived Duxford
609	PR:L	R7680	In use May, 1942

Mk IB

Sqn	*Unit Code*	*Example*	*Dates/notes*
1	JX	R7861	October, 1942
56	US:L	R7679	In use 11.42 with white nose/black stripes
56	US:L	DN307	In use 12.42; acquired under wing stripes
181	EL:U	R8831	In use 1.43; fighter-bomber aircraft
183	HF	DN242	In use 1.43; formed Church Fenton 11.42
193	DP	R7684	In use 1.43; formed Harrowbeer 12.42
197	OV	DN264	In use January, 1943
198	TP	DN249	In use January, 1943
257	FM	R8632	In use 7.42; equipped at High Ercall
486	SA:S	R8714	In use 11.42; equipped August, '42
609	PR:L	R7680	In use 9.42. R7646, first IB served for a time as PR-E (and also with 56 Sqn) prior to fighter-bomber trials at AAEE

Although this chapter has been mostly concerned with the Typhoon, it was mainly with older types of fighters that Fighter Command was still equipped. Spitfire Vs dominated it, and they were at a great disadvantage when facing the Fw 190. Mostly the Spitfires were Mk VBs fitted with two cannon and four machine guns, but in the closing months of 1941 the Mark VC with the Universal Wing of 'C' Wing which permitted the fitting of up to four cannon or two cannon and four machine guns or eight machine guns, came into use. The four-cannon version was not common, but frequently seen were VCs with the position for the extra cannon 'plugged'. During 1942, Mk VCs (usually with two cannon) were in service alongside VBs in many squadrons, including Nos 19, 66, 91, 92, 122, 130, 131, 152, 167, 234, 303, 310, 312, 313, 315, 317, 402, 501, 609, 610. Most VCs were sent to the Middle East.

The next major version was the Mk VIII, ultimately diverted overseas because an interim version, the Spitfire IX, proved itself a good enough match for the Fw 190. It was destined to serve in improved forms until long after the war. The Mk IX was a refined VC with stronger engine mounting for the Merlin 60 series engine, and a stiffened rear fuselage. Thus it was possible to modify Vs into IXs. This happened in a number of cases and early Mk IXs were such conversions made by Rolls-Royce. AB505, the first of these, arrived at Duxford on April 26, 1942, for tactical trials. Apart from its longer nose, four blade propeller and twin radiators—which became a good recognition feature—its most striking feature in flight was the engine note which somewhat resembled that of the American Allison. Gone was the gorgeous purr and whistle of the old Spitfires. AB505 returned to Hucknall on May 8, 1942, credited with an excellent performance. More conversions soon followed, and Mk Vs on the production lines were soon being converted to IXs, as IXA, IXB and IXC.

No 64 Squadron at Hornchurch was the first to take the Mk IXB into action, which it did during a *Rodeo* on July 28, 1942. No 611 Squadron was soon after equipped and the principle was now to keep Mk IXs in 11 Group and to rotate squadrons from time to time, the aircraft changing hands as needed, until sufficient IXs were available for retention by squadrons not in the South. Nos 72 and 402 Sqns also used Mk IXs in July, 1942, and soon after Nos 133 and 401 had them.

Another Spitfire variant brought into use in 1942 was the high-altitude fighter Mk VI (with Merlin 47—high-altitude version of the Mk 45) fitted with 'pointed' wing tips, pressure cabin and four-bladed propeller. No special camouflage was applied to these machines in home squadron use in 1942, and those which at any time wore any were rare. X4942, the prototype, had an 'A' wing, but most had the 'B' wing. 100 were built and they formed in varying quantities the equipment of these squadrons: Nos 124 and 616 (fully equipped); Nos 66, 91, 129, 164, 234, 310, 313, 421, 501, 504 and 602—some 'rotating aircraft,' in the manner of the Mk IX units. Nos 124 and 616 Squadrons received the aircraft during the period May-July, 1942, operated them over France, usually for high-cover work, and attempted to intercept Ju 86P high-altitude raiders over Britain in August and September, 1942. They remained in use for about a year with these two units, intercepting PR aircraft.

Hurricane development had meanwhile continued, and in 1942 the 'Hurribomber' came into its own for operations by and over the Channel, including the 'Channel Dash' by the German capital ships on February 12, 1942. Hurricane IIB losses became heavy, but they and Mk IICs were still in use for Operation *Jubilee*, the Dieppe landing. By the end of the year losses were prohibitive, but the Typhoon was then in service in a fighter-bomber role, first with 181 Sqn, following trials with R7646 carrying 2 × 500 lb bombs.

Through 1942, Hurricanes performed a useful role as night-intruders for which they were either all-black, or had black under surfaces and some side surfaces. Red codes were usual, also red serials.

Fighter Command throughout 1942 continued its coverage of coastal shipping and, in increasing numbers, the Spitfires, Typhoons and Hurricanes flew across the Channel, tempting the Luftwaffe to battle. Its aircraft lacked range, however, so Fighter Command was fighting at a disadvantage such as the Luftwaffe had known in 1940. Large-scale escort was given to Bostons and Blenheims.

To attempt any detailed survey of the squadrons and their equipment would prove too vast for inclusion here, but the following survey covers a number of relevant aircraft types and squadrons.

Spitfires in use with home-based squadrons in 1942:

Sqn	*Unit Code*	*Example*	*Dates/notes*
609	PR:B	W3238	January, 1942; Mk VB
452	UD:D	AA911	February, 1942; Mk VB
72	RN:C	AA945	February, 1942; Mk VB
130	PJ:X	BL712	April, 1942; Mk VB
81	FL:V	BM158	May, 1942; Mk VB
91	DL:W	AA976	May, 1942; Mk VC
164	FJ:S	W3569	May, 1942; Mk VB
64	SH	BR600	July, 1942; Mk IXB
332	AH	AB269	Used over Dieppe 19.8.42; VB
124	ON:Y	AA920	September, 1942; Mk VB
133	MD:N	BS133	September, 1942; Mk IXB
616	YQ:P	BS111	September, 1942; Mk VIB
71	XR:K	EN737	September, 1942; to 334 Sqn USAAC 29.9.42; Mk IXB
164	FJ:O	BL368	October, 1942; Mk VB
401	YO:R	BS104	December, 1942; Mk IXB
611	FY:B	EN133	December, 1942; Mk IXB

Hurricanes in use with home-based squadrons in 1942:

Sqn	*Unit Code*	*Example*	*Dates/notes*
87	LK:Y	Z3779	January, 1942; Mk IIC, all black
247	ZY:S	BD336	January, 1942; Mk IIC, all black
253	SW:P	Z3171	January, 1942; Mk IIC, all black, red codes
402	AE:S	BE479	January, 1942; Mk IIB. Day camouflage
1	JX:Y	Z3778	February, 1942; Mk IIC, all black, red codes
3	QO:F	Z3068	February, 1942; Mk IIC. Day camouflage
175	HH:S	BE478	May, 1942; Mk IIB. Day camouflage
1	JX:E	BE581	May, 1942; Mk IIC. Day camouflage
3	QO:P	BD687	Lost fighting near Dieppe 19.8.42. Mk IIC. Day camouflage

New home-based fighter squadrons formed during 1942 were:

No 121 (fmd 5.42, coded AV, eg. Spitfire VB BM509:AV-R; became 325 Sqn USAAC on 29.9.42). **No 164** (fmd Peterhead 6.42, coded FJ), **No 165** (fmd Ayr 6.4.42, coded SK, eg M:AR408 Mk VB), **No 167** (fmd Castletown 3.4.42, coded VL), **No 174** (fmd 3.42 at Manston, coded XP; Hurricane IIB), **No 175** (fmd 3.42 at Warmwell, coded HH). **No 195** (fmd 11.42 at Hutton Cranswick, coded JE; used Typhoons), **No 332** (fmd 1.42, coded AH, eg, S:BL430 Spitfire VB), **No 421** (fmd 4.42 Digby, coded AU; Spitfire VB); **No 486** (fmd 3.42, Kirton-in-Lindsey, with Hurricane IIB, coded SA).

Chapter 9

1942-43: Night fighters supreme

BY MAY, 1941, six squadrons were flying Beaufighter IFs for home night defence, wearing a thick super-matt black finish, as related in Chapter 5. Their code letters and serials were very light grey. For the rest of 1941 they were supplemented by Defiants, Havocs, Bostons and Hurricanes. From August, 1941, the Defiant NFII with a Merlin XX was in use, and ultimately served from 1941 to mid-1942 with the following squadrons: No 96 (ZJ, eg, AA540), No 151 (eg, DZ-V: AA436 in use mid-1942), No 256 (eg, JT-?, AA546) supplemented in 1941 by a few Hurricane IICs as were some other Defiant squadrons (V3995: JT-Y in use summer-autumn 1941), No 264 (eg, PS:AA400). Dull red codes came into general use on home-based night-fighters circa September/October, 1941, and at about the same time larger diameter fuselage roundels were introduced, presumably to improve identity during the winter months.

Another new variant which came into service in 1941 was the Merlin engined Beaufighter Mk IIF. Although R2058, the first one, flew in July, 1940, it was April, 1941, when deliveries to squadrons commenced. Delay arose through various aerodynamic difficulties. Lower power was available for take-off on the Merlin version, which had a pronounced swing. Fear of a shortage of Bristol Hercules engines was, however, sufficient to promote a large order (for 450 Mk IIFs) despite the fact that the need for Merlins was increasing with the large orders placed for the Lancaster bomber. The Mk IIs delivered between April, 1941, and mid-1942, bore the serials R2270-84, R2300-49, R2370-2404, R2430-79, T3009-55, T3070-3107, T3137-83, T3210-3227, T3356-89, T3410-47, V8131-70, V8184-8218. Mk IIs served with many existing Beaufighter squadrons in small numbers, R2270 flying with 604 Sqn in 1942 and R2277 with 25 Sqn, but for the most part they fully equipped squadrons, replacing other types. The principal users, and examples of their aircraft, were:

Sqn	*Unit Code*	*Serial*	*Notes*
96	ZJ	V8138	In use 9.42
125	VA	T3148	In use 5.42
255	YD	R2402: A	In use 2.42; red codes, large fuselage roundel
307	EW	T3009	In use 3.42
406	HU	R2404	In use 12.41
409	KP	R2331	In use 3.42
410	RA	T3387	In use 8.42

Sqn	*Unit Code*	*Serial*	*Notes*
456	RX	T3151	In use 3.42
488	ME	T3385	In use 9.42
600	BQ	R2276	In use 1941

In addition, Mk IIFs formed various portions of the strengths on Nos 51, 54 and 63 fighter OTUs.

As the Mk II was entering service, opinion was divided as to how best to tactically employ the British twin-engined night-fighters. In the case of the Beaufighter II two machines R2274 (used by the FIU and 406 Sqn) and R2306 (used by 29 Sqn) were fitted with four-gun Boulton-Paul turrets immediately aft of the pilot's cockpit, both to cure nose-up tendency when the usual four cannon were fired and also to permit engagement of the enemy from other than astern. Tests were also made at the Fighter Interception Unit using a Havoc fitted with a battery of six upwards firing guns, and two Mosquito fighters later briefly appeared with turrets, prescribed at this period of trial. Both modified Beaufighters, Mk Vs, were black overall and had modified exhaust stacks to reduce glare.

Spring, 1942, saw the introduction of the Beaufighter VIF to the night-fighter squadrons. Its Bristol Hercules VI engines conferred on it better performance at higher altitude. Most Beaufighters so far used by squadrons carried 'bow and arrow' type A.I. radar aerials, but another change much evident in 1942 was the operational use of centimetric radar employing a dish scanner placed in a thimble-like nose radome. The all-black X7579 with yellow 'P' prototype markings was one of the trial machines fitted with this new A.I. Mk VII radar, superseded in service by A.I. Mk VIII which was fitted in some Beaufighters until the end of the war.

Examples of Beaufighters Mk I/VIF and the squadrons which used them between May, 1941, and October, 1942, were as follows:

Sqn	*Unit Code*	*Serial*	*Mk*	*Notes*
25	ZK	X7617	IF	In use 1.42; used IF until October, 1942
29	RO	R2192	IF	In use 5.41; used Mk VIF from 8.42
68	WM	R2099	IF	In use 10.41; operated Mk IF from 6.41; VIF received 1.43
125	VA	X7931	VIF	In use 9.42; this Mk replaced IIF in 9.42
141	TW	X7545	IF	In use 9.41, with A.I. Mk IV
141	TW	V8265	IF	In use 8.42, with A.I. Mk VII Mk IF in use from 6.42 to 6.43
219	FK	X7557	IF	In use 9.41. Mk VIF came into use 10.42
219	FK	V8451	VIF	
255	YD	X7931:A	VIF	In use 4.42, the month when VIF replaced Mk IIF
256	JT	X7845:G	IF	In use 10.42
307	EW	X8106	VIF	In use 5.42, when Mk VIF came into use on sqn
406	HU	X8229	VIF	In use 7.42. Mk VIF came into use 6.42
409	KP	X8153	VIF	In use 6.42, when squadron was equipped with VIF
456	RX	X8251	VIF	In use 6.42, when squadron was equipped with VIF
604	NG	R2136:N	IF	In use 4.42
604	NG	V8275:B	IF	In use late 1942

The Mosquito arrives

It is an interesting exercise to consider what fundamental effect upon the war the introduction of the Mosquito in 1940—which would have been quite feasible, had its fantastic potential been realised earlier—would have had. Indeed, in retrospect one may reasonably argue that the war would have been shortened, and pursuance of the fast unarmed bomber concept would have increased bombing effectiveness and cut casualties. This is hardly the place to argue this case, but in May, 1941, when the Luftwaffe ceased its major blitz on Britain this event ironically coincided with the first flight of the all-black Mosquito prototype night-fighter, W4052. Accent was then on the reconnaissance version of the Mosquito, the most versatile military aircraft ever produced. With the competent Beaufighter in widespread service the Mosquito was now developed as a fighter to succeed it. Production lines were established at the SAG factory at Leavesden from where the first Mosquito fighter, an NFII, emerged in January, 1942. So revolutionary was the aircraft on account of its speed and tactical flexibility that it was decided to build Mk II (Dual Control) aircraft as well as normal Mk II fighters. Initially these machines interspersed on the line wore standard black finish. From late 1942 they were finished in dark green and two shades of grey with a Sky Type S tail band and yellow stripes along the wing edges.

On January 26, 1942, the first Mosquito II (DC) was delivered to No 157 Squadron specially formed to work out any snags with the new type at Castle Camps. In April, 1942, Mosquito fighters became operational there and with No 151 Squadron at Wittering. All of their machines had the thick RDM2 black finish which de Havillands abhorred—more so when they found that it reduced the aircraft's speed by about 15 mph. In mid-summer they had it replaced by Night finish, ie, the usual matt black. Red codes and serials and the usual roundels were applied changed on the fuselage to Type C1 in July when the fin stripe was also altered to embrace a narrow white band. DD712:YP-R of the third Mosquito fighter squadron had such markings.

Hitler sanctioned the 'Baedeker' raids on April 23, 1942, and a few nights later the Mosquitoes went into action although some weeks passed before they made any claims. These, with the other night-fighters available (which even still included Spitfires used on 'Fighter Nights' yet part of day fighter squadrons in 1942 and Typhoons in 1943), were employed to intercept mixed forces mainly composed of Dornier 217 E4s and Ju 88 A4s and A14s. Following this series of raids the Luftwaffe limited its efforts to small scale attacks on a wide variety of targets.

Summer, 1942, witnessed experiments to change the camouflage of night-fighters. Black always had produced a silhouette effect against a light sky, the Northern Lights and clouds. Various combinations of grey-green-blue grey and brown were experimented with, particularly at RAE. Finally it was decided to use dark green and medium sea grey, the latter extending over the lower half of the aircraft as well as forming part of the upper surface camouflage. Code letters remained dull red and serials were now Night, although some Beaufighters after repainting retained red serials certainly into 1944. Advantages of the new scheme were that it was ideal for daylight operations over the sea (particularly over the Bay of Biscay

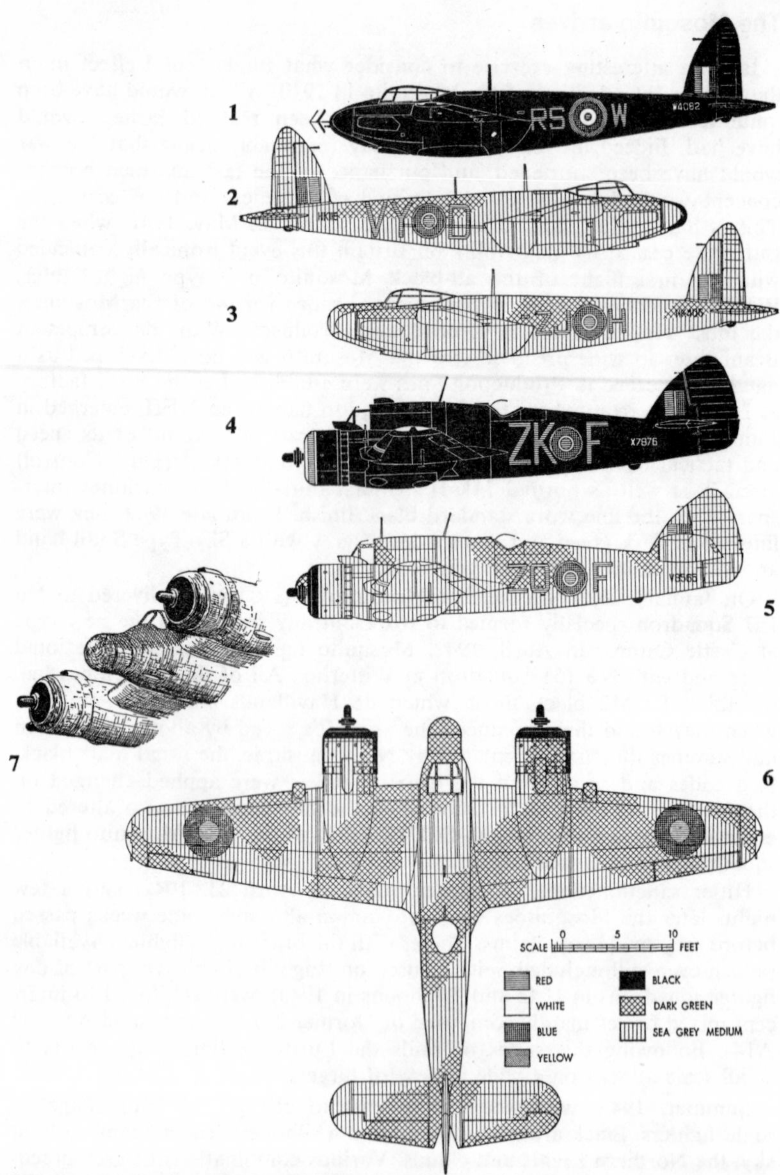

Figure 11: Mosquito and Beaufighter night-fighters, 1942-43. *(1) Mosquito NFII W4082 as used by 157 Sqn between March and August 1942. Size of coding on the squadron's aircraft varied, this being slightly smaller than some. After a spell with 85 Sqn, during which it acquired the grey-green finish, it returned to 157 Sqn between December 1942, and July 1943. (2) Mosquito NFXII HK118 arrived at Marshalls from Leavesden on February 2 1943, as a Mk II and after conversion there joined 85 Sqn in April 1943. It was lost on October 23 1943. (3) Mosquito NFXIII HK406 as used by 96 Sqn between November 1943, and July 1944. It destroyed three V-1s. (4) Beaufighter NFIF X7876 as used by 25 Sqn between March 1942, and the end of the year. Red codes and serials and the Type C1 roundels illustrate the machine in late summer markings. (5) Beaufighter NFVIF V8565 of the Fighter Interception Unit, as recorded at Wittering on April 29 1944. A.I. VIII fitted in the nose radome. (6) Plan view of the Beaufighter VIF with nose radome showing typical camouflage pattern, applicable to V8565. (7) Fitting of the 'thimble nose' to accommodate A.I. Mk VIII radar.*

where *Instep* patrols were made to interfere with German fighters and Condors observing Allied shipping), and suitable for daylight operations when the weather was poor, also for aircraft engaged on *Rangers* which began in February, 1943. When they were withdrawn from night-fighting duty in about August, 1944, the Beaufighters were still wearing this camouflage. On Mosquitoes it was retained until 1954 when Meteor night-fighters took over—and still wore similar markings for a time.

When Mosquito IIs began their service with No 100 Group of Bomber Command at the end of 1943 they had their undersurfaces and parts of the sides Night, the colour terminating in a wavy line. Vertical tail surfaces remained grey and green. Serials were black—red if they were painted on black areas. Radomes were invariably over-painted in the appropriate camouflage colour at this period.

The grey-green scheme also applied to Boston/Havoc intruders of Nos 418 and 605 Squadrons, the latter's aircraft thus marked including W8263:UP-V and W8399:UP-X in January, 1943. Both were Boston IIIs with clear noses. W8266:UP-H featured a belly gun tray. Bostons were phased out of 605 Sqn in February/March, 1943. Grey and green camouflage was also applied now to the Turbinlite machines. AH510, a Boston used by the 2 TAF Comm Flt 1943 and with Fighter Command Comm Flt later, had this camouflage scheme.

The OTUs

This book has naturally concentrated on aircraft in operational formations, but the contribution of the OTUs cannot be overlooked. Their aircraft (often ex-squadron machines) wore standard markings applicable to the period or one earlier.

On July 31, 1944 the equipment at No 51 OTU Cranfield included Beaufighter IFs X7672 and X7675 in standard colours and with dihedral tailplanes. V8254 with them carried a letter 'O' forward of the roundels and looked most unusual in that its entire upper surfaces were a very bright shade of dark green. Serial numbers were black, and the latter aircraft had a 'thimble nose' radome, with A.I. Mk VIII. R2151 had similar radar fitted. Also in use were a number of Beauforts. W6538 wore the overall grey/green scheme for night-fighters with 'H' in black ahead of the roundels, whereas another was grey/green with Sky under surfaces. N1019 also grey/green had black under sides, whereas W6467, which I clambered over at the time, had dark sea grey upper surfaces and white sides and under surfaces. Her serial was in ocean grey, others were black. A curious feature of the upper surfaces was that, when touched, a white powder came off, possibly due to weathering. Alongside was a Mosquito II DZ655 with YX-G in yellow (YX aft on starboard and forward on the port side). Its under surfaces were black. For radar training some specially converted Wellington XVIIs were available, including MP523 and MP525/G. Their extreme upper surfaces wore the usual sickly grey and green of Coastal Command aircraft, otherwise they were white. Their noses had been overpainted. Some Hurricane IICs, their guns removed, were used for practice interceptions of the Wellingtons. In the usual colour schemes but uncoded they included PG436 and PG437.

Mosquito variants

Between 1942 and 1945 the process of refining radar and night-fighters progressed hand-in-hand with tactical requirements of Fighter and Bomber Commands. One special need arose to combat German high-flying Ju 86P bombers which appeared over Britain in August-September, 1942. Although the Spitfire HFVI was available it was really an interim machine preceding the HFVII with its two-speed supercharger Merlin. Nothing was available that could catch the raiders until de Havilland rapidly converted the Mosquito pressure cabin prototype bomber into a fighter by lightening it, extending the wing tips and fitting to it a fighter nose, cut from DD715 which was then being modified into the prototype of the Mosquito fighter with nose radome and scanner radar. The machine, in two-tone grey and dark green, was prepared in the amazing time of one week. Enemy bombers never offered it a chance of combat before the weather broke and precluded high level raids.

Fears remained that the enemy might either resume the raids later, or use the machines for reconnaissance and perhaps for nuisance night raids. Accordingly four more special Mosquito XVs were ordered, and built and delivered in the winter of 1942/43, finished first in PR Blue then in a special deep blue shade known as Deep Sky before delivery. Between March, 1943, and August, 1943, these and the special prototype served with 85 Sqn wearing Night finish. In August they reverted to Deep Sky ready for possible high-altitude attacks, this time on Scotland. These never materialised.

The last major Beaufighter night-fighter variant, the VIF, remained in front-line night defence service until 1944. Both Mk Is and VIs adopted the grey/green finish although there were the usual exceptions to the scheme. All-black Beaufighters were still occasionally seen in 1944 at least. Both marks featured the dihedral tailplane, first fitted to R2057 and principally to Coastal Command aircraft. This modification made the machines more stable, and fighter pilots preferred the older type with its increased agility. Beaufighters in use with FIU at Wittering on April 29, 1944, included ZQ-E: MM857 (red codes, black serial and nose radome) with dihedral tailplane, ZQ-O: R2243 (black serial, dihedral tailplane, nose radome) and ZQ-G: V8329 red serial, level tailplane).

Filton's final batch of 250 Mk VIFs had nose radomes accommodating A.I. Mk VIII and a late batch from Rootes also featured this. Meanwhile, Mosquito production was at a high rate. Doubts had been harboured about the Mosquito's suitability for service in regions of temperature extremes and high humidity; consequently the Beaufighters were considered more suitable for overseas use.

At the start of 1943 Mosquito IIs began to arrive at Marshalls works at Cambridge, where their machine-gun equipped noses were replaced by black radomes accommodating A.I. Mk VIII, and they were redesignated Mk XII. These first entered service with No 85 Sqn at Hunsdon in February-March, 1943. They were followed by the Mk XVII, similar but with American SCR 720/729 radar known to the RAF as A.I. Mk X.

Mk II production was followed by that of the Mk XIII which entered squadron service in time to join Mk XIIs and XVIIs, and take a major part in the 'Baby Blitz' of 1944 during which period the Mk II withdrew.

Some XIIIs had the same shape radome as the XII, but a new 'Universal Nose' was designed to accommodate all the scanner type radars early in 1943 and was the usual type fitted to the Mk XIII.

Next came the Mk XIX initially schemed as a long-range version for Coastal Command. In the event it was delivered in quantity to Bomber Command squadrons of 100 Group, and used overseas. Very few problems were encountered with the Mosquito at any time in its career, but initially the exhaust shrouds gave trouble. Final Mosquito fighter development was of a line of aircraft with the Merlin 72/76 and 113/114 two-stage engines, and once more the exhaust system brought many snags. Although these machines came into service in the middle of 1944 it was many months before they could be effectively used. In the last six months of the war they gradually replaced many of the earlier marks in defence and bomber support roles in the version known as NF30.

Full details of the equipment of Mosquito night-fighter squadrons appears in the book *Mosquito* (Faber & Faber). Its complexity is such that no comprehensive record could be given justice here. However, the following listing of night-fighter squadrons using Beaufighters and Mosquitoes from late 1942 until the end of hostilities gives some illustration of the versions used:

Sqn	*Code*	*Type*	*Mk*	*Serial*	*Date/Notes*
23	YP	Mosquito	II	DD683:U	Sept '42. All black, no A.I.
23	YP	Mosquito	VI	RS596:M	Jan '45. Grey-green-black, ASH radar on nose
25	ZK	Mosquito	II	DZ689	July '43. Grey-green
25	ZK	Mosquito	17	HK288:X	Feb '44. Grey-green
25	ZK	Mosquito	30	NT360:A	Mar '45. Grey-green
29	RO	Mosquito	12	HK169:C	May '43. Grey-green
29	RO	Mosquito	13	HK413:D	Jan '44. Thimble nose
68	WM	Beaufighter	6F	V8619	Oct '43. Thimble nose
68	WM	Mosquito	17	HK348	Dec '44. Grey-green
68	WM	Mosquito	30	NT317:J	Mar '45. Grey-green
85	VY	Mosquito	12	HK172:Z	June '43. Grey-green
85	VY	Mosquito	17	HK245:X	Jan '44. Grey-green
85	VY	Mosquito	30	NT494:N	Mar '45. Grey-green
96	ZJ	Mosquito	13	HK499:A	Feb '44. Grey-green
125	VA	Mosquito	17	HK301:U	Feb '45. Grey-green
141	TW	Beaufighter	1F	V8253:T	Jan '43. Thimble nose. A.I. Mk VII
141	TW	Mosquito	II	DD717:M	Mar '44. Black underside
141	TW	Mosquito	30	NT500:K	April '45. Grey-green
151	DZ	Mosquito	II	W4097	May '42. All black; A.I.
151	DZ	Mosquito	12	HK193	Jan '44. Grey-green
151	DZ	Mosquito	19	MM494	May '44. Grey-green
151	DZ	Mosquito	30	MT500:J	Dec '44. Grey-green
157	RS	Mosquito	II	W4094:H	May '43. Grey-green
157	RS	Mosquito	19	MM650:J	June '44. Grey-green-black, full AEAF stripes
157	RS	Mosquito	30	MV551:W	Apr '45. Grey-green-black
169	VI	Mosquito	II	W4085:A	Mar '44. Grey-green-black
169	VI	Mosquito	19	MM645:U	Feb '45. Grey-green-black
219	FK	Mosquito	17	HK260	Mar '44. Grey-green
219	FK	Mosquito	30	MM790:G	Dec '44. Grey-green
239	HB	Mosquito	6	PZ226:B	Sept '44. Grey-green-black
239	HB	Mosquito	30	NT362:S	Mar '45. Grey-green-black
256	JT	Mosquito	12	HK131	July '43. Grey-green
264	PS	Mosquito	II	DD727:D	Jan '43. Grey-green

Sqn	*Code*	*Type*	*Mk*	*Serial*	*Date/Notes*
264	PS	Mosquito	13	HK479:F	June '44. Grey-green; full AEAF stripes
307	EW	Mosquito	II	DZ741:E	Nov '43. Grey-green
307	EW	Mosquito	12	HK109:V	Mar '44. Grey-green
307	EW	Mosquito	30	MT497:O	Dec '44. Grey-green
406	HU	Beaufighter	6F	ND222:Y	Nov '43. Grey-green, thimble nose
406	HU	Beaufighter	6F	ND221:P	June '44. Grey-green Thimble nose and full AEAF stripes
406	HU	Mosquito	12	HK164:N	July '44
406	HU	Mosquito	30	NT283/G:V	Jan '45. Grey-green
409	KP	Mosquito	13	MM560:F	Oct '44. Grey-green
410	RA	Mosquito	II	DZ292	Dec '43. Grey-green
410	RA	Mosquito	13	HK466:P	Feb '44. Grey-green. Universal nose (most usual form)
410	RA	Mosquito	30	MM744:I	Jan '45. Grey-green
418	TH	Mosquito	6	SZ962:U	Mar '45. Grey-green-black
456	RX	Mosquito	2	DD739:K	Aug '43. Grey-green
456	RX	Mosquito	17	HK286/G:A	Jan '44. Grey-green
456	RX	Mosquito	30	NT241/G:W	Jan '45. Grey-green
488	ME	Mosquito	12	HK121	Jan '44. Grey-green
488	ME	Mosquito	13	MM466:R	Aug '44. Grey-green
488	ME	Mosquito	30	NT372:B	Mar '45. Grey-green
515	3P	Mosquito	6	PZ249:Z	Mar '45. Grey-green-black
604	NG	Beaufighter	6F	V8557:R	Oct '43. Grey-green; thimble nose radome
604	NG	Mosquito	12	HK181:J	Mar '44. Grey-green
604	NG	Mosquito	13	MM503:B	May '44. Grey-green
605	UP	Mosquito	II	DZ657:F	Feb '43. Grey-green-black
605	UP	Mosquito	6	SZ993:A	Apr '45. Grey-green-black

For operations from June 5/6, 1944, which took night-fighters over the south of Britain, and over France, etc, full AEAF black/white stripes were applied to the machines. These were reduced in about September, 1944, to stripes on the under bellies of the aircraft. This applied to 100 Group aircraft too. From January, 1945, a narrow white ring often was to be seen added to upper surface wing roundels of Mosquitoes.

Chapter 10

1941-43: Fighters in the Desert

THE WAR IN AFRICA abruptly changed when Rommel arrived on February 12, 1941, to take charge of the Axis forces. He arrived during a British advance which took our troops as far west as El Agheila. On February 24 they were retreating and on April 8 were back at Tobruk. Overhead flew Hurricanes of Nos 3 (RAAF) and 73 Squadrons giving front line protection. Reinforcements rushed out from home were being diverted to Greece where, too, the war was going badly. On September 5, 1940, six Hurricane Is had arrived in Egypt from Takoradi, West Africa, and the following month there was sufficient to equip Nos 73 and 274 Squadrons. On arrival at the MUs in Egypt the machines were found to need thorough overhauls after the long flight. Many of these early deliveries were lost in the winter months, then came a delivery of 50 Hurricanes to Alexandria in May, 1941, supplemented by others from Takoradi. By this time the Curtiss Tomahawk was available, and these two types bore the brunt of the fighting over the desert in 1941.

Tomahawks joined the desert squadrons early in 1941, No 3 (RAAF) Sqn receiving them in April, 1941. It took to them slowly, and first operated them against French forces in Syria in June, 1941, for bomber escort and ground attack duties. In May, No 250 Sqn was equipped with them. Subsequently they were to serve with Nos 94, 112, 208, 260 Squadrons and Nos 2 and 4 SAAF Squadrons. No 208 used them partly in the Army/Air Component role, using a Hurricane for fighting and covering the Tomahawk engaged on fighter-recce work.

July, 1941, saw Rommel's forces at the Egyptian border, with Tobruk holding out far behind the front. There were engagements still, but the late summer was mainly devoted by the British to a build-up for a coming offensive, Operation *Crusader,* launched October 14, 1941. Available in the Middle East were 14 Hurricane long-range squadrons, two short-range and three tactical recce squadrons which, between them, flew 140 sorties in the first two weeks of the assault, and were supported by the Tomahawks. On November 20, 1941, No 80 Squadron took its Hurribombers into action for the first time, each carrying 8 × 40 lb bombs. All seemed well with the offensive when Rommel cunningly struck eastwards on November 24. The army had to fall back and once more Tobruk was besieged.

December saw yet another British attack with the army racing across the desert. Soon our supply lines were impossibly long, and diversion of equipment to the Far East brought about great difficulties. Unaffected by the plight in the Far East were Kittyhawk deliveries which commenced via Takoradi and the Cape at the end of 1941. No 3 (RAAF) Squadron took them into action for the first time on January 1, 1942, near Antelat. A month later 112 Sqn was receiving Kittyhawks. Engine troubles plagued the entry of the new type which, like the Tomahawk, proved none too easy to handle.

When the enemy counter-attacked in January, he was able to advance rapidly once more. St Valentine's Day found the 8th Army back at Gazala. Here the front line was to remain for some three months. If the army position could be regarded as static this was far from true of the air force. The Hurricane I was now quite outclassed and as yet there were few Mk IIs in the desert. Tomahawk deliveries had now ceased, and there were few Kittyhawks as yet. March, 1942, saw the decision to form three Hurribomber squadrons and have 35 short-range fighter squadrons, 15 of them flying Spitfires. By the end of May, 1942, only No 80 Sqn had Hurribombers and three Kittyhawk squadrons were flying fighter-bomber sorties with 250 lb bombs. No 73 Sqn was now using all-black night-fighter Hurricanes and 208 was watching enemy troop movements until replaced by No 40 Sqn, SAAF, later in March. The Desert Air Force fighters were now based at Gambut, El Adem and used the ALG at Gazala.

Meanwhile, the Lutwaffe and the Italians had begun to pulverise Malta and its people in the hope of submission. It aimed also to cut the supply lines to Egypt and the Far East via Suez and in the event almost did so, for the cost of defending the island in shipping and aircraft was great—not to mention the tragic casualties of the islanders matched only by their great heroism. This was the time of the great Malta convoys, and on March 6 the first 15 Spitfires flew off HMS *Eagle* and were soon joined by another 16. The arrival of the Spitfire in this theatre had been delayed due to the need for a special air filter to prevent sand and dust entering the engine. Most of these Spitfires were destroyed by mid-March, leaving 185 and 229 Hurricane squadrons to bear the brunt of the fighting. On April 18/19 the USS *Wasp* flew off 47 Spitfires to Malta, but by 23rd, 17 had been destroyed on the ground, 29 damaged beyond repair—and others lost in battle. There were now only six serviceable fighters on the island. A second load of 64 Spitfires (mainly Mk VB) flew off HMS *Eagle* on May 9, was immediately dispersed and in action one hour later ! These aircraft flew 74 sorties that day. Another 17 came off *Eagle* later in May, by the end of which month the first six Spitfire VBs had arrived in the desert for 145 Sqn to be used to give high cover for the Hurricanes.

As the Malta battle was furiously waged, Rommel struck again on May 26 and heavy fighting ensued; 250 and 450 Squadrons were using Kittyhawks now, operating as fighter-bombers, and between May 27-31 our fighters flew 1,500 sorties. Fifty of the 250 machines used were lost. Bir Hakim fell after a valiant fight and our resources were yet again stretched beyond their limit. In June the army had to fall back. Tobruk fell and still Malta was being blasted. By now, 20 more Spitfires were in the desert. French and Greek Hurricane Squadrons were there and Nos 252 and 272

Beaufighter squadrons in Africa. No 92 Sqn began to operate Spitfires over the sands and 94, 417 and 601 Sqns were equipped with them, leaving 126, 185 and 249 to fight in Malta with Spitfire Vs.

German forces entered Egypt on June 24 and advanced to El Alamein where they were halted. Between May 24 and July 7, 1942, 202 RAF fighters had been lost, some Kittyhawk squadrons bearing 100 per cent losses. In the middle of July, 1942, a count showed 11 fighter squadrons were at only half strength; five still had Hurricane Is or Tomahawks. By the end of the month, Kittyhawk losses were far from made up and the newly arriving Mk IIs with Packard-Merlin engines disappointingly went to the US Army squadrons now in the theatre. Of 513 Kittyhawks scheduled to arrive between April and August, 1942, only 251 had arrived by the end of August; and then only 58 were ready to fight.

Throughout the summer, indeed until late October, Malta underwent its torment. An answer to the entire situation was meanwhile being forged in Britain, a massive offensive under that glamorous skilled leader, Montgomery, from El Alamein and the establishment of a 'second front' in North-West Africa in which American forces were to take a large part. Thus, the remaining weeks of summer were devoted to logistics as large supplies of aircraft and equipment were taken to the Mediterranean. *Furious* and *Eagle* were busy delivering Spitfires to Malta during July and in the two years since August, 1940, 670 Hurricanes and Spitfires were flown into the island in the course of 19 operations. By September 30, 1942, 337 Spitfires had been delivered to the Middle East and 42 more from the Cape, diverted from Australia. Defence of the Nile Delta region was to be left in the hands of Beaufighters, 284 of which had come to the theatre. Some were now being used by Nos 46 and 89 Squadrons, particularly for night-defence, and No 1435 Flight in Malta. By the end of September, 830 Kittyhawks had been delivered for the coming onslaught, to support the large numbers of Bostons delivered directly or flown in from Britain, and large numbers of Martin Baltimores.

A tremendous artillery barrage opened Montgomery's attack from El Alamein on the night of October 23/24, 1942, and the carefully planned massive assault began. Hurricanes, Spitfires and Kittyhawks were all actively engaged at dawn and by November 8, Rommel was retreating fast. It was then that news broke that the Allies had landed on the beaches of the wide sweeping Algiers Bay. Preparations for the landing had been comparatively rapid, and in only nine days 122 Hurricanes and Spitfires (mainly VB and some VCs) had been assembled at Gibraltar. The campaign, too, was conducted fast. By 9 am, 18 Hurricanes of No 43 Sqn had landed on the captured airfield at Maison Blanche, followed soon after by Nos 81 and 242 Spitfire squadrons. The same day, Nos 72, 93, 111 and 152 Spitfire squadrons, No 225 with Hurricanes, 255 flying Beaufighters, and Spitfires of the US 31st and 52nd Fighter Groups were in North Africa. For a markings enthusiast the sight must have been a joy to behold since the fighters exhibited an amazing assortment of roundels and stars, US flags applied to tails, and fin stripes in a multitude of combinations. Furthermore, the two-tone brown and blue of the desert fighters was there, mixed with the better known greys and greens of home-based fighters. Codes ranged from white through sky to dull red. Some of the American fighters had yellow surrounds to their fuselage insignia as was customary then in Europe, and numbers of RAF and indeed RN aircraft wore American stars—painted over their British roundels.

Operation *Torch* brought an Axis answer, an unhindered move into Vichy France's Tunisia, but it was eventually to little avail. In North-West Africa the Allies rapidly leapt ahead by establishing forward bases, dropping paratroops, and putting skeleton forces into position. Thus they were soon near Tunis and Nos 72, 81, 93, 111 and 152 Squadrons moved into Souk-el-Arba, only 60 miles from the city. The 8th Army was halted at the Mareth Line as in Algeria incessant rain turned dust into mud whilst enemy supplies poured in by sea, and spectacularly by air, to Tunisia. First supplies of Spitfire IXs became available at this time, so No 72 Sqn returned to Gibraltar to equip with them in February, and 225 Sqn received Spitfire Vs with clipped wings for low-level recce duty.

On March 20/21, 1943, the 8th Army successfully attacked the area around the Mareth Line, whilst overhead roared waves of Kittyhawks and Hurricane IID strike fighters with Spitfires giving high cover. The enemy line really broke on March 26/27, and Bizerta and Tunis were now being heavily bombed.

During one memorable engagement, American P-40s and RAF Spitfires came upon about 100 escorted Ju 52s near Cape Bon. Most of the transports were destroyed, for the loss of only seven Allied fighters. Later that day another large toll was taken and on April 22, 21 Me 323s were massacred by 7½ squadrons of Kittyhawks and Spitfires. Between April 5-22, 432 enemy transports were claimed for the loss of 35 fighters, perhaps an inflated total. Certainly the enemy lost a major part of his entire transport force. There was still much tough land fighting to follow before he capitulated on May 12/13, 1943. The desert war was over, the tide of war had without doubt swung in favour of the Allies.

Desert colours

By the end of 1940, 87 Hurricanes had arrived in the Middle East. 274 Sqn was in the desert and 73 had just arrived from Britain. Hurricanes being delivered at this time wore the same colours as home-based fighters. T9530 had the usual dark green-dark earth-Sky scheme and a black spinner, whereas W9320 also in Egypt in February, 1941, had similar camouflage but had in addition a sky spinner and fuselage band. Squadron codes were grey. Tomahawks also wore these colours, basically unchanged until the summer.

After experiments, particularly at RAE, a new scheme more suited to the desert terrain came into use in August, 1941, at about the same time as Fighter Command changed to grey and green aircraft. Some Tomahawk squadrons introduced the new scheme early in August, but in the case of the Hurricane the 'Middle East (ie, Desert) Camouflage' was approved on August 22, 1941. On the red dope base which taughtened the fabric were applied 'Midstone and Dark Earth', aircraft undersides being sprayed Azure Blue. Night-fighter machines were all-black with light grey codes and serials. Code letters were usually very light grey or white, but later red was quite a common feature. Perhaps because of the conditions of war, Nos 43, 213 and notably 112 Squadron applied individualistic squadron colours and 274's aircraft also featured a special fuselage 'lightning

81 *Spitfire IX LZ949 in Italy in 1945 still painted in earth and midstone but with her sky fuselage band painted out, probably in azure, the under surface colour. Codes are white.*

82 *Mosquito FBVI YP-Y of No 23 Squadron taxies out in Malta. Grey/green finish, black under surfaces, red codes and serials.*

83 *A Beaufighter VIc EL457 fighter-bomber over the Eastern Mediterranean in June 1944. Desert colour scheme, white 'J'. The unit to which it belongs is not known* (A. Northcott).

84 *Spitfire Vc JK926:1, a tropicalised machine, serving with No 73 OTU in the Middle East late in 1943. It is in the then current grey/green/grey 'temperate' colour scheme with sky spinner and fuselage band and white number* (Alan Green).

85 *The earliest Coastal Command fighters were Blenheims in squadrons transferred from Fighter Command. This is Blenheim If L1336 of 248 Sqn in green-brown/black-white finish with grey codes in winter 1939-40* (IWM).

86 *EL223/G a trials Beaufighter VIc with torpedo attached. Grey-green-sky finish; note the two styles of roundel* (IWM).

87 *Coastal Command Blenheim IVFs of 235 Sqn, V5735:Q Y-D is nearest. Drawing of another machine of the squadron is given in Figure 14* (IWM).

88 *LX803, an early Mk X, showing the two slate colours and sky finish adopted for Coastal Command. Like the other early Mk Xs it does not have a rearward firing gun. The machine is shown new on delivery from the factory* (IWM)

89 *Two Mosquito VIs of 333 Sqn, both of which seem to have sea grey medium under surfaces and white or sky codes. KK-K banking away has standard Mosquito fighter-bomber colouring, whilst KK-Q nearest would seem to have dark grey upper surfaces of more than one shade* (Luftforsvaret, via Gunnar A. Lindaas).

90 *Mosquito VI NE-D:RS625 of 143 Sqn, Coastal Command, with black codes outlined in white.*

91 *NE788, a Beaufighter X with fuselage and wing bomb racks, of No 455 Sqn at Langham in 1944. Codes have been placed forward. Full black and white AEAF striping is carried* (IWM).

92 *Beaufighter X MB-T:NT950 of 236 Sqn, Coastal Command, banks away to show rockets and rails and placing of AEAF 'invasion' stripes* (IWM).

93 *A line-up of Typhoons of 193 Sqn. The stripes for special identity may be seen* (IWM).

94 *Typhoons of 183 Sqn wearing nose markings applied for Exercise Spartan* (IWM).

95 *EN133:FY-B. A Spitfire IXC of 611 Sqn, in use at the end of 1942* (The Aeroplane).

96 *BS435:FY-F of 611 Sqn in Type S smooth camouflage. The glossy finish is well portrayed* (The Aeroplane).

97 *BS142 a Spitfire HFVII in glossy Type S camouflage* (IWM).

98 *Four Spitfire XIVs of No 610 Sqn, DW-D:RB159, E:RB167, A:RB150 and G:RB166. They each exhibit slightly different camouflage patterning and the nearest has the leader's motif by the cockpit. The paint shows slight reflective qualities* (IWM).

99 *A formation of Spitfire XIIs of No 41 Sqn, including EB-B:MB882, D:MB858, H:MB794, J:MB840, E:MB862, all in glossy finish* (IWM).

100 *Spitfire XII MB882:EB-B showing under-wing markings, ventral long-range tank, yellow outer wing leading edge and serial partly obscured by codes* (IWM).

flash'. Some of the Spitfires used for *Torch* had colours as used in NW Europe, for the terrain was mixed.

This is perhaps a suitable moment to mention that Hurricane markings for naval service were also finalised officially in August, 1941. In their case Extra Dark Sea Grey replaced Midstone and Dark Sea Grey replaced Dark Earth. Sea Hurricanes IB, IIB, IIC (to quote instructions) were to have Sky under surfaces, also applied to hooked Hurricanes. Whereas the later Mks IIB, IIC and Sea Hurricane IA had the usual RAF size serials, the other versions had ROYAL NAVY in 4 inch letters with a gap of 8 inches between the words, and serials 4 inches high, 2½ inches wide, and ½ inch apart in Night. Changes to Type C1 roundels, etc, were made in the Middle East at the same time as they were introduced in Europe and applied also to naval aircraft. Late in 1942 a yellow surround was applied to under wing roundels on some Kittyhawks.

Initially, Beaufighters adopted desert markings when they operated from Egypt, with blue under surfaces being usual. Some, however, had black under surfaces, and red codes seem to have been usually applied on night-fighters. Such markings adorned the Mosquito intruders of No 23 Sqn which operated from Malta.

Desert squadrons

Development of the Hurricane IIB/C has already been dealt with in this book. IICs were used in the desert, but their cannon suffered from sanding up. Main deliveries were made mid-1942, 21 IICs destined for India being diverted in June, 1942, and 20 more in July. A new version that served with distinction in the desert was the Mk IID. Production aircraft appeared early in 1942 and No 6 Sqn, first to use them, was ready for action by May 31, 1942. Each carrying two 40 mm anti-tank guns, they proved highly successful. Mk IIDs also formed part of the equipment of five of the 22 Hurricane squadrons in the Middle East. In common with most Hurricanes, they had a special nose air filter.

Delivery of the Kittyhawk began in late Autumn, 1941, with the Mk Is AK571-AL230. These were bought outright, but Mk IAs, similar and supplied under Lend-Lease, were ET100-999 and EV100-699. The Kittyhawk IIA (Packard-Merlin V-1650-1) was delivered in the summer of 1942, examples being FL219-368. FS400-499 were diverted to the USSR and USAAF. Kittyhawk IIIs (first delivery Sept, 1942: FL710-730, FL875-905, FR779-872, FR111-140, FR210-361, FR385-392, FR412-521) had Allison engines and lengthened fuselages. The first 21 were P-40Ks and the remainder P-40Ms with the long fuselages.

Examples of squadrons and their equipment in the 1941-1943 North Africa Campaign:

Sqn	*Unit Code*	*Example*	*Type*	*Date in use/Notes*
6	JV	BN677:V	Hurricane IID/Trop.	6.42
43	FT	HV408:X	Hurricane IIC/Trop.	11.42 NW Africa
43	FT	BR288:F	Spitfire VC/Trop.	2.43 NW Africa
46	Nil	X7746	Beaufighter IF	7.42 in Egypt
73	Nil	BM975:G	Hurricane IIC	7.42, all black
80	?	Z4636	Hurricane I/Trop.	11.41 in desert
87	?	W9173:V	Hurricane I/Trop.	12.41 in desert
89	Nil	V8219	Beaufighter IF	11.42; A.I.VII, in Egypt

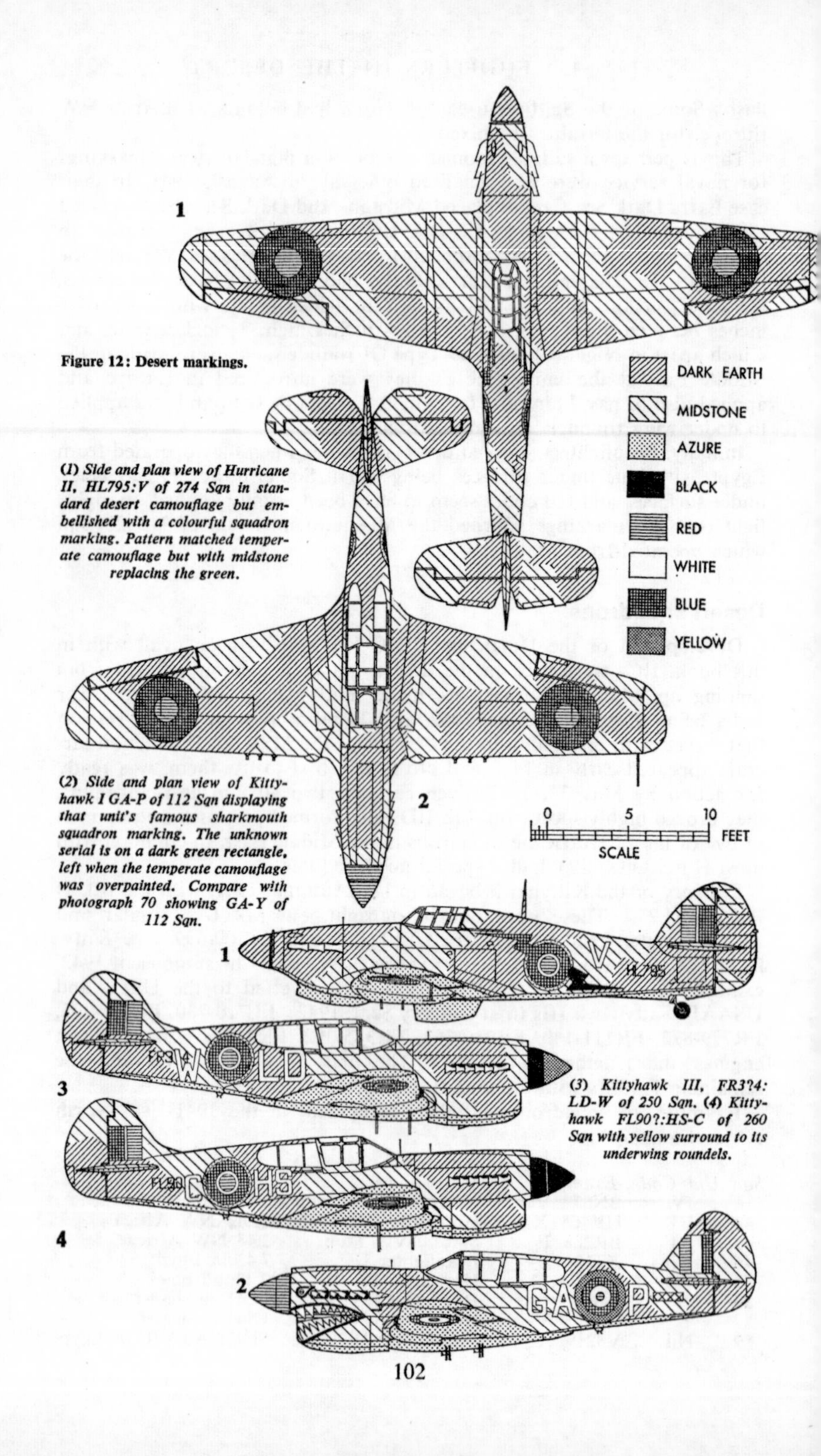

Figure 12: Desert markings.

(1) Side and plan view of Hurricane II, HL795:V of 274 Sqn in standard desert camouflage but embellished with a colourful squadron marking. Pattern matched temperate camouflage but with midstone replacing the green.

(2) Side and plan view of Kittyhawk I GA-P of 112 Sqn displaying that unit's famous sharkmouth squadron marking. The unknown serial is on a dark green rectangle, left when the temperate camouflage was overpainted. Compare with photograph 70 showing GA-Y of 112 Sqn.

(3) Kittyhawk III, FR3?4: LD-W of 250 Sqn. (4) Kittyhawk FL90?:HS-C of 260 Sqn with yellow surround to its underwing roundels.

Sqn	*Unit Code*	*Example*	*Type*	*Date in use/Notes*
92	QJ	BR580	Spitfire VC/Trop.	8.42; EP659 VB in use 12.42
93	HN	ER769	Spitfire VC/Trop.	1.43
112	GA	AK461:A	Tomahawk IIB	10.41 in desert
112	GA	ET265:K	Kittyhawk I	3.42 in desert
127	YN ?	Z5263:T	Hurricane II/Trop.	9.42 in desert
145	ZX	BR325:T	Spitfire VB/Trop.	2.43 in desert
185	GL	BR387	Spitfire V/Trop.	1943, Malta. Unit still had UK coding
208	GZ	W9357	Hurricane I/Trop.	11.41; BP166 IIB 10.42; IIC BN127 also
213	AK	W9290:B	Hurricane I/Trop.	6.41; BM966:T (IIB mid '42); BP123:S (IIC mid 1942); All long-range
225	WU	ER808:X	Spitfire VC/Trop.	4.43 in NW Africa
249	T	BR111:M	Spitfire VC	7.42 in Malta
250	LD	FR243:I	Kittyhawk III	2.43 in desert
253	SW	LZ836:D	Spitfire VB/Trop.	6.43 in NW Africa
260	HS	FL274:V	Kittyhawk IIA	12.42 in desert
261	Nil	P3731:J	Hurricane I/Trop.	In use 1941; used 1940: N2701, N2717
450	OK	AK636	Kittyhawk I	3.42 in desert
600	BQ	V8388	Beaufighter IF	1943; example given coded 6-Y
601	UF	EP455:Y	Spitfire VC/Trop.	12.42 in desert

Other squadrons which participated in the African war, unit codes, aircraft types, etc, included: *No 30** (RS:Hurricane IIC, BP586:X, black codes late 1942), *33* (?; Hurricanes I/IIA/IIB/IIC long range 1941-42), *72* (?; Spitfire VB/C 1942/43), *81* (FL:Spitfire VB/VC 1942-43), *94** (?; Kittyhawk), *111* (JU:Spitfire VB/C 1942-43), *126* (TD:Hurricane, Spitfire; Malta), *154* (Spitfire VC, eg, ER249 1942-43), *153* (?; Beaufighter, eg, X7872; late 1942), *229** (?; Hurricane IIA/B, Spitfire V 1943), *237** (GO later DV; Hurricane IB/C some uncoded), *238** (KC ?; Hurricane I/IIA/B), *241* (RZ:Hurricane IIB/C; Spitfire VC in 1943), *242* (LE:Spitfire VB/C 1942-43), *252** (probably nil; Beaufighter I; T4982 Idku late 1942), *255* (YD:Beaufighter, eg, Q:MM924 late 1943), *272** (Nil; Beaufighter, eg, V8079:L in 9.42), *274** (Nil—NH allotted; Hurricane I/II), *335** (Nil; Hurricane I/II, eg, BP279 in 10.42), *336** (Nil ? Hurricane II), *349** (GE Hurricane), *417** (Nil ?; Hurricane IIC later Spitfire VC), *451** (?; Hurricane), *603* (T:code also used by 249 Sqn in Malta too; Spitfire V). Commonwealth squadrons included: SAAF Nos 1* (Hurricane), 2* (Kittyhawk), 4* (Kittyhawk), 5* (Tomahawk, Kittyhawk:GL) and RAAF Nos 3* (Kittyhawk) and 7* (Hurricane I/II/IID).

* Squadrons operating Western Desert.

Some units retained UK codes, some carried none, others had a single letter or number. Units operated exclusively in the East could duplicate those of home-based units since squadron letters were applied for use within one theatre. Hence, RS applied to 157 Sqn in the UK and 30 Sqn in the Middle East. Generally, squadrons which left the UK for Africa retained previous codes if no duplication arose. Single letter codes may have been issued for security reasons.

Chapter II

1943-44: Middle East and Italy

NORTH AFRICA was ours, and Malta held firm. The fighters now paused briefly arranging themselves to step into Sicily and stride on to the toe of Italy. From Malta harassing attacks multiplied, Mosquito IIs of 23 Sqn in desert camouflage and black under surfaces keeping up a nightly campaign against Italian and German occupied airfields. Busy in the fighting were DZ230:YP-A, DD687:YP-E and DZ233:YP-T. The main assault on Pantelleria came between June 7-11 made by British fighters and fighter-bombers, mediums of the Desert Air Force and heavies provided by the USAAF. Next the small island fortress of Lampedusa fell on June 12. An airstrip on Gozo was now prepared, and into Malta for the coming Sicilian invasion vast supplies were now arriving. Gozo, Pantelleria and Malta soon housed 40 fighter/fighter-bomber squadrons.

Before the invasion Mediterranean Air Command obtained command of the air over and around Sicily and neutralised its defences, then gave close support and cover to the landing forces as they sailed to the island and fought on its beaches. Once a foothold was established the air forces concentrated on close support.

As the airborne forces made their night assault, all-black Hurricane IICs of 73 Sqn were there to see that all searchlights were extinguished. During the daylight hours the seaborne invaders were fully protected by Spitfires and Kittyhawks.

When darkness fell on July 10, the first day of the invasion of Sicily, Beaufighters of No 108 Sqn and Mosquitoes of No 23 continued harassment and protected the beaches. Fast behind the soldiers came an RAF unit laying down provisional runways. On July 11 a 72 Sqn Spitfire in need of fuel became the first RAF aircraft to land in Sicily. By July 13 the first Spitfires of No 244 Wing arrived from Malta and after another three days six more Spitfire squadrons were ashore based about Comiso. Numbers rapidly increased as more Spitfires moved in from Malta, into a world of oranges and lemons and olive oil. Despite successful enemy ground resistance Spitfires, Beaufighters, Mosquitoes and the American Warhawks ranged the skies supreme, although the Luftwaffe tried to intervene usually with heavy loss. Withdrawal was eventually made into the NE corner of the island around Catania, a region subjected to intensive fighter-bomber attacks. Repeatedly the Lutfwaffe marshalled its bomber forces making some successful counter attacks, particularly on maritime targets. By August 17 only Messina remained in enemy hands, to be evacuated at the risk of the Kittyhawks' bombs and the Spitfires' guns. Sicily fell during that day. The end for Fascist Italy was near too.

Straight from the desert sands and stony dry wastes of Tunisia there came principally Kittyhawk IIs and IIIs, and Spitfire VCs, the former types mainly for the fighter-bomber role. Colours remained those of the desert war, two tones of fawn and the unusual blue shade on under surfaces. Roundels were standard. Sky bands and spinners were not ordered, but there were certainly Spitfires in grey-green finish wearing either or both, yet few in number. Code letters were laid down as white at this period, but an increasing number of squadrons used red. Among them was No 43 whose Spitfires had their codes outlined white by the autumn of 1943, perhaps before. 'Treble One' opted for plain white on its aircraft well into 1944. Some squadrons had flight colours on spinners, but many Spitfires retained black or the camouflaged colour in which they were delivered. Spitfires supplied to the US forces during 1943 bore similar colours, a red letter above the RAF fin stripe identifying the Group. At this period RAF fin stripes and yellow surround to the fuselage US insignia was still usual, and a grey star often featured. Malta-based Beaufighter night-fighters usually had black under surfaces in place of the blue, a colour also carried by Mosquitoes of No 23 Sqn and the other Mosquitoes which came into the theatre.

Squadrons involved in the Sicilian campaign, and the 1944 Italian campaign, and examples of their aircraft were:

Sqn	*Code*	*Example*	*Type*	*Notes*
6	JV	KW716:A	Hurricane II/IV	Later probably uncoded
23	YP	HJ737:R	Mosquito VI	Malta, dets. later 30.8.43 '737' flew 1000th sortie from Luqa
43	FT	MH997:J	Spitfire V/IX	Red codes outlined white. Mk IX rec'd in 8.43
72	RN	JL368	Spitfire V/IX	
73	Nil	JK741 MJ341:C	Hurricane IIc/ Spitfire Vc/IXc	Hurricanes used as intruders
81	FL	EN190:X	Spitfire Vc/IXc	
92	QJ	JF502:4	Spitfire V/IX/VIII	Mk VIII received 7.43 at Pachino, Sicily. LF VIII came into use in 1944
93	HN	JK468	Spitfire Vc/VIII	Nos 73, 93, 111, 243 formed No 324 Wing. Example used 6.43. JF560 (VIII) in use 12.43
111	JU	MA728:B	Spitfire V/IXc	Example in use 1.44
112	GA	FR495:W	Kittyhawk III	Fighter-bomber squadron. In use 1.44
126	TD	?	Spitfire Vc	
145	ZX	LV729:M	Spitfire VIII	Example in use 8.44 as ftr-bomber
152	UM	MT948:N	Spitfire VIII	Used some early VIIIs with pointed wing tips
153	?	JL179	Spitfire IX	Used Beaufighter again later, KV921 in use Jan. 1944, fitted with A.I. VIII

Sqn	*Code*	*Example*	*Type*	*Notes*
154	?	JK518	Spitfire Vc	In use 5.43
185	GL	?	Spitfire Vc/VIII	
219	FK	V8868	Beaufighter VIF	
225	WU	JK112:A	Spitfire Vc/IXc	
227	?	EL270:N	Beaufighter VIF	
229	?	BD692	Spitfire/Hurricane IIc	Example of latter given
232	EF ?	EF526	Spitfire V/IXc	Example used in Italy 6.44
241	RZ	KX109	Hurricane	Spitfires in use by 12.43, eg MH608 and RZ: V-MH425, and LF IX
243	?	MJ712	Spitfire 1X	
249	GN	LZ811:P	Spitfire V/IX	
250	LD	FR304:W	Kittyhawk	Fighter-bomber sqn Desert colours
255	YD	V8847	Beaufighter VIF	Home-based NF colours
256	JT	HK229:G	Mosquito XII/XIII	Mk XII grey-green-black Red serials and codes
260	HS	FR358:B	Kittyhawk	Fighter-bomber sqn Desert colours
417	AN	JF827:M	Spitfire Vc/VIII	Desert colours
450	OK	FR796:K	Kittyhawk III	Fighter-bomber sqn
600	6/BQ	V8388:6-Y	Beaufighter VIF	Reverted to BQ code in 1944
601	UF	MK551:T	Spitfire V/IX	Fighter-bomber sqn

The following Commonwealth squadrons also took part: SAAF Nos 1, 2, 4, 40 using Spitfires and No 5 with Kittyhawks; No 3 Sqn RAAF using Kittyhawks.

Available for operations in the Eastern Mediterranean were SAAF Squadrons 3, 4 and 7. RAF squadrons were:

Sqn	*Code*	*Example*	*Type*	*Notes*
33	?	HV585	Hurricane NFIIc	
46	FH ?	X7746	Beaufighter I/VIF	
74	?	EP692	Hurricane/Spitfire Vb/IX	
89	Nil	X7849	Beaufighter IF/VI F	Example in use 4.43
94	?	MH705	Hurricane/Kittyhawk /Spitfire IX	
108	Nil	V8691:P	Beaufighter/Mosquito	MM442:M Mosquito in use 4.44
123	XE	KZ673	Hurricane IIc	In use 4.44 as ftr-bomber
127	YN ?	KZ431	Hurricane/Spitfire	Hurricane IIc ftr-bomber quoted in use 11.43
134	?	HW127	Hurricane IIb	In use 10.43. Spitfire JK118 in use 7.43
213	Nil/AK	HL941:V	Hurricane IIc	AK-V quoted in use 1943
237	Nil	HL928	Hurricane IIc	Tropicalised, desert colours
238	?	BS342	Hurricane/Spitfire IX	Spitfire quoted (HFIX)
274	Nil	BN113:Z	Hurricane IIc	Tropicalised, desert colours
335	Nil	HL599:W	Hurricane IIb	Tropicalised, desert colours
336	Nil	HL712	Hurricane IIb/IIc	
451	?	BN518	Hurricane IIc	In use 5.43. Spitfire Vc/IXc later

NB. Not all squadrons carried squadron code letters.

The fall of Italy

As the fate of Sicily was sealed heavy bombers were already engaged upon a heavy onslaught on Italian communications centres. Soon the Italians sued for an armistice. The Germans were far from ready for defeat and used vast resources to defend Italian soil. On September 3, the armistice was secretly signed, and the Eighth Army landed on the toe of Italy under the umbrella of the old Desert Air Force. On September 9, 1943, came the Salerno landing. Fighter cover from Sicily was difficult to maintain. Even carrying drop tanks, Spitfires had only about 25 minutes loiter-in-target time. Thus it fell to long-range USAAF Lightnings and carrier-based Seafires to provide cover and support. By night it was the task of the Sicilian based Beaufighters. The Luftwaffe did all it could to attack the support ships using Hs 293 and PC 1400 FX radio controlled AP weapons, but achieved only limited success. Orders were given for building, in the face of intense resistance, four landing strips near Paestum, all completed by September 15. These were short and on unsuitable soil, but on September 12 Seafires became the first to land. The three Spitfire squadrons of 324 Wing followed soon after. Fighting was intense and army progress very slight. The Luftwaffe now operated at night giving the Beaufighters and Mosquitoes the chance to show their supremacy.

To leave the Greek islands in enemy hands at this time seemed ill-advised, for an invasion of Greece sooner or later had to take place. In any case it would divide the German resistance. Amongst the forces to be used were three Spitfire squadrons, two of Hurricanes and four Beaufighter squadrons. First came an airborne assault on Kos in which Spitfires of No 7 Sqn SAAF took a major part but had to be reinforced by those of 74 Sqn, for the enemy fiercely counter-attacked forcing our small force to withdraw on October 3. They soon withdrew from other islands in the Aegean despite heavy Allied bomber attacks. Arrival of Nos 47 and 603 Beaufighter squadrons did little to alter a humiliating reverse.

In Italy the advance was very slow, although the evacuation of Sardinia by the Germans allowed the stationing there of Spitfires and a detachment of 23 Sqn Mosquitoes. Corsica, too, was given up, more fields becoming available for our fighters. After a tough struggle Naples fell on October 1 and a complex of airfields around Mount Vesuvius (which nastily joined the German side some months later) was established as a region of great importance. Of equal value was the large complex of airfields in the Foggia region, useful for long-range attacks on the Balkans and the underbelly of Europe. Occasionally the Luftwaffe still mounted unpleasant night attacks, sometimes with extremely uncomfortable results, but a greater nuisance was the winter rain which turned so many airfields into quagmires. Nevertheless close daylight support of our troops was maintained and the 'cab-rank' idea of line astern standing patrols (officially code-named *Rover David*) was evolved.

On the ground the armies lost their initial momentum, held up by a combination of enemy strength, bad weather and long supply lines. So, under close cover, it was decided to leap-frog the front line with a landing further on at Anzio which took place on January 22, 1944. Despite the initial surprise and massive air support the beachhead soon was contained. There followed the controversial bombing of the Cassino Monastery and the slow advance to Rome, entered on June 4, 1944. Two days later the whole visage of the war in Europe was changed, as the Allies landed in Normandy.

When the Italian invasion began Spitfires—now in use as fighter-bombers too—retained the desert colours. These predominated into 1944, evidenced by JU-U:JL325, which had the large tropical nose filter and white codes, positioned as on home-based Spitfires which was usual in the Middle East. It had 8-inch serials, but Spitfires in this theatre often had much smaller serials, probably hurriedly applied after the removal of Sky trimmings, as on EP653. Other VCs in desert trim were JU-K:ER171 and JK329:JU-S in use in January, 1944, at Capodichino with Mk IXCs and EN138:JU-M and LZ833:JU-X. 'Treble One' had received its first IXs in Malta in June, 1943.

For a short time it operated three Mk VIIIs JG925:JU-Q, JG937 (from July, 1943, until September) and JG941:JU-C; the latter retired in January, 1944.

Fighters in Italy

The first Spitfire initially planned to have a two stage Merlin engine was the Mk VII, production of which for home use began August, 1942. It was a high-altitude fighter with pointed wing tips and a pressure cabin. It was not tropicalised and did not operate in the Middle East. Externally, however, there were Spitfires with similar features. These were Mk VIIIs. Success achieved by fitting a Merlin 61 into a Mk V airframe and naming it Mk IX overshadowed the Mk VIII and only 1,658 VIIIs were built.

Mk VIII production began November, 1942, and reached its peak a year later, by which time about half had been built. The VIII was the ultimate Merlin Spitfire from which the XIV with a Griffon stemmed and later the Spiteful. The VIII had the 'C Airframe' specially designed to easily accommodate the Merlin 61 series and 4-cannon armament. It had reduced span ailerons and usually the standard wing plan form, although the early examples had extended wing tips like the Mk VII in both the 'F' and 'HF' VIII versions. Wing plan, as with other Spitfire marks gave no clue to precise form, which was entirely dependent upon engine mark. The FVIII had the Merlin 61 or 63, HFVIII the Merlin 70 and LFVIII the 66 series. All had a Vokes Vee tropical filter or air intake fitted in the usual position beneath the wing root leading edge, thus avoiding weight and other penalties of the bulky type. Other similarities with the Mk VII included the redesigned cooling system featuring the enlarged port wing air intake, stronger engine bearers and the increased rudder area which resulted in a 'pointed fin' on some aircraft featured also by some Mk IXs and many of the XVIs. The Mk VIII entered service in June, 1943, just in time for the Sicilian campaign, due to a very slow production build-up. Change-over in production of any mark of fighter was not the simple business one might assume and it plagued the Spitfire programme. Their serial number batches were as follows: *JF*274-300, 322-364, 392-427, 443-485, 501-528, 557-592, 613-630, 658-676, 692-716, 740-789, 805-850, 896-902, 926-967. *JG*104-124, 157-204, 239-275, 321-356, 371-387, 404-432, 456-500, 527-568, 603-624, 646-695. *MD*214-256, 269-303, 315-356, 369-403, *NH*614-636, *MT*502-527, 539-581, 593-635, 648-689, 703-748, 761-802, 815-846 (except

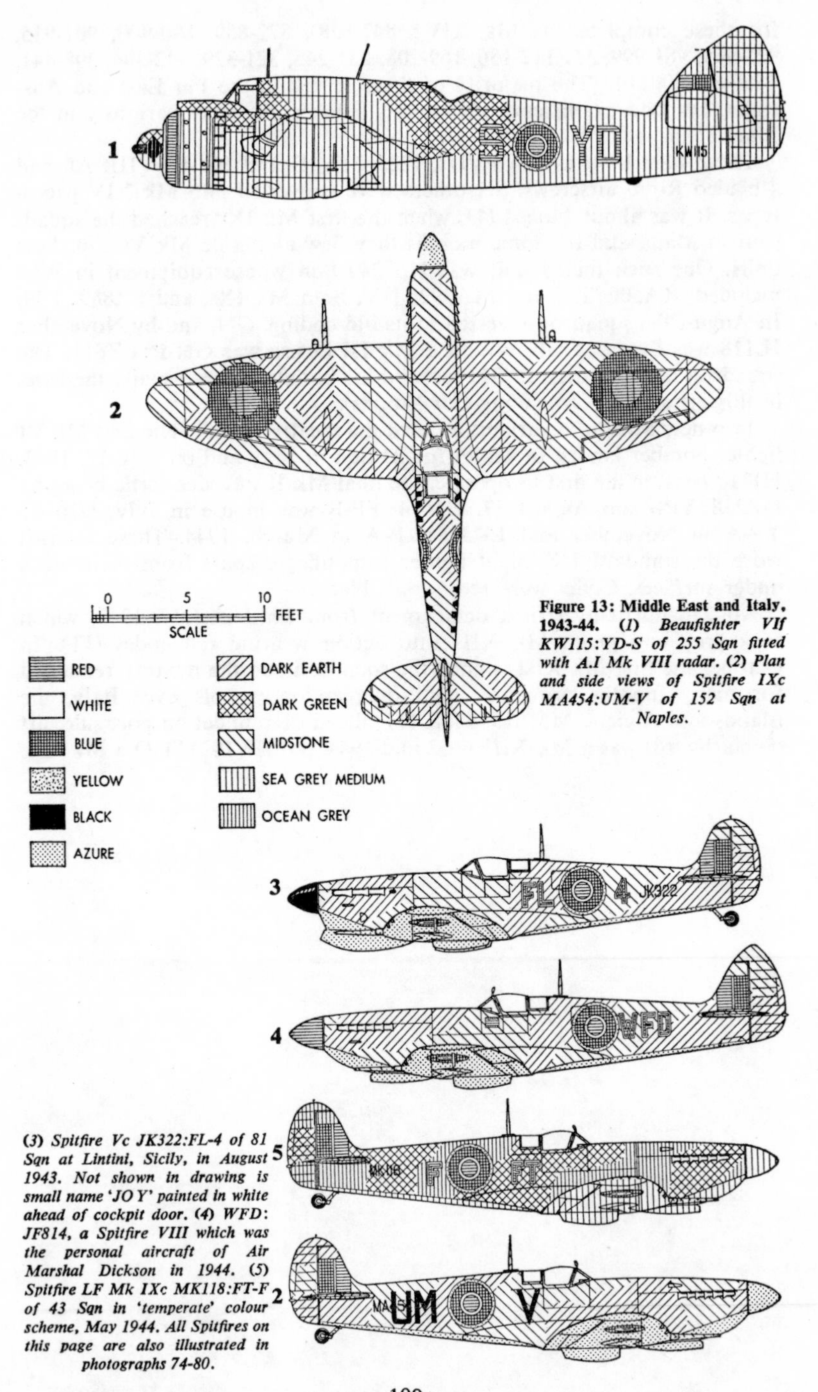

Figure 13: Middle East and Italy, 1943-44. *(1) Beaufighter VIf KW115:YD-S of 255 Sqn fitted with A.I Mk VIII radar. (2) Plan and side views of Spitfire IXc MA454:UM-V of 152 Sqn at Naples.*

(3) Spitfire Vc JK322:FL-4 of 81 Sqn at Lintini, Sicily, in August 1943. Not shown in drawing is small name 'JOY' painted in white ahead of cockpit door. (4) WFD: JF814, a Spitfire VIII which was the personal aircraft of Air Marshal Dickson in 1944. (5) Spitfire LF Mk IXc MK118:FT-F of 43 Sqn in 'temperate' colour scheme, May 1944. All Spitfires on this page are also illustrated in photographs 74-80.

for these completed as Mk XIV: 847-858), 872-889, 890-900, 901-915, 925-969, 981-999, *MV*112-156, 169-208, 231-245, 321-329, 342-346, 398-441, 456-487, 500514. (The majority of these served in the Far East and Australia, but odd examples from various batches did serve variously in the Middle East.)

These were built as 276 FVIII, 1225 LFVIII and 160 HFVIII. All had 4-bladed Rotol airscrews. Six others were converted into Mk XIV prototypes. It was about June, 1943, when the first Mk IXs reached the squadrons in Malta and for some months they flew alongside Mk VCs in these units. One such mixed unit was No 249 Sqn whose equipment in June included MA500:T-Z and MA392:T-V, both Mk IXs, and LZ889:T-N. In August the squadron reverted to its old coding, GN, and by November JL118 was flying as GN-W and a Mk IX in use was GN-P:LZ811. The squadron leader's aircraft '311' carried his initials as was usually the case, in this instance EN-W (Wing Cdr Woods).

Two new Mosquito variants entered the theatre as well. The first Mk VI fighter-bomber landed in Malta for 23 Sqn in May and on July 17, 1943, HJ710 became the first to operate, the final Mk II intruder sortie being by DZ238:YP-Z on August 17. HJ674:YP-B was in use in July, HJ676: YP-A in November and LR308:YP-A in March, 1944. These aircraft wore the standard UK night fighter camouflage, apart from their black under surfaces. Codes were red, serials black.

No 256 hurriedly sent a detachment from Ford in July, 1943, which took grey and green Mk XIIs into action wearing red codes (JT). In October the first Mk XIIIs joined the squadron and the mixture remained for many months providing night-interception patrols over Italy, the islands and Algiers. MM615:JT-R (JT ahead of roundel on port side, aft on starboard) was a Mk XIII used mid-1944 and HK162:JT-O a Mk XII.

Chapter 12

1941-45: Coastal Command Fighters

WHEN THE SECOND world war began, fighters were envisaged only for the interceptor role. There was no type set aside exclusively for night-fighting, and another item missing from the RAF's inventory was the long-range fighter. Nearest approach was the planned cannon-fighter (the Whirlwind) delayed by armament and engine development work. In any case, this was a short range aircraft, unsuitable for bomber escort and lacking the duration needed for convoy protection work. For the latter task—uncatered for in the re-armament planning—the Blenheim was somewhat hastily chosen in the early months of hostilities, and squadrons, mainly of fighter Mk IVs, came into Coastal Command in February and March, 1940. They did their best until the Beaufighter with sufficient range and great fire power—not to mention good development potential—was ready as an inspired item to prove an outstanding one for patrol and shipping strike duties. In the closing months of the war it was joined in the latter role by that most amazing aeroplane the Mosquito, itself originally planned in one scheme purely as a convoy escort fighter—and argued into production partly on its obvious superiority over the Fw 200 convoy raiders.

September, 1939, found Coastal Command equipped with flying-boats, Ansons and a few Hudsons with which it policed the inshore convoys. Such brushes as occurred were on a limited scale and the aircraft of the Command acquitted themselves surprisingly well. Even the Ansons—particularly those of 500 Sqn—for all their leisurely gait, put up some good fights.

When the air war broke in all its fury in spring, 1940, the position had much changed. Chapter 2 of *Fighting Colours* relates how, in the closing weeks of 1939, rapid expansion of Fighter Command had occurred with new squadrons equipping with Blenheims and Battles. During February and March, 1940, by which time SEF fighter production had built up considerably, several of the Blenheim squadrons were passed to Coastal Command.

These Blenheim squadrons had been flying Mk IFs wearing green/brown and black/white finish without under-wing roundels, with Type A fuselage roundels and Type B above the wings. Codes were medium grey. This version remained in operational use until summer, 1940. Replacement by the Mk IVF fighter with long-range tankage, as carried by the Mk IVL, likewise painted green/brown: black/white and fitted with a four-gun belly tray, began in February, 1940.

For several months, Bomber Command Blenheims had been wearing the greenish shade of Sky, recorded variously officially as 'light green', 'duck egg green', and 'duck egg blue', and even 'a special shade of light grey'. Coastal Command Blenheim fighters began to appear in the greenish tint of Sky in June, 1940, and during the next few months all those that I saw had this tone. Varying sizes of Type C fuselage roundels and fin stripes characterised the IVFs which retained grey codes until their retirement in 1942 to Nos 1, 2, 3, and 5 OTUs.

Blenheim fighters gave close cover to coastal convoys on a large number of quite uneventful sorties, but they made some strikes on enemy shipping and indulged in short range reconnaissance flights over the North Sea and Europe. By the end of 1940 some had acquired black under surfaces—mostly the prerogative of Coastal Command's Blenheim bombers in the hands of Nos 53, 59, 233, and 86 Sqns. Examples of the latter's aircraft in use April, 1941, are BX-D: V9393 and BX-S: V5392, both with Sky under surfaces.

During 1941, the Beaufighter established itself as a highly effective night-fighter and examples were delivered to Nos 252 and 272 coastal fighter squadrons, the first reaching No 252 Sqn in March, 1941 (eg, T3228, '3232 and '3248) and 252 Sqn a few weeks later (eg, T3300, T3273). Losses on the Blenheim squadrons had been heavy in 1940 and demands were made for a replacement type, met by the Beaufighter IC ('C' for Coastal). Extra fuel tanks, and a navigator's table and instruments, characterised the IC, R2152 being the trials installation aircraft. An order for 80 ICs followed, the aircraft being delivered in the green-brown-sky scheme still in use for coastal patrol/strike aircraft including Ansons, Beauforts and Hudsons. In line with other fighters, incidentally, Coastal Command's aircraft had Type A under-wing roundels from the summer of 1940 and retained them until the mid-war years.

The Beaufighter VIC was an adaptation of the Hercules VI powered Mk VIF, useful for forays over Biscay (known as *Insteps*) to prevent escort being given to returning U-boats and patrols by Fw 200s. The range these Beaufighters possessed was useful for *Rover* patrols, and by 1942 they were giving ideal cover to the remaining Beauforts on strikes around the European mainland. VICs came into use on 235 and 248 Squadrons in May, 1942, and soon after on 236 Sqn, examples being respectively T5106, T5102 and T5108. Probably the best known exploit by a Coastal Command Beaufighter of this period was the dropping of a tricolour flag on the Arc de Triumph, Paris, by Flt Lieut Gatward and Sgt Fern in ND-C: T4800, a Mk IC of 236 Sqn on June 12, 1942..

By late 1941 it was obvious that the Beaufort's usefulness as a torpedo-bomber was expiring. Plans were discussed for a successor, a cross between the Beaufort and Beaufighter which eventually emerged as the Brigand. Bristol, meanwhile, suggested a torpedo-carrying Beaufighter VIC; X8065 was quickly modified into the trials installation aircraft, beginning trials in April, 1942. Despite destruction soon after in a flying accident, tests had proved the scheme feasible and 16 more aircraft were ordered for conversion and delivered to No 254 Sqn from December, 1942. These included JL615, '616 and '618. In January, 1943, first deliveries were made to No 144 Sqn whose machines included JL610, '653 and '655.

Whereas the Hercules VI of the Beaufighter VIC was ideal for medium altitudes, it meant that this version was slower at low levels. Engines were therefore modified, becoming Mk XVIIs and, fitted with these, the Beaufighter TFX arrived with provision for torpedo gear and the Mk XIC with the torpedo gear omitted as on JL876-915, 937-948, JM105-136, JM158-185, JM206-250 and 262-267. These latter were used mainly by Nos 404 and 143 Squadrons, examples including JM111 to '115 used by No 404 and JM158 and '159 used by 143 Sqn. Other users were No 9 OTU and the Central Gunnery School (eg, JM178, '179).

Eventually the order for Mk VI (ITF—or Interim Torpedo Fighter) was expanded to 60 (serials JL583, 593, '610-618, '629-638, '649-659, '713-722, '827-835, '849-857 and JM104) fitted with Hercules VI or XVI engines. Apart from Nos 144 and 254 Sqns, its principal users, the VI (ITF) flew with Nos 1 and 2 Torpedo Training Units, and Nos 2, 5, 9, and 132 OTUs.

A usual feature of the Mk VIC and later Coastal Command Beaufighters was the fitting of a rearward-firing Browning gun in the aft cupola. The thimble nose of the Mk VIF with A.I. Mk VII or VIII radar was adapted to contain ASV radar on later Mk Xs. Increased dihedral tailplane was then needed to cure stability problems associated with the increased load. Thus, a long fin fillet appeared on late production Mk Xs being built when the war ended. In all, 2,095 Mk Xs were completed (JM268-291, '315-56, '379-417, LX779-'827, '845-86, '898-914, '926-56, '972-99, LZ113-58, '172-201, '215-47, '260-97, '314-46, '359-84, '397-419, '432-65, '479-95, '515-44, NE193-232, '245-60, '282-326, '339-386, '398-446, '459-502, '515-59, '572-615, '627-69, '682-724, '738-79, '792-832, NT888-929, '942-71, '983-99, NV113-58, '171-218, '233-76, '289-333, '347-90, '413-57, '470-513, '526-72, '582-632, RD130-76, '189-225, '239-285, '298-335, '348-96, '420-68, '483-525, '538-580, '685-728, '742-89, '801-36, '849-67, SR910-919).

The Mk X entered production in the spring of 1943 and was soon serving with Nos 143 (eg, LX847), 144 (LX781), 235 (LX807), 248 (LX806), and the other strike squadrons.

Trials began in September, 1942, with the firing of eight rocket projectiles from beneath the wings of EL329. In November, 1942, a special mixed strike wing of Beaufighters was established to operate with torpedo, cannon and a 500 lb or 1000 lb bomb slung beneath each wing and sometimes the fuselage, too. 143 (fighter), 236 (fighter-bomber) and 254 (fighter and 'Torbeau') Squadrons made up the first Wing at North Coates which, after a none too successful operation on November 20, took time off to work up and begin a campaign destined to last from April 18, 1943, until the end of the war. The leading Beaufighters would first rake enemy shipping and engage any fighters not attended to by the fighter cover—later they were to fire rockets at the ships—then came the 'Torbeaus' and bombers to sink the ships. Outriders aided navigation, form-up and station keeping. 1944 found the expanded forces busy along the entire enemy coastline. From September, 1944, efforts were concentrated against shipping in Norwegian waters to prevent the shipment of iron ore south from Narvik, and the supply of German forces in Norway. A concentrated campaign was waged against E-boats, U-boats and smaller submarines in the closing weeks of the war.

The Mosquito was first introduced to the Command by the Norwegian-manned 333 Sqn. In pairs, its Mk IIs made recce flights along the Norwegian coast. Later in the war its Mk VIs (eg, HP904:E, HP910:L)

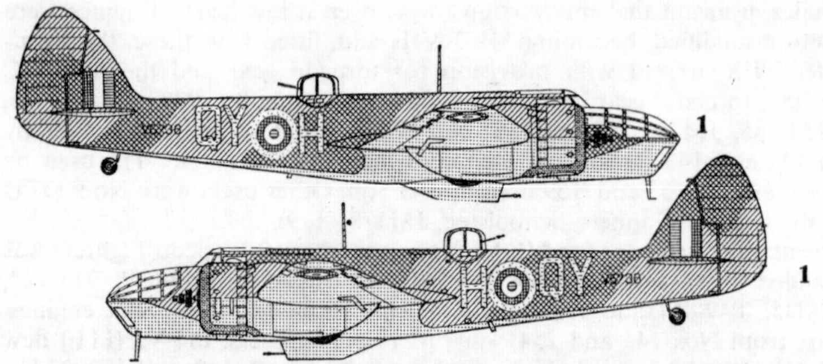

Figure 14: Coastal Command fighters. *Side and plan views of (1) Blenheim V5736: QY-H which flew with 254 Sqn from February 26 1941 until it was posted missing on July 9 of that year.*

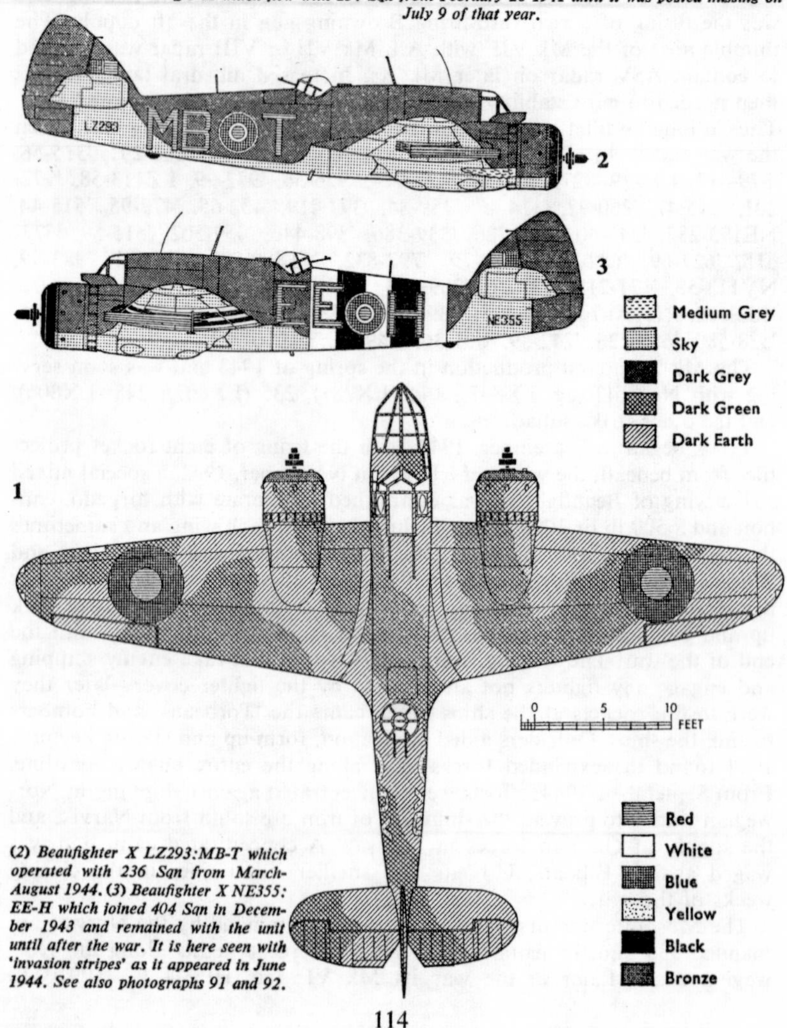

(2) Beaufighter X LZ293:MB-T which operated with 236 Sqn from March-August 1944. (3) Beaufighter X NE355: EE-H which joined 404 Sqn in December 1943 and remained with the unit until after the war. It is here seen with 'invasion stripes' as it appeared in June 1944. See also photographs 91 and 92.

performed very usefully as strike wing outriders and navigation leaders. Mixed formations of Beaus and Mossies operated from September, 1944, in increasing frequency, mainly from Scotland. Usually the Mosquitoes had cannon, but from October 26, 1944, they, too, pumped rockets into suitable targets. Progressively Nos 333, 248, 235, 143 and 404 forsook their Beaus for Mosquitoes, but the end of the war ended the re-equipment scheme.

After that the Brigand, scheduled to replace the Beaufighter, appeared but never entered any squadron in Coastal Command, No 42 (and 254 from which it was formed) sticking to the well-tried Beaufighter. And soon that wartime innovation, the torpedo fighter, was only history. One thing was to stay from wartime ideas, the heavily armed fighter-bomber, and in retrospect one may argue that today's hefty fighter machines stem from the Beaufighter concept rather than the wartime single-seaters.

Coastal Command's primary role was patrol. Finding and striking came second, but in all these the long-range fighters and heavily-armed machines of the later period were employed. It is not easy to distinguish squadrons by roles where the fighter element is concerned. The following listing, however, encompasses the squadrons employed, and examples of their equipment and its dating. Unlike most squadrons, Coastal Command's sometimes changed their unit code letters.

Sqn	*Type*	*Code*	*Example*	*Date*	*Notes*
143	Beaufighter	HO	T3243 (IC)		Formed 6.41 with
	Beaufighter XIC	HO	JM180	In use 6.43	Beaufighters. Based at
	Beaufighter X	NE	K:LX808	In use 6-7.44	North Coates, Manston, Banff, etc.
	Mosquito VI	NE	N:HR373		Fitted with R.P.s; ocean grey/sky, black codes outlined yellow.
144	Beaufighter X	PL	N:LZ216	In use 1.44	Previously used
	Beaufighter X	PL	O:LZ225	In use 6.44	Hampden. Beaus from
	Beaufighter X	PL	R:NV138	In use 12.44	early 1943. Operated
	Beaufighter X	PL	A:RD393	In use 3.45	from Banff, Dallachy.
235	Blenheim IF	QY	L6790	In use 3.40	Transferred to C.
	Blenheim IVF	QY	P:L9261	In use 3.41	Cmd from Ftr Cmd on
	Blenheim IVF	QY	D:T1830	In use 1941	27.2.40. Main bases
	Beaufighter IF	LA	A:R2269	In use 5.42	North Coates,
	Beaufighter VIC	LA	Q:X8084	In use 11.42	Chivenor, Banff.
	Beaufighter X	LA	LX401	In use 7.44	
	Mosquito VI	LA	HR131	In use 7.44	
236	Blenheim IF	ND	L6804	In use 7.40	Reformed 31.10.39.
	Blenheim IVF	ND	R2797	In use 5.41	Based North Coates
	Beaufighter VIC	ND	C:X8239	In use 6.42	9.42 to 5.45.
	Beaufighter X	MB	T:NT950	In use 10.44	
	Beaufighter X	MB	J:RD562	In use 4.45	Fin fillet, radome.
248	Blenheim IF	WR	E:L1336	In use 2.40	To Coastal Cmd on 20.6.40.
	Blenheim IVF	WR	K:N6239	In use 3.40	
	Blenheim IVF	WR	N6233	In use 9.40	
	Blenheim IVF	WR	J:L9454	In use 1.41	
	Beaufighter IC	WR	K:T3332	In use 8.41	First Mosquito strike squadron.
	Beaufighter VIC	WR	R:T5142	In use 6.42	
	Beaufighter X	DM	Q:JM348	In use 1.44	
	Mosquito VI	DM	Q:HR632	In use 2.45	
252	Blenheim IVF	PN	L8407	In use 2.41	Reformed 11.40.
	Beaufighter IF	PN	B:R2198	In use 2.41	
	Beaufighter IC	—	T3248	In use 3.41	

Sqn	*Type*	*Code*	*Example*	*Date*	*Notes*
254	Blenheim IF	QM	L8176	In use 8.40	Formed Bircham
	Blenheim IVF	QM	R2779	In use 9.41	Newton 1.40. Based
	Beaufighter VIC	QM	T5106	In use 6.42	North Coates.
	Beaufighter X	QM	LZ412	In use 11.43	Used 'Torbeaus'.
	Beaufighter X	QM	M:RD439	In use 4.45	
272	Blenheim IVF	?	L9252	In use 1.41	Formed 8.40 at
	Beaufighter IC	?	M:T3915	In use 1941	Aldergrove, to M.E.
333	Mosquito II	—	L:DZ711	In use 3.44	First Coastal Cmd
	Mosquito VI	KK	N:HP262	In use 2.45	Mosquito fighter sqn
404	Blenheim IVF	EE	H:N3525	In use 1941	
	Beaufighter IIF	EE	W:V8152	In use mid-1942	Grey-green/grey finish
	Beaufighter XIC	EE	X:JM136	In use 7.43	
	Beaufighter X	EE	F:NE354	In use 6.44	
	Beaufighter X	EO	R:NV428	In use 1.45	
	Mosquito VI	EO	C:RF842	In use 5.45	
455	Beaufighter X	UB	C:RD332	In use 3.45	Beaufighter X received 12.43. First op 6.3.44.
489	Beaufighter X	P6	X:NE210	In use late 1944	Beaufighter received late 1943. Ops from Leuchars, Langham, Dallachy.

Examples of machines used by the training units are: 9 OTU JM117: 4-T ('4' was squadron code) Mk XIC: T5155:2-L ('2' was squadron code), Mk VIC 132 OTU RD689:9Y-L (yellow letters outlined black) in use 6.45, Mk X.

Camouflage and markings

Four stages in the wartime camouflage of coastal 'strike fighters' may be conveniently listed. Firstly, there was the dark green and dark earth of the Blenheims with their white and black under surfaces. Then came the period June, 1940, to June, 1942, when brown and green upper surfaces were supplemented by what is best called 'duck egg green' under surfaces. Squadron letters remained medium grey on the Blenheims and were usually sited with the unit letters aft on both sides of the fuselage. National insignia consisted of Type B upper wing roundels, Type A under wing roundels and Type A or C fuselage roundels according to period. Blenheims (IVF) WR-E:L9394 and WR-Q:T2078 of 248 Sqn, recorded June 16, 1941, wore the laid down schemes, both having the 'B' camouflage pattern prescribed for the type (ie, the fuselage 'striping' was pointing aft in the patterning). EE-C:T1950 and EE-A:P4847 which I recorded on October 10, 1941, had the standard colours, P4847 having 'A' Pattern, mirror image on the other.

About June, 1942, Beaufighters of Coastal Command appeared in dark slate grey and extra dark sea grey, and retained their duck egg green under surfaces and underwing roundels. Code letters were now ordered to be either red or grey, and two wearing the latter in a very pale shade that I then took to be Sky Type S and recorded in September, 1942, were EL264:WR-D and T4711:WR-W, JL832 of the Coastal Command Development Unit typified those with red, having a letter 'A' forward of its roundels in the autumn of 1943. In August of that year other red coded examples included EE-V:JM122 and LZ173:EE-W, both of 404 Sqn.

101 *A Spitfire HFVI, BR579:ON-H of 124 Sqn with its serial almost obliterated by the codes and freshly painted fuselage band* (IWM).

102/103 *Two views of Tempest II MW742 show its grey and green upper camouflage and special white identity markings. A sky band and spinner are features, also the yellow leading edge stripe. Undersides are light sea grey* (Hawker Siddeley).

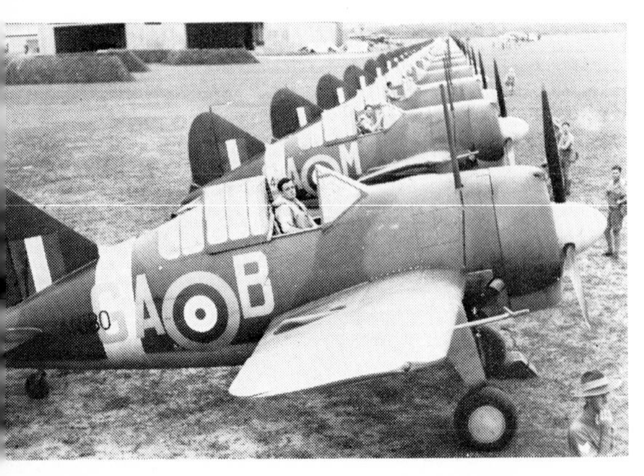

104 *A line-up of Buffaloes in green/brown/sky finish.*

105 *A Thunderbolt 1 in SEAC finish coded AD-R; possibly 113 Squadron,* (D. Reeves).

106 *The inscription on the bomb dates the photograph here of another Thunderbolt as circa December 1944. White bands and codes are well shown* (IWM).

107 *Spitfire XIV MV363:N in 1945 SEAC finish. Camera port is covered over and name 'MARY' is in white. Aircraft is from 11 Sqn* (N. T. Wilkinson).

108 *A line-up of Spitfire VIIIs in 1944 SEAC finish prior to application of the white stripes shown in photographs 107 and 109* (IWM).

109 *Spitfire VIII, AF-Z:JG534, in 1945 SEAC markings. Compare with picture 107* (IWM).

110 *Thunderbolt II KL859 of No 60 Sqn in natural finish with black identity bands and bars, also black codes T:MU, and standard SEAC roundels in two shades of blue. Fuselage top decking is olive drab.*

111 *Immediate post-war trim on Spitfire XIVs of No 132 Sqn. FF-B:RN133, the squadron commander's aircraft, is nearest, carrying his pennant marking. RN190:FF-J is in the far distance. As with many SEAC roundels the fuselage marking on RN133 shows that it is the European type suitably doctored* (IWM).

112 *A closer view of a SEAC Spitfire, in this case the Mk XIV flown by Sqn Ldr 'Ginger' Lacey when CO of 17 Sqn at Seletar in 1945. The white codes are thinly outlined in black and the mailed fist emblem of the squadron is on the nose. Beneath the cockpit is the customary squadron leader's pennant and an impressive display of crosses and 'rising sun' emblems recording Lacey's great record as a World War 2 fighter ace* (N. T. Wilkinson)

113 *Another view of Sqn Ldr Lacey's aircraft shows the pennant and 'kill' markings in greater detail* (N. T. Wilkinson).

114 *Line-up of 17 Sqn Spitfire XIVs at Seletar in 1945 shows RN150:YB-W nearest with fuselage serial overpainted and a small white serial on the fin. Outline of C type roundel can just be seen with the white showing through the worn SEAC roundel. Name 'Miss Freda' is painted in white script forward of the cockpit* (N. T. Wilkinson).

115 *Back in Europe can be seen Tempest V JF-Z of No 3 Sqn with serial number almost obliterated by AEAF stripes* (IWM).

116 *Spitfire IX PT462:C of a Free French RAF squadron wearing under-belly AEAF stripes and French rudder stripes and roundels. Under-wing roundels appear to be absent. Photo circa January 1945* (IWM)

117 *Spitfires of No 412 Sqn on the Continent in early 1945 in the usual late-war Spitfire finish. VZ-J, nearest, shows traces of once having had AEAF stripes. VZ-L is MJ452* (IWM).

During February, 1943, instructions were given that Beaufighters in Service hands should now have dark sea grey upper surfaces and sides replaced by extra dark sea grey from mid-June, 1943. It was at this period that a few Beaufighters engaged on Biscay patrols had white sides and under surfaces. Code letters were ordered to be red. Aircraft were leaving the production lines, according to Bruce Robertson's book, *Aircraft Markings of the World 1912-67,* in dark sea grey and sky finish from October, 1943. It seems likely, however, that they served in extra dark sea grey or perhaps ocean grey. I noted many Beaufighters in 1944 and '45 in the slightly blue tone associated with ocean grey, and also that from late 1943 'the under surfaces on the Beaufighters are a lighter shade', to quote from my diary of December 12, 1943. This may well have been Sky Blue. Also, I recorded in 1944 and '45 many Coastal Beaufighter Xs with 'dark grey and dark green' upper surfaces and sides, but it was not until the autumn of 1944 that I was able to record one in close-up, NE576: MB-0.

A mid-1944 innovation was entire code letter positioning on the fuselage over the mainplane to prevent over-painting by AEAF markings by some squadrons; MB-T: NT950 wore these, like UB-E: NT947 of 455 Sqn. Both had very dark grey/Sky finish and the former had red and the latter light grey codes applied as 'UB-E' in hyphenated form. No date seems to have yet been discovered for the removal of under-wing roundels, but I noted that from the spring of 1944 until mid-1945 they were absent. Indeed many post-war Beaufighters of Coastal Command did not carry them.

By Christmas, 1944, the Mosquitoes of the Command seem generally to have acquired dark grey upper surfaces (extra dark, probably) and had either Sky or medium sea grey under surfaces. Code letters were now placed forward usually, yet sometimes no squadron letters were used, only the aircraft letter ahead of the roundel. PZ446 of 143 Sqn featured grey/ Sky paintwork with forward codes and RP racks. Beaufighters RD354: MB-W and RD509: MB-U, both RP aircraft in use February, 1945, also had the dark grey/Sky finish with forward placed hyphenated red codes. Yet on March 24, 1945, MB-O passed my way in very dark grey and green upper decks and Sky under surfaces, with codes placed in the style of 1943 and in red! RD432: PL-L^1 and RD425: PL: F^1 at this period demonstrated another variation—the small 1 on the forward-placed hyphenated codes revealing them as 'C' Flight aircraft of 144 Sqn. In photograph 89 is shown Mosquito KK-K in standard night-fighter colours with very light coloured Sky codes. In May, 1945, this, HP862, and HP858: KK-O, arrived at Cambridge for major inspections—both extra dark grey and Sky with the KK coding (unusually) ahead of the roundel and Type A1 upper wing roundels—introduced to the Command generally in January, 1945.

When one writes about aircraft markings the scope is vast, and the exceptions to consider are many. Mixing business with pleasure at Rotol's Staverton works on August 22, 1945, I came across JM281, a Mk X in standard grey-green night-fighter finish with 'A' in white aft of the roundels. Although she had served on the squadrons, somewhere something odd had happened—but then, it always does, to make aircraft markings so fascinating.

Chapter 13

1943-44: New marks, new types

THROUGHOUT 1943, Fighter Command and squadrons which, from June 1, 1943, formed part of the Second Tactical Air Force, waged a ceaseless offensive by day and night against enemy forces in North-West Europe. With the Luftwaffe fighting desperately in Russia and the Middle East, fighters now rarely found the foe over Britain. Exceptions were the Fw 190 fighter-bombers making fast sneak raids on coastal towns and including lightning strikes on Canterbury, and a tragic sortie to the London area. Typhoons flew standing patrols against them, for the enemy flew in beneath radar cover, and the black and white under-wing stripes on the Typhoons proved a useful distinguishing feature to friend and foe. These operations took place in the first six months of 1943, formations usually comprising about twenty aircraft. They ceased when the Fw 190s began nuisance night raids. Squadrons which faced them included Nos 1 and 486.

Several modified versions of existing fighter aircraft were introduced, or were about to be so, in 1943. Clipped wing Spitfire Vs appeared on the squadrons late in 1942, their wings cropped and the tips plugged to improve low altitude handling. With some pilots they were unpopular, but at low levels they were a useful item in the armoury. Mk IXs were similarly modified, and the clipping of wings soon affected LF, HF, and FIX variants. This produced a profusion of interest completely spoiling the apparent external order. The HF clipped machines had now an improved medium level performance. 'Pointed' or other tails—it mattered not; the distinguishing feature was the engine. And here there was another change for, at last, the Rolls-Royce Griffon on the drawing boards at Derby even before the war, could be heard beneath the new-look cowlings of the Spitfire XII and XIV. Gone was that lovely Spitfire whine and whistle; in its place the throaty chuckle one can still hear in the existing Mk XIXs.

The prototype Mk XII was DP851, a grey-green-yellow machine which served variously as a Griffon test installation aircraft and for various gun combinations. Mk XIIs in ocean grey and green/medium grey finish filtered into 41 Squadron in March, 1943, in whose hands they remained until late 1944. 91 Squadron was the other operator, using them until spring, 1944. Their camouflage was standard, and they had the slightly shiny 'smooth' finish. They were not really low altitude fighters for much of their work was at medium altitudes. To prove their all-round usefulness they opened their campaign by chasing a high-flying raider over Anglesey on April 3, 1943. Their first claim was a Ju 88 off Belgium on April 17. Conversion to the Mk XII was quite a lengthy process, but soon XIIs were escorting bombers, giving support to 'Bomphoons' and tackling those Fw 190 raiders. In 1944 LF XIIs proved very useful against the flying-bombs. Their small number (only 100 were built) was probably due to engine supply bottlenecks and the effectiveness of other Spitfire variants.

One of the latter was the Mk XIV based on the Mk VIII. Development took place largely in 1943. A few trickled into service in January, 1944. Soon they equipped Nos 91, 322 and 610 Squadrons. A curvaceous tail, long nose housing the Griffon and a five-bladed propeller were unmistakable features. The first I was able to closely examine was JF316, a prototype, on a lorry near Cardington. It was in the usual operational Spitfire colours including a rich blueish shade of ocean grey, and had a 'P' prototype marking. This one retained the broad chord or 'pointed' fin fitted when it was a Mk VIII airframe. It had no Sky adornments, and the spinner was black when I cautiously noted its impressive features on April 19, 1944.

Already No 610 Squadron was working-up on XIVs at Castle Camps where I had noted (distantly and uncoded) RB169 and RB172. I had to wait until July, 1944, to examine closely a squadron aircraft. It was RB174:DL-T (DL forward on the port side, aft on the starboard) with provision for four cannon but carrying two only in the outer ports. Only under its fuselage did it have the black and white 'AEAF stripes'. I was told it had been chasing flying-bombs. Questioned on its use the pilot told me that the XIVs had been maintaining patrols over the South Coast during the build up of the invasion fleet.

A lesser known version of the Spitfire now in use was the HFVII. It resembled the VI apart from having a Merlin 61-series engine and a pressure cabin of refined form, and replaced the former in Nos 124 and 616 Squadrons in the spring of 1943. It was serving with Nos 131 and 616 Squadrons in 1944. Some VIIs acquired deep sky finish for their high-altitude role (eg, a few on 131 Sqn). Generally they had standard paintwork, and pointed wing tips. No 154 Squadron had them from late 1944 until March, 1945.

By 1943 the Hurricane was outdated for cross-Channel ventures. Some Mk II fighter-bombers were still in use early that year, which saw the introduction of the Mk IID and IV in home-based units. Mk IID delivery had begun at the start of 1942, but it was December and January, 1943, when No 184 Squadron took on charge Mk IIDs like HW684, KX142, and KX304, mainly for operational trials pending the next version, the Hurricane IV. Delivery of this commenced in May, 1943, and soon Nos 137, 164, 184, 438 and 439 Squadrons had the new mark. They used it for offensive operations begun on July 23 by 137 Squadron's KX827, KW918, KZ661 and KZ662. The two Canadian squadrons had them until shortly before D-Day. A special wing permitted a variety of stores to be carried —bombs, rockets, or 40 mm cannon. When I recorded BR-A:KX407, BR-J:KX194 (IIc), BR-S:KZ554 and BR-X:KZ193 in 1943, all had RP rails fitted.

An entirely new shape of 1944 was the Hawker Tempest V, delivery of which began to the squadrons in January, 1944. To an extent the Tempest supplemented the Typhoon, and in some measure replaced it. Again the camouflage, etc, was standard. Some teething troubles on 486 Sqn resulted in JN792 being an early write-off and taking a lorry ride which brought to me a good close view of her. I recorded in my diary that 'the mainplanes looked huge for a fighter, and had a very glossy finish'. A close look showed traces of black and white stripes under the wing centre section as painted on Typhoons until about March, 1944. On April 14 I visited Castle Camps to see 486 Squadron's new mounts. All that I saw had the under-wing stripes. No 3 Squadron also had Tempests by this time.

Typhoons were now showing a new look, their cannon having been supplemented by four rocket rails beneath each wing. They were waging a sustained onslaught on the Luftwaffe. Wehrmacht, radio and radar stations, and bridges likely to be useful on reinforcement routes to the invasion lodgement area. From the start of May, 1944, they were joined in operations by the Tempests.

Mustang IIIs began to arrive in Britain in large quantities at the end of 1943. These, too, wore the usual finish of ocean grey-dark green and medium sea grey with standard Sky and yellow adornments. On account of their range they proved most useful as escort aircraft. They were fast, too. FZ105 was used in attempts to improve the view by Malcolms. As a result most Mk IIIs were fitted with the bulged canopy, popularly known as the 'Malcolm hood'.

Type S finish

New types formed only a small part of the 1944 fighter force, the backbone of which was a large armada of Spitfire IXs and a sizeable number of Mk Vs. The accent on the early war years had been on disguise, now it was upon performance. With the Luftwaffe rarely over Britain it was decided in 1942 to introduce the shiny Type S camouflage with a smooth and slightly reflective glossy finish. This was slow to make its appearance on squadron aircraft, but picture 96 shows two of 611 Squadron's Spitfires taken at the end of 1942 in this finish. With a spot of polishing it could give up to 10 mph increased speed at a vital time of the war. On the Spitfire VII, XII and XIV, many Typhoons, and the Tempests, the new paintwork was applied from the start of their lives. On others it appeared retrospectively as convenient.

Type S finish was well in evidence when I called on No 1 Squadron at North Weald on April 15, 1944. The squadron was just re-equipping with the Spitfire IXs, its Typhoons including JX-N: MN513 and JX-T: EJ974 being parked in their very shiny coats to one side. MK725: JX-N was a IXB that particularly took my fancy for it was spotlessly clean, which was unusual for a wartime aeroplane. Nearby stood JX-O: MK998. All the Typhoons were very clean, and each had a four-bladed propeller and a 'teardrop' canopy. There was no evidence here of any under-wing stripes, but all had yellow wing leading edges.

At Wittering on April 29 there were fighters galore for various trials with the AFDU. Typhoon XP-D (codes in standard position): EJ488 was one of the shiny ones. It had a teardrop canopy and a three-bladed propeller. Spitfire IXB MH413: ZD-M featured the bulged canopy of many later Spitfires and RB179, a Mk XIV, had the shiny finish too. Spitfire Mk VC BR372 was on a dispersal, interesting as the machine used for dive bombing trials and in that it had dark sea grey and dark green upper surfaces which, years before, had preceded the ocean grey finish. P8160: AF-I of the demonstration flight had white codes like P8282:AF:E, there being no trace of blue or green in their codes, which showed up well against the other Sky Type S trim. Neither of these had a shiny finish.

Identity markings

The use of markings to denote special exercise forces has long been in vogue. Before the 1939-45 war one could see Wellingtons wearing them for large-scale exercises, and from time to time they cropped up in the war years. The most important exercise held was *Spartan,* in which tactical air forces combined with the army in the development of techniques, attempted at Dieppe, needing full exploitation prior to detail planning of the landings in France. *Spartan* took place in early March, 1943. Attacking forces had the port under surfaces or wings of their aircraft distempered black. Typhoons, Spitfires, Mustangs and Tomahawks had these markings. As a further identity they featured a white stripe about eighteen inches wide from the spinner to the cockpit entry door. At Bottisham on March 9 I noted the oft-pictured Mustang I AL995, now with 'S' aft as its only coding, and wearing these new markings. Three of 613 Squadron's Mustangs landed, O:AP294, P:AP295 and L:AP254 all wearing black port wing undersides and the white stripe.

Defenders wore standard markings as on the Spitfire VIs of 124 Sqn, then detached for a few days to Duxford. ON-P, W, S, V, R, F, A, were among them. For moving the fighter squadrons' stores and personnel there were Harrows of No 271 Sqn, still on charge. These were now plying to and fro, movement being vital for any tactical campaign. It is interesting to read from my notes that I recorded their under surfaces as 'painted in that old deep green which we used to call duck egg green'. K6993 with BJ-L (BJ ahead both sides) was one, but when I saw it a year later it had the usual brown-green upper surfaces yet azure blue on its under surfaces. Codes were red.

Operation 'Overlord'

It was evident in the spring of 1944 that the attack on the European mainland would come soon. Increasing numbers of transport aircraft were seen; bombing of rail targets was an obvious prelude. Then there came the massed movement of gliders to the south from their storage bases in eastern England. Behind the scenes secrecy of the precise date was maintained, although May or early June with long evenings for massive day fighter cover suggested themselves as likely times.

Special identity markings were promulgated to distinguish the Allied tactical forces directly supporting the landings. They were related distantly to the black and white stripes of the Typhoons and Tempests, and to those used in *Spartan*. From dawn on June 5, fighters could be seen wearing three white and two black stripes chordwise around each mainplane and around the rear fuselage where the last band was adjacent to the Sky band. Each stripe was eighteen inches wide and on the mainplane the bands were theoretically placed to begin six inches inboard of the roundel. These measurements were roughly adhered to, and whilst they did not usually blot out the serial number, the same cannot be said for squadron letters. Usually the stripes circumscribed them, sometimes they were painted over them. In some cases Sky codes were applied on them or even on the aircraft fins. FF-G:MK367 and FF-W:MH758 retained their usual codes with the stripes. Mk VB (clipped) FF-D:W3560 also did so. Some NF Mosquitoes had them, like MM625 which had NG in red but no individual letter. Mustang III PK-D:FB182 being part of ADGB did not wear them. It had PK forward on both sides. BR160 had a V after and no other codes. Tempest JF-P:JN743 of ADGB was also without stripes. An interesting rarer sight was Spitfire VB (clipped) AB180 with ocean grey and dark green upper surfaces, and Sky under surfaces bearing a tapering black line upon them from the spinner to the rudder. This was an ASR machine. MN946:TP-Y was a fully striped Typhoon with codes as usually sited. Some of that squadron wore their unit letters on the cowling. ZY-Y: MN363 had them and was fitted with RP racks. Both had four-bladed propellers and teardrop canopies when I recorded them in July, 1944.

To list all the squadrons employed and their aircraft would demand space beyond that available, but the following list includes a large proportion of them:

Sqn	*Code*	*Example in mid 1943*	*Type*	*Example in mid 1944*	*Type*
1	JX	Q:MN115	Typhoon 1B	R:MK798	Spitfire IXB
2	Nil ?	X:AM112	Mustang 1	A:FD567 *	Mustang 1A
3	QO	MN123	Typhoon 1B	J:EJ768	Tempest V
				(Tempests coded JF)	
4	Nil ?	AM207	Mustang 1	PL764 *	Spitfire PR XI
19	QV	AB467	Spitfire VB	H:FB113 *	Mustang III
26	Nil	AL966	Mustang 1	MB953 *	Spitfire XI
63	?	AL965	(Reformed 5.44)	E:BS239	Spitfire IX
56	US	W:JR442	Typhoon 1B	D:ML293 *	Spitfire IX
63		AL965	Mustang 1	G:BL232	Spitfire
64	SH	AR424	Spitfire VB	H:MH729 *	Spitfire IX
65	YT	BM491	Spitfire VB	FZ151 *	Mustang III
66	LZ	K:W3719	Spitfire VB	?	Spitfire IX
91	DL	EN230	Spitfire XII	RB173	Spitfire XIV
118	NK	BL718	Spitfire LF VB	FZ139	Mustang III
122	MT	BM269	Spitfire VB	FZ177	Mustang III
124	ON	H:BR579	Spitfire HF VI	C:MB808	Spitfire VII
126	5J	—	—	T:MJ623 *	Spitfire IXB
127	9N	—	—	MK680	Spitfire IXE
129	DV	F:MJ664	Spitfire IX	D:FB364	Mustang III
131	NX	B:AD411	Spitfire VB	MD120	Spitfire VII
132	FF	U:EN922	Spitfire VB	H:MK367 *	Spitfire IXB
137	SF	W:P7119	Whirlwind	Z:JR261 *	Typhoon 1B
164	FJ	KZ193:0	Hurricane IV	J:JP437 *	Typhoon 1B
165	SK	M:AR508	Spitfire VB	H:MK362	Spitfire IX
168	Nil	FD444	Mustang II	AM112 *	Mustang 1
174	XP	R:JP671	Typhoon 1B	H.MN992	Typhoon 1B
175	HH	E:JP394	Typhoon 1B	R:JR501 *	Typhoon 1B
181	EL	Q:EK211	Typhoon 1B	N:MN311 *	Typhoon 1B
182	XM	L:R7677	Typhoon 1B	Z:JP705 *	Typhoon 1B
183	HF	L:JR128	Typhoon 1B	A:MN529	Typhoon 1B
184	BR	B:KZ611	Hurricane IV	Z:JR337 *	Typhoon 1B
193	DP	JR240	Typhoon 1B	E:MN886 *	Typhoon 1B

Sqn	*Code*	*Example in mid 1943*	*Type*	*Example in mid 1944*		*Type*
197	OV	N:DN494	Typhoon 1B	Z:JP504	*	Typhoon 1B
198	TP	P:EJ930	Typhoon 1B	R:MN813	*	Typhoon 1B
222	ZD	MH428	Spitfire IX	X:MH765		Spitfire IX
229	9R	—	—	A:MH813		Spitfire IXC
231	MV ?	AH798	Tomahawk 1	(Disbanded 15.1.44)		
245	MR	S:JP660	Typhoon 1B	J:MN371	*	Typhoon 1B
247	ZY	N:DN252	Typhoon 1B	G:MN373	*	Typhoon 1B
257	FM	L:EJ926	Typhoon 1B	F:MN645	*	Typhoon 1B
263	HE	N:P7102	Whirlwind	B:MN769	*	Typhoon 1B
266	ZH	L:R8937	Typhoon 1B	Z:MN712	*	Typhoon 1B
274	JJ	—	—	K:MH603		Spitfire IXC
302	WX	AA928	Spitfire VB	F:MA843		Spitfire IXC
303	RF	EN173	Spitfire IX	?		Spitfire IXC
306	UZ	L:EP116	Spitfire VB	U:FB393		Mustang III
308	ZF	K:EE742	Spitfire VB	K:MH671		Spitfire IX
309	WC	AL964	Mustang 1	F:LF363		Hurricane IIC
310	NN	V:EE661	Spitfire VB	P:BS249		Spitfire IXC
313	RY	BL255	Spitfire VB	P:ML261		Spitfire IX
315	SZ	BR631	Spitfire IX	R:FB181		Mustang III
316	PK	K:EN172	Spitfire IX	O:FB229		Mustang III
329	5A	—	—	F:PL379		Spitfire IX
331	FN	H:EN572	Spitfire IX	MK924		Spitfire IX
340	GW	O:P8748	Spitfire LF VB	T:MK183		Spitfire IX
341	NL	BS123	Spitfire IX	M:MH497		Spitfire IX
345	2Y	—	(Formed 12.2.44)	L:AD227		Spitfire V/IX
349	GE	?	Tomahawk II	H:MK192		Spitfire IX
401	YO	BL486	Spitfire LF VB	N:MA897		Spitfire IX
403	KH	BR637	Spitfire IX	MH614		Spitfire IX
416	DN	BM204	Spitfire VB	U:BS411		Spitfire IX
421	AU	BM306	Spitfire IX	Y:MK121		Spitfire IX
438	F3	—	—	W:MN375		Typhoon 1B
				(Formed 15.11.43)		
440	I8	—	—	K:MN535		Typhoon 1B
453	FU	BR624	Spitfire IX	F:MK258		Spitfire IX
486	SA	K:JP853	Typhoon IB	S:JN766		Tempest V
501	SD	M:W3702	Spitfire VB	S:BL632		Spitfire V/IX
504	HX	?	Spitfire VB	R:EN907		Spitfire V/IX
				(Reformed 1944, coded TM)		
602	LO	BL310	Spitfire V	F:MJ881	*	Spitfire IXC
609	PR	F:DN406	Typhoon 1B	Z:MN701	*	Typhoon 1B
610	DW	Y:EE745	Spitfire VB	A:RB150		Spitfire XIV
616	YQ	X:MB768	Spitfire VII	?		Spitfire IX

* AEAF stripes known to have been carried.

The above lists many of the squadrons but, as pointed out, it is not complete. Spitfire XIIs bore serials MB829-863, '857-882 delivered first, and EN221-238, '601-627.

Chapter 14

1941-45: Fighters in the Far East

THE CAMPAIGN in the Far East presents one of the saddest stories in Britain's history. Everywhere it was a case of too little too late, or a wrong conception of the needs for defence—and its message for today is all too obvious. Inconceivably it seems that Singapore was entirely without any fighter protection until May, 1941, and that in India a few Blenheims and a host of biplanes were all that were available. The reverses in Europe in 1940 prohibited reinforcements going to the East, a region of almost no action. Overseas re-deployment was instead to the Middle East, preventing planned Hurricane deliveries further east. For defence the RAF looked towards North American supply.

Japanese strength and standard of equipment was obviously under-estimated. Four Allied squadrons had been equipped with the outdated, under-armed Brewster Buffalo, which had to face a carrier force equipped with the legendary Zero fighter.

When the battle broke on December 7, 1941, the RAF had in Malaysia five fighter squadrons. These, it was argued, could be reinforced by others from the USA and the Netherlands East Indies. Britain's force had been planned to rise from 88 obsolete or obsolescent aeroplanes to 336 modern machines for which a string of new bases was being prepared. Radar and observer links were required and additional bases in Burma and Ceylon. The 40 Buffaloes, and 12 Blenheim 1Fs of No 27 Sqn, could hardly provide effective defence.

By late November, 1941, relations with the Japanese had deteriorated so that attack seemed likely against Siam and perhaps Malaya—and remotely against Singapore. In consequence squadrons moved to war stations to support a possible British advance into Siam. RAAF Hudsons and three Catalinas of No 205 Sqn meanwhile were to watch for 'enemy' shipping. Too late they came across Japanese transports off Malaya. At this time No 21 Sqn RAAF, and No 27 Sqn were deployed for Operation *Matador* against Siam, leaving Nos 243, 453 and 488 to defend Singapore.

At first light on December 8, 1941, enemy troops began to land on the beach of North Malaya and Blenheims were ordered to shoot them up at once. Operations by the fighters began at 03.00 hrs. Two Buffaloes strafed enemy barges near Kota Bahru and at 04.00 Singapore had its first raid by carrier-based aircraft. Attacks soon began on airfields with the object of putting them out of use but not of destroying them. In a matter of hours Nos 21 and 27 Sqns had only four aircraft each and withdrew to Butterworth. Their efforts had been ineffectual.

Short endurance prevented the Buffaloes from being of much help to the bombers. For 453 Sqn an even more demoralising situation awaited. Their task was to patrol over HMS *Repulse* and HMS *Prince of Wales;* they arrived to find both mighty warships had been sunk, and had only their destroyer escort to look after. Such was the enemy success that Nos 21 and 27 Sqns had again to retreat south to Ipoh over difficult forested territory. Meanwhile, Buffaloes of No 3 PRU flew useful reconnaissance sorties off the coast. A few days later, 453 Sqn moved forward to Ipoh, losing five of its number to crashes en route, and only six Buffaloes reached the field. Japanese raids soon reduced a revived 21 Sqn and 453 Sqn to a strength of four aircraft each. On December 23 all were withdrawn to Singapore. 21 and 453 Sqns had been very handicapped by lack of attack warning and poor facilities in general, although their presence was at least a morale booster for the troops.

State of the fighters on December 24 was as follows: 21 and 453 Sqns re-organising at Sembawang, 243 Sqn had 14 Buffaloes at Kallang where 488 Sqn also had 14 and a Dutch squadron had nine, with 27 Sqn also there sorting itself out. Desperate messages had gone to Britain for reinforcements which by January 8 should have included 51 crated Hurricanes diverted from the Middle East with 24 pilots. These were to operate from Kallang, and they arrived amid great excitement on January 13, for it was considered these could provide effective defence.

Meanwhile the Buffaloes soldiered on, facing the continued heavy Jap attacks. Twelve of them escorted Blenheims attacking barges in the River Linggi on January 15. Next day 15 Buffaloes shot up road movements between Tampin and Gemas. Four shot up troop barges on the Muar River, attacks repeated by half-dozen others escorting Vildebeestes there on January 17. The attacks were repeated on the 18th when 14 aircraft operated. PRU Buffaloes were watching the repair of airfields and the build-up of Japanese squadrons upon them. No 27 Squadron's Blenheim fighters unsuccessfully attempted to halt raids on Singapore where the Hurricanes were being hastily assembled on dispersed sites. They entered combat on January 20, flown by pilots of No 17 Sqn and some from 135 and 136. With ground crews they were formed into 232 Sqn at Kallang.

From HMS *Indomitable* another 48 Hurricanes were soon to be flown off and 39 more in crates were on the way. Buffaloes were continuing their straffing operations and patrolling around Muar, intercepting bombers when practicable. Roads and the beachhead were also strafed. Some of the Hurricanes were at Seletar by the 25th, their intended airfields having been overrun. Then came the landings at Endau. Fifteen Buffaloes and eight Hurricanes escorted bombers to the spot, and a second wave of Vildebeestes had four Buffaloes as escort. The slow biplanes proved a headache for the escorters who, nevertheless, claimed 12 Zeros.

Next came a period of heavy raids on the Singapore airfields. Nos 21 RAAF and 453 Squadrons were being mainly used for army support, leaving 232, 243 and 488 Sqns to defend the island. On their first day of operations, incidentally, the Hurricanes claimed eight unescorted bombers

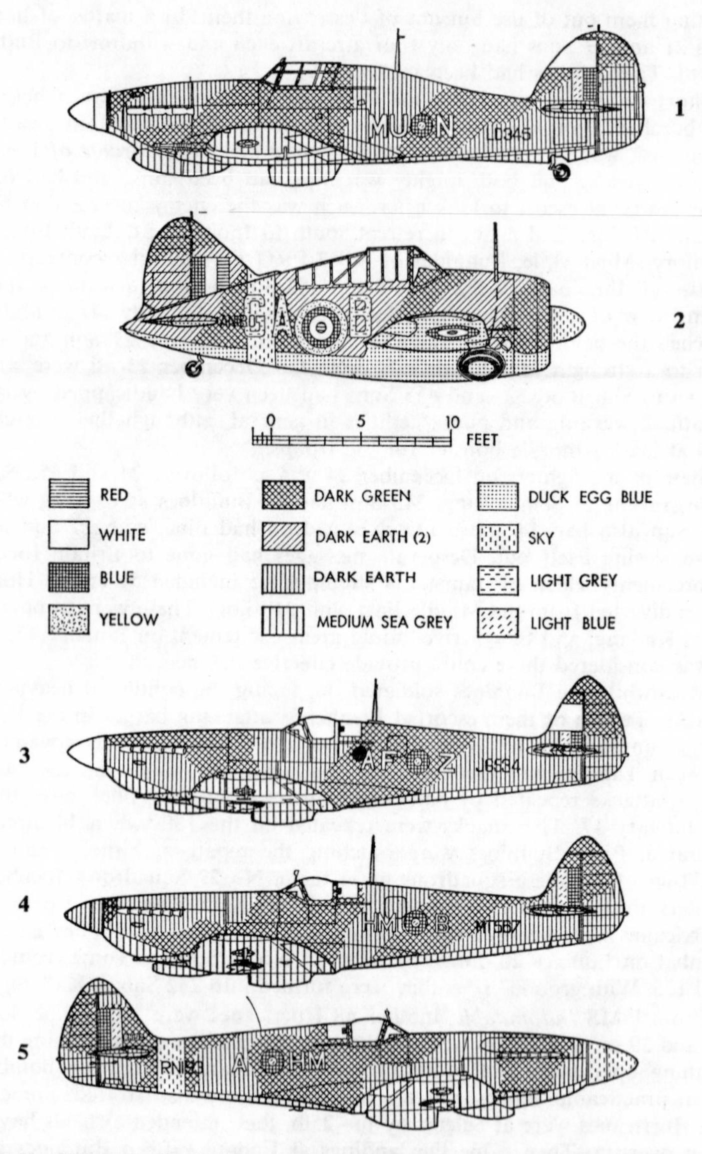

Figure 15: SEAC fighters. *(1) Hurricane Mk IIC LD345:MU-N of No 60 Sqn, complete with white wing identity bands and other white trim. The squadron codes were 15 inches high and fin band 18 inches deep. An interesting feature of this and all the Spitfires illustrated here is that the fuselage and wing roundels had an outside diameter of 15 inches; the inner pale blue ring was of 6 inches diameter. (2) Brewster Buffalo AN180:GA-B of 21 Sqn RAAF has the earlier colours similar to those of home-based fighters. Its camouflage pattern appears to have been non-standard for a single-engined fighter, but this applied to other Buffaloes. Note that the Sky band and spinner differs much in shade from the duck egg shade (blue or green) of the under surfaces. (3) Spitfire VIII JB534:AF-Z of 607 Sqn in late war colours with white trim and wing and tail fin and tailplane bands. It has a non-standard camouflage pattern. (4) MT567:HM-B of 136 Sqn has the usual pattern and is in 1944 finish. (5) RN193, a Mk XIV of the same squadron has the post-war scheme, and is of interest in that it has a small white fin serial.*

without loss . . . if only there had been more Hurricanes. Usually the bombers were escorted, and against these formations the Hurricanes were flying three to five sorties daily. When fighting the Zeros, however, the Hurricanes were at a disadvantage. Their desert filters deprived them of about 30 mph although at over 20,000 ft they were superior in speed and climb but could be outmanoeuvred. Seventeen had been lost by the 28th and only 21 Hurricanes were available for fighting. No 27 Squadron had been withdrawn to the Netherlands East Indies and when the army fell back to Singapore Island only Kallang could be used, for all the other fields were on its north side. By the end of January, only eight Hurricanes of 232 Sqn and six Buffaloes of 453 were left on the island, the reinforcement Hurricanes being taken direct to Sumatra. After flying about 100 sorties the PR Buffaloes were finally knocked out on February 7.

On Sumatra No 258 Sqn was established with 15 Hurricanes. It had come from the Middle East in *Indomitable* on January 26 and flew some sorties from Singapore. During the first ten days of February the Hurricanes were almost continuously airborne. When Singapore fell on February 15, it was claimed that fighters had destroyed 183 enemy aircraft. A total of 30 later credited to the Buffaloes seems reasonable. Hurricanes claimed 100 destroyed for the loss of 45 to themselves.

A mixture of Hurricane Is and IIBs had so far reached the East. To improve the IIBs performance its outer four guns were removed. Thirty-nine more Hurricanes arrived on February 12. Two days later a massive airborne assault was launched on Palembang when the Hurricanes were airborne and out of W/T range. Soon the task was the escort of Blenheim bombers to prevent the Japanese from capturing the island, but on 15th withdrawal was forced and Sumatra was captured.

Finally came the attempt to hold Java. Fighters were now located at Tjililitan where 232 Sqn and the newly-arrived elements of No 605 Sqn were established with 25 Hurricanes. No 605's IIAs went into action on February 23 and they fought until Java was overrun.

The aircraft and their colour schemes

All the fighters engaged in the period December, 1941, to February, 1942, were similarly painted. They had dark green and dark earth upper surfaces with Sky (duck egg green shade) under surfaces except perhaps some Hurricanes with lighter shades of Sky. Code letters (when carried) were medium grey placed with the unit letters forward on the port and usually aft on the starboard side of the fuselage. Serials were black, spinners and rear fuselage bands Sky. Roundel types were as for home based fighters.

Relatively little has, not surprisingly, survived concerning the aircraft engaged in the campaign, but there follows a listing of some aircraft used:

No 21 Sqn Royal Australian Air Force: Buffaloes used included AN170, AN171, AN174. Unit probably coded GA (and if so GA-B: AN180 may be added to the list).

No 243 Sqn, examples used being W8147, W8179, W8199, W8238.

No 453 Sqn possibly coded FU; formed October, 1941. Examples W8160, AN184, AN211.

No 488 Sqn formed October, 1941. Examples used included NF-U: W8198, NF-O: W8138 and AN187, '189, W8135, '8171, '8186, '8191, '8195, '8200.

No 27 Sqn; no details known. Used Blenheim IF.

No 232 Sqn coded EF, No 232 Sqn briefly existing before becoming part of 242 Sqn probably coded LE, and No 258 Sqn coded ZT.

Burma and India

Japan's onslaught on Burma began around Christmas, 1941. Two terrible raids on Rangoon killed over 7,000 of its inhabitants. To defend Burma, seven airfields had been built, reinforced by six landing grounds. For the fighters there was a serious disadvantage since mountains to the east prevented early warning. Defence lay entirely in the hands of the 16 Buffaloes of No 67 Sqn which included W8135, '8138, '8168, '8191, '8195, '8198, along with American P-40s guarding the Burma Road to China. Object of the Japanese attacks was its entry point, Rangoon, and the aim was to cut supplies to China. During those frightful raids the fighters fought well and claimed 36 of the enemy, an amazing achievement considering there was only one radar station, virtually no early warning and the most primitive communications system. Thirty Hurricanes were hastily brought in during January, and No 67 Squadron re-equipped for exhaustive fighting next month defending Rangoon. But the Japanese could not be held anywhere in the East and soon struck into Burma. Rangoon fell and all that remained of the fighter force—three Buffaloes and 20 Hurricanes—was forced to withdraw to India under terrible conditions. Here the defensive force was re-organised and included Nos 17 and 67 Squadrons using Hurricanes based for a time on the forward base on Akyab which was heavily raided on March 27. After this, only 13 Hurricanes remained. By April the fighters were committed to the defence of Calcutta.

Indomitable ferried more reinforcements in the form of Hurricane Is and IIs of Nos 30 and 261 Squadrons for the defence also of Ceylon from Ratmalana, Trincomalee and Colombo. These bases gave fighter cover to the Royal Navy. A tremendous fight was waged over the island on April 5, when 18 enemy aircraft were claimed for the loss of 18 of the 36 Hurricanes (Mks I and IIB) of Nos 30 and 258 Squadrons. The Navy took a hammering and 261 Sqn fought another fierce battle around Trincomalee on April 9, but the island was clearly going to hold out.

Radar units had now been set up in India so that when the Japanese began raids on April 6, the Hurricanes had early warning. Soon the situation calmed as the Japanese reached the border of India and paused for breath. For many months the fighters stood by to repulse another great attack but the summer came and went with nothing major materialising. By June, 1942, Hurricanes equipped Nos 17, 30, 67, 79, 135, 146, 258 and 261 Sqns, in India and Ceylon.

A few Japanese bombers had made a night raid on Calcutta in January, 1942, and caused panic amongst its inhabitants. At once a few Beaufighters arrived to halt the night raids, going into action on January 15/16. Four nights later, with sore losses to heal, the enemy raids halted. Against the A.I. equipped machines the enemy was powerless to achieve anything.

Throughout 1942 the Middle East war, swinging to and fro over the desert sands, dictated to a large extent the strength of the forces in India. Supplies intended for the Far East often went no further than North Africa where Rommel's prowess had shaken the British. All that could still be spared for India were Hurricane IIs, a type largely withdrawn from offensive operations over NW Europe. The supply of Spitfires was still insufficient to allow any to go to India except for PR duties. Eventually the defensive strength there was set at six Hurricane squadrons; 1943 saw the deployment of Beaufighter VIs for night-fighter duties.

The fighter squadrons came much into their own when Wavell launched his First Arakan Campaign, the aim then being to capture Akyab. Hurricanes distinguished themselves in close support work, but the strength of enemy land forces nullified the army's efforts. Meanwhile, other fighters supported the Wingate enterprise when the Chindits first campaigned, an exciting aspect of operations, halted when the June monsoon came. Hurricanes had given useful escort to the supplying Dakotas.

Hurricane deliveries were now sufficiently large to permit them to replace such aircraft as Blenheims, and they were ideally suited to the tough conditions of operation, using guns and bombs. Nos 11, 34, 42, 60 and 113 Squadrons were equipped with them. Early in October, the first Spitfire VCs arrived for Nos 136, 607 and 615 Squadrons. At last the Mohawks of No 5 Sqn (eight had been India's sole defence force at one time) could be replaced after they had put up some stiff fighting. Another Buffalo squadron, No 143 (eg, AN124, W8246), received Hurricanes, too.

Greatest of the needs in this theatre of operations was for transport aircraft and these were now arriving in the form of Dakotas. The fighter types sent there were essentially schemed for operations in the defence of Britain. They lacked range and needed to be tropicalised and also to be backed by early warning stations, etc. One of the great success stories was that of the Beaufighter which immediately proved successful and soon became known to the Japanese as 'Whispering Death' on account of its quiet approach.

The arrival of the Spitfire was, perhaps, the most successful event of all for it took such a heavy toll of enemy fighters and bombers bold enough to venture near or over India. Then the Japanese brought along strong fighter cover at high altitudes—only to find that in January, 1944, the Spitfire VIII had arrived. It had a top speed of over 400 mph and could fight at up to 40,000 feet. British air superiority was now unquestionably gained, and by what was possibly the most refined Spitfire of all.

Our strength was well apparent in the Second Arakan Campaign when Hurricanes Mk IIB, IIC, IID of No 20 Sqn and the Spitfires fought so well. The Japanese provided a strong distraction in the Imphal and Kohima regions in March and April, 1944, and in only 16 days 2,200 sorties were flown by Hurricanes of four squadrons in the ground attack role against the 31st Division at Kohima. Around Imphal the Hurricanes of Nos 11, 28, 34, 42, 113 Squadrons fought a bitter battle. Then came the support for the Second Chindit Campaign and massive support for the second thrust into Burma which, despite the monsoon, led to the capture of Rangoon. And still it was the Hurricanes that were bashing away at the enemy whilst Spitfire VIIIs maintained air supremacy. Battles to clear Burma continued far into 1945.

By then the picture of equipment had changed. The Republic Thunderbolt was at hand, for in 1944 seven squadrons equipped with the type, Nos 79, 123, 134, 135, 146, 258 and 261, and others were to follow. Nos 67, 136, 273 and 607 all had Spitfires by mid-1944 and 60 Sqn was flying Hurricane IVs. Three, Nos 17, 20 and 28, were to soldier on another year with a mixture of Hurricane IICs and IVs. Thunderbolts proved useful in the role the Hurricanes had adopted and Spitfires, too, sailed in as fighter-bombers as the war reached its concluding months. There was no need to invade Malaya; the arrival of the nuclear age halted the fighting in time. And still Nos 17, 20 and 28 Squadrons had Hurricanes.

When production permitted, the Spitfire XIV made its debut in the East and in the spring of 1945 the FRXIV reconnaissance fighter with a rear fuselage oblique camera.

SEAC markings

Once the Buffaloes and early Hurricanes had ceased to exist, a change in colouring was soon apparent. Hurricanes, Spitfires and Thunderbolts in SEAC appeared with dark earth and dark green upper surfaces with deep blue or more often medium grey under surfaces. Many aircraft had been switched from the Middle East and these often retained their azure blue under surfaces. Others, perhaps intended for operations in coastal regions, had dark grey and green camouflage with lighter grey under surfaces. This latter scheme gradually replaced the green and brown so that by the war's end this was common. Stocks of American paints are known to have been drawn upon, so that fighters had shades other than those specified for British aircraft. The use of Sky trim seems to have been erratic, but it became usual about the end of the war. Spinners were sometimes in Flight colours, but usually they were white.

In 1943, large code letters were replaced by a smaller size often 18 inches high, sometimes only a foot high and white. In June of that year—officially on June 24—a blue and white roundel was adopted which frequently appeared as roundel blue or a paler shade of blue 16 inches in diameter with a 6 inch white/off-white centre disc. Two fin stripes, blue and white, were applied two feet high on the single-engined fighters. Code letters were positioned as was usual on home-based fighters.

As a further aid to identity, white nose, wing and tail bands were applied. Thunderbolt instructions required 28 inch wide bands around the inner wing section, 18 inch wide bands around the tailplane and across the fin and a stripe around the cowling leading edge 17 inches wide. Hurricanes and Spitfires had similar markings, but usually only their spinners were white. These markings first came in with the entry of the Thunderbolt in February, 1944, but it seems that the Hurricanes and Spitfires did not wear them until much later.

Thunderbolts were being supplied in natural finish during the final months of the war. In place of white trimmings these wore black and had black codes and anti-dazzle panels. Sometimes these latter were olive green. Dark Blue was officially prescribed for the wing, nose and tail trim of the Thunderbolts, and there is no doubt that some machines wore this colour. Another feature of some of them was the repetition of the serial number in black in various positions on the fin in small characters.

A green-brown-light grey Spitfire VIII used was JG412:DG-L with white codes and blue-white small roundels which, on its under surfaces, embraced a small red centre disc somewhat strangely featured on quite a number of Spitfires. Hurricane HV945 in the grey-green scheme was shorn of all white bands by June, 1945. Hurricane IIC LB557, coded EG-N (with N two feet high and aft of the roundels) meanwhile had white spinner, white wing bands which did not overlap the flaps and a white stripe across the top of the tail's dark blue and lighter blue stripes. It had grey-green camouflage and belonged to the last Hurricane squadron to operate in SEAC. Many Beaufighters were now in use as strike-fighters. NE807:F (aft of the roundels) and of 27 Sqn in 1945, had white bands around its mainplanes and across the fin and rudder. Others similarly marked and in use in January, 1945, with 27 Sqn included C:NV245, F:NV253 and U:NV256. After the war, fighter colours came gradually into line with those on home-based aircraft.

It would be impossible here to list all the fighters that were sent to South East Asia Command. Most of the Spitfire VIIIs were shipped there, and almost all of the Thunderbolts. Mk I aircraft with the old 'razor back' carried the serials FL731-850 and HB962-HD181. Mk IIs with teardrop canopies were HD182-301, KJ128-367, KL168-347, KL838-887.

The squadrons

Listed here are the relevant fighter squadrons which operated in the Far East and their respective equipment:

Sqn	*Unit letters*	*Type*	*Serial*	*Notes*
5	?	Mohawk IV	AR650	12.41 to 6.43
		Hurricane IIC	HW801	6.43 to 1944
	OQ ?	Thunderbolt I/II	HD140	1944-45
11	?	Hurricane IIC	B-LB796	1943
		Spitfire VIII	?	1944
		Spitfire XIV	MV319	1945
17	YB	Hurricane IIC	BN540	in use 1943
		Hurricane IVC	HV798	
20	?	Hurricane IIB	BN699	in use 1943
		Hurricane IID	HW676	
28		Hurricane IIB	BH134	
30	RS	Hurricane I, II	LD573:X	
		Thunderbolt I, II	HD286:G	
34		Hurricane IIA, B	LB999	
		Thunderbolt I, II	KL200	
42	AW	Hurricane IIC	KZ244:C	in use 12.43
		Thunderbolt II	KJ316:Y	in use late '44
60	MU	Hurricane II	LE354:M	Mk IIC listed
		Thunderbolt	KL859:T	in use 7.45
67	RD	Buffalo	W8280:U	
		Hurricane II	BN871	
		Spitfire VIII	JG183:S	
79	NV	Hurricane IIC	BN569	
		Thunderbolt I, II	KL231:L	
113	?	Hurricane II	KZ373	
		Thunderbolt I, II	HD173:N	

Sqn	*Unit letters*	*Type*	*Serial*	*Notes*
123	XE	Hurricane II	BP114	in use 6.43
		Thunderbolt I	HD106	in use 12.44
		Thunderbolt II	KJ241	in use 3.45
131	NX	Spitfire VIII	?	
		Thunderbolt II	KL194	
132	FF	Spitfire XIV	RN133:B	
134	GQ	Hurricane IIA/B/C	BN957	
		Spitfire V/VIII	JK118	in use 7.43
		Thunderbolt	KL339:GQ-B	
135	WK	Hurricane I, II, IV	?	
		Thunderbolt I	HB975:L	
136	HM	Hurricane II	?	
		Spitfire VIII	MT507:B	
		Spitfire XIV	RN193:A	
146	NA ?	Buffalo	AN124	
		Hurricane I/II	BN927	
		Thunderbolt I, II	KJ330	FL793 Mk 1
152	UM	Spitfire VIII	MT958	
155	DG	Mohawk IV	BS798:B	in use 1943
		Hurricane II	HW420	in use 11.43
		Spitfire VIII	LV735:Q	
258	ZT	Hurricane IIA/B/C	BD881	
		Thunderbolt I/II	HD185	
261	FJ	Hurricane II	AP935:A	in use to late '44
		Thunderbolt II	KL849:G	in use '44 to 8.45
273	MS	Fulmar	X8773	few used
		Hurricane I/II	Z4952:K	
		Spitfire VIII	MD254:R	in use 1944
607	AF	Hurricane IIB/C	HL783	
		Spitfire VIII	JF781:P	in use 1944
615	KW	Hurricane II	HV828	Mk IIC
		Spitfire V/VIII	JL108	Mk V given
		Thunderbolt I/II	KJ141:W	

118 A good close view of late-war Spitfire camouflage on an old Mk Vc, EP829, seen freshly painted at a Middle East MU in late 1944. This particular aircraft had earlier shot down the thousandth enemy aircraft over Malta, as inscribed beneath the cockpit. Not featured on this aircraft, however, are the yellow wing leading edges usual in Europe (Alan Green).

119 *Non-standard changes to Spitfire finish can be seen on this Mk IX, AU-Y, in early 1945. AEAF stripes have been removed, as have the yellow leading edge stripes. Squadron badge has been added on the nose* (IWM).

120 *As the 2nd Tactical Air Force moved forward in Europe it occupied airfields shattered by attacks of both sides. Typhoon MN606 of 247 Sqn has black and white belly and wing stripes, and retains a yellow leading edge* (IWM).

121 *Mustang III, QV-D:FB201 of No 19 Sqn and part of ADGB in the summer of 1944. It has white nose and wing bands, sky codes and fuselage band. Home based, the machine has no AEAF stripes* (IWM).

122 *Mustang III, FZ120:F of 316 Sqn, showing post-war Mustang trim on one of the Polish squadrons which existed many months after the end of the war in Europe. Has underwing serials, white nose, and sky band.*

123 *More non-standard finishes appeared in SEAC after the war. This is an interesting Beaufighter X, NV11?, in SEAC standard finish of green/brown/grey and white bands, but with the fuselage roundel converted to red/white/blue form by crafty re-painting. Code P is probably in red with a white outline. Squadron is not known* (N. T. Wilkinson).

124 *Tempest V EJ555 at Dedelsdorf, Germany, in September 1945 in the hands of No 274 Sqn. Drawing of this aircraft appears in Figure 18* (Stuart Mackay).

125 *Identity markings were removed from RAF Mustangs after the war. This is a Mk IVA in grey/green/light grey finish at Luqa, Malta in late 1945. Serial is KH759 repeated in usual peace-time style under the wings* (Howard Smith).

126 *Another post-war style on Mustang IV KH816 of 213 Sqn. Finish is silver, spinner probably red. Outlining and positioning of codes (which may be yellow) is interesting* (B. C. Morrison).

127 *Peace-time Spitfire finish typified by a Mk XVIII of 208 Sqn in Palestine in 1946. Grey/green/light grey colour scheme with white codes and with sky fuselage band retained in this instance* (Barry Nevill).

128 *At the same period Spitfires in service were being shorn of camouflage. This is a Mk IX BS467:RG-C of 208 Sqn in natural finish with black anti-dazzle panel on cowling. Another Mk IX, NH487, stands beyond it still in camouflage* (Barry Nevill).

129 *Another 208 Sqn Spitfire Mk XVIII in 1946 (being recovered after a crash) was RG-J, the squadron leader's machine which carries his pennant under the cockpit. Note the red/white/blue C type roundels on the upper wing, also seen in picture 128* (Barry Nevill).

130 *Mosquito T3, RR307, in silver finish with 'T' bands (usual on these aircraft) in use with No 141 Squadron whose white crest appears on a black fin disc. Note the D type roundels. Period was 1948-49.*

131 *Hornet 1 PX237 wearing light grey/blue finish and Type B roundels. It has black underwing serials without roundels there. It bears traces of Type C1 fuselage roundel. Photographed in 1946.*

132 *Hornet PX277:EB-W in grey/blue finish has silver spinners and Type D roundels. There are no underwing roundels. This is an interesting picture showing very early application of Type D roundels— September 1947.*

133 *Vampire 5 VV451:XC-E of No 26 Sqn. Squadron badge on nose, silver aircraft with black codes, 1950. Vampires in camouflage finishes are shown in Figure 20.*

134 *Tempest TT5, EJ758:B used as a target tug at Sylt in 1951. It is silver with yellow and black target tug stripes and yellow fuselage band* (A. Jones).

135 *Meteor 8s of 74 Sqn, 4D-K:WA874, L:VZ540, D:VZ512, B:VZ547. Silver with black codes and tiger motif on nacelles, corresponding in finish to the Vampires shown in picture* (MoD).

136 *Squadron colours return, Meteor 8s of 41 Sqn in silver with red and white squadron colours 1952. A:WB111, S:WE867, G:WE943, D:WA962.*

137 *An interesting picture taken when camouflage was re-introduced. Meteor night-fighters in the new scheme are shown with earlier machines in the old night-fighter finish in this formation of NF12s (light grey and green) and NF14s (with three-tone camouflage).*

Chapter 15

1944-45: Fighters in Europe

THE INVASION OF NORMANDY was the major stepping stone to victory in Europe. Stretched to its utmost defending the homeland, and fighting on so many fronts, the Luftwaffe was barely evident. It was nevertheless, putting up a tough struggle particularly over Italy.

Here the going was hard throughout 1943 and '44. Progress became possible mainly as a result of audacious coastal landings under day and night fighter cover. German faith lay in Fw 190 fighter-bomber strikes and small scale night raids by Ju 88s on shipping and communication centres. Against the former the RAF pitted Spitfire VIIIs and IXs variously in the 'F', 'LF', and 'HF' versions and also put to good use Spitfire fighter-bombers. Spitfires in Italy by 1945 were generally painted in the grey-green-grey schemes sometimes with Sky adornments. Red codes continued to be outlined frequently in Sky or white and spinners were often in flight colours.

Spitfires of No 145 Sqn with blue spinners and no Sky bands included ZX-T: MT686, ZX-W: MT551 and ZX-R: MT664—all Mk VIIIs with red codes outlined in white. By 1945, and perhaps before, there were a number of Spitfires in use—Mustang IIIs as well in 1945—with Sky under surfaces; and from about March, 1945, there were Mustangs flying in natural finish as in Britain. Beaufighters with A.I. VIII were gradually phased out early in 1945 as the Mosquito XIX took over. The latter in the usual grey-green camouflage with red codes, as in Britain, had black serials, and on 255 Sqn they included TA127: YD-Z, TA128: YD-L and TA437: YD-S.

Few entirely new squadrons formed after the middle of the war but three worthy of mention are Nos 326 (coded 9I), 327 and 328 (S8), all commissioned on December 1, 1943, to fly Spitfires during the operations over the South of France.

In the Balkans, Spitfires equipped Nos 335 and 336 Squadrons of the Greek Air Force. Their aircraft had blue-white-blue roundels, officially from February, 1945. MH298 was one of 335's thus painted. Two squadrons also wore the red star imposed over RAF roundels, signifying Yugoslav association. These were Nos 351 Y Sqn which began to group itself in April, 1944, at Benina and officially formed on July 1, 1944, and No 352 Y Sqn. They trained on Harvards and then Hurricane IIs and IVs working up to give support to Tito's partisan forces from Italy. One of

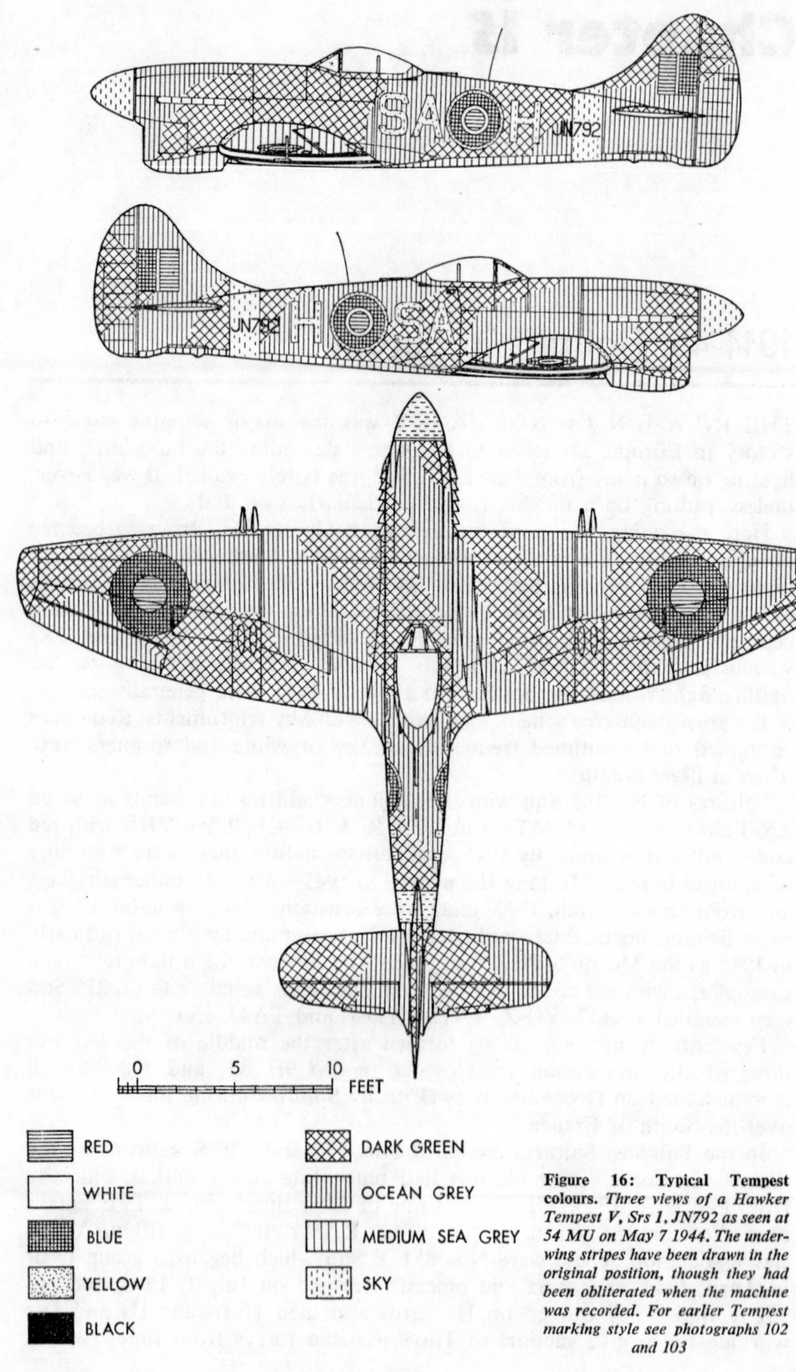

Figure 16: Typical Tempest colours. *Three views of a Hawker Tempest V, Srs 1, JN792 as seen at 54 MU on May 7 1944. The underwing stripes have been drawn in the original position, though they had been obliterated when the machine was recorded. For earlier Tempest marking style see photographs 102 and 103*

352's Spitfires was JK544:M (aft) in Sky and with full Sky trim on its grey-green-grey finish.

After the war ended and occupation forces moved into Austria the grey-green Spitfires retained their red codes outlined Sky and some had Sky bands, eg, RK855:FT-C with red spinner, red codes outlined Sky, Sky bands and above its rudder stripes a small black and white series of checks signifying 43 Sqn. By 1947, 111 Sqn had settled for Sky codes, no fuselage bands, grey spinners and Type C wing roundels which came into use in Italy about March, 1945. Gone now were the desert colours and in the post-war period day and night-fighters in the Middle East wore home-based styles of marking.

North-West Europe

Daylight over Normandy's beaches revealed a bitter struggle for beach-head positions. Overhead flew massive formations of Allied fighters—mainly Spitfires—despite the inclement weather. Typhoons like MN630 and MN517 of 609 Sqn hammered at enemy positions, Tempests including JN751, JN743 and JN752 flew overhead cover, Spitfire Vs of 26 Sqn in pairs spotted for the naval guns, in which role they had the help of Mustang IA/IIs of No 2 Sqn, including FD567 and FR908. Typhoons, including JR513, JR134 and R8850 of No 181 Sqn, were at hand to deliver rocket salvos where needed. In the evening, Hamilcar gliders were escorted to the Caen area by Mustang IIIs—useful on account of their lengthy duration.

Landing strips were soon hacked from the fertile farmland to allow fighter aircraft to refuel and operate from them. On June 10, Nos 441, 442 and 443 Squadrons were already based in France. By the time Typhoons were moving in, dust was rising causing blocked filters and calling for rapid modifications. Fuselage and wing black and white stripes were carried by a wide assortment of aircraft now, whether they were Hurricanes delivering beer or mail, Spitfire fighter-bombers or Tempests operating from home bases. By the third week of the campaign, 31 squadrons were operating from French soil.

A vain attempt to halt the advance was made by panzer forces which the Typhoons hideously decimated around Falaise. Soon the route to the Seine was under way. Already, however, a new development long awaited was employing the forces of Air Defence of Great Britain, the flying-bomb attack.

Against the V-1s some of the finest fighters were pitted—Spitfire IXs, Mk XIVs of 91 Sqn, including RB161, 196, 173, 182, and 185 which each destroyed a V-1 on June 18, Mustang IIIs and the highly successful Tempests. JN761 of 3 Sqn on June 16 was the first of these, in all probability, to destroy a flying-bomb, closely followed by JN809 of 486. At night the Mosquitoes took over, and in August came the Meteors.

No 616 Sqn (YQ) was the first to have them and equipped with a dozen in July, 1944. At the end of that month a squadron detachment moved to Manston from where, on July 27, the first anti-V-1 patrol was flown. The first kill was made on August 4 by EE216 and 13 flying-bombs were in all claimed by the Meteor squadron. The first Meteor to join the squadron, incidentally, was EE219:YQ-D and it was not until March 23, 1958 (as 5897M), that it was delivered for scrapping at Bath's yard at Kirkby. EE227 was another used in August, 1944, coded YQ-Y.

In an attempt to halt the V-1 attack, large forces of Lancasters and Halifaxes were soon engaged to destroy the V-1 supply depots and storage areas in France. To ensure safety they had the cover of Spitfires and Mustangs of ADGB, and for many home-based squadrons this was a pattern for their employment until the end of the war. For the long-range Mustangs another role was the escort of Mosquitoes and Beaufighters of Coastal Command attacking shipping off Norway and targets in Denmark. Principal users of the Mk III were these squadrons: No 19 (QV-D:FB201 in August, 1944, QV-H:FB113 in June, 1944), No 65 (YT:FZ166 in use on D-Day), No 118 (NK-F:KH519), No 122 (MT:FB213), No 126 (5J-B: FX122), No 129 (DV-D:FB364), No 234 (AZ-P:FB184 in use 1944), No 306 (UZ-J:FB120), No 309 (WC-V:FZ111 in use 1945), No 315 (SZ-R:FB181 in use April, 1945), No 316 (PK-O:FB229 in use April, 1945) and No 441 (9G:FB184).

A look at Typhoons in the middle of 1944 revealed them in a wide assortment of states. EJ829 with teardrop canopy and three-bladed propeller had OV ahead on the port and aft on the starboard sides of the fuselage, and individual letter A, as recorded on June 11. It had no AEAF stripes. FM-T:EK172 was similarly marked and fitted out when noted on June 18. EK485 with teardrop canopy and three-bladed prop had AEAF stripes under the wings only on June 25, and was uncoded. July 5 revealed EJ955:ZH-Q with codes in the usual positions, three-bladed propeller, framed canopy but no invasion stripes. That day I also came across P5216, now unarmed, painted green-brown and with yellow under surfaces. The spinner was painted Sky. Four days later I recorded XP-B, the individual letter on the port side being on a black band as an outline only in Sky. DP-M had her squadron letters aft on both sides of the fuselage in white with 'M' in Sky. She had a teardrop canopy and three-bladed propeller. All of these machines had a non-shiny finish—perhaps the shine had worn off, for none were in a clean state. Not so though for Spitfire IXB BS434:AP-A (codes in usual position) noted at Wittering on July 26 in very smooth, semi-glossy finish as supplied by Titanine under the Type S designation. Mustang UZ-U:FB393 had the small red and white Polish insignia on its cowling and two-foot code letters forward of the roundels on both sides of the machine.

A noticeable change in August, 1944, concerned the removal or overpainting of AEAF stripes which eventually were carried only under the rear fuselage and sometimes extended to the foot of the code letters. On January 3, 1945, 2nd TAF ordered removal of Sky rear fuselage bands and coloured spinners were now to be black or in a camouflage shade. Scent of victory had caused some units to paint spinners brightly. Another feature was the introduction of Type C roundels above the wings both on 2nd TAF and ADGB fighters. About March, many squadrons added a thin yellow surround to these, but no specific order seems to have been given to do this. The order concerning spinner colours also seems to have been overlooked after a short time. Yellow leading edge stripes remained and stayed for many months after the war.

On March 20, I first recorded a 'silver' Mustang IV with only Type C1 roundels and black letters 'FY' ahead of the fuselage roundels. Officially it was March 31, 1945, when the order was given that camouflage could be removed from RAF day-fighters, although it was many months before the silver machines could be seen in numbers. Production aircraft still left the factories camouflaged and from about this time the finish seemed generally to have been far more glossy than hitherto. Early Mustang IVs wore camouflage. The first arrived in September, 1944, although the type largely came into squadron use during February, 1945. Units which operated them from Britain were: No 19 (QV-Q:KH689), No 65 (YT: KH647), No 118 (NK:KM236), No 122 (MT-M:KH642), No 126 (5J-J: KM649), No 154 (KH651), No 234 (AZ:KH251), No 303 (PD-A: KM186), No 442 (Y2:KH661) and No 611 (FY:KH645).

Once the war in Europe was over there was a rapid decline in the size of the fighter force. Typhoons in particular were rapidly withdrawn and some replaced by Tempests. Squadrons of the latter now included Nos 3, 56, 80, 174, 222, 274 and 501.

Typical of the aircraft in use at the end of the war were the following: Typhoon MN514:TP-Y with codes in usual position had a teardrop canopy and four-bladed propeller and still retained full AEAF stripes. On April 8, I recorded Mustang III SH-A:FX957 with white spinner, nose and chordwise wing bands, which features the Mustang IIIs generally had and retained long after the war. This one had Type C wing roundels and Sky rear fuselage bands. Two days later I noted that Typhoon ZH-Y: RB451 had all roundels of the Type C1 variant. She had a Sky band, four-bladed prop and teardrop canopy. Her spinner was red as also were the wheel discs and the inside of the wheel wells. Another Typhoon seen had a yellow spinner. ZH-Y had another striking feature—a very light shade of green in her camouflage which was certainly not due to fading. Paint colours did vary considerably and one batch of which I obtained a good sample was extremely dark green and far removed from the usual shade. Certainly colours weathered, but not to the degree some pundits would have us believe.

EK210 was a Typhoon in use May, 1945, with a blue spinner and Type C roundels. HF-Z:JR263 had a black spinner, three-bladed prop, teardrop canopy, Type C wing roundels and RP racks.

Too late to see operational employment in the war came the de Havilland Hornet. Production examples began to leave the factory in March, 1945. Initially they were finished in light grey with PR Blue under surfaces and were intended as high-altitude interceptors. On April 18, I noted PX211 light grey overall with Type B roundels on the fuselage and above the wings. The fin flash was red-white-blue. Hornets entered service in the former scheme which also briefly applied to some of the first Vampires. The latter type went into service in ocean grey-dark green-sea grey medium with Sky boom bands but did not have the yellow leading edge stripe. Delivery began in April, 1945.

Special instructions covered the markings to be applied to another new type which entered service too late to fight, the Tempest II. Although the instructions were issued in May, 1944, it was nearly the end of that year before the first machine left the production lines wearing ocean grey-dark green-sea grey medium finish. Retained was the Sky fuselage band, but the spinner was white. A two-foot wide white band encircled the nose and one a foot wide was painted across the fin and rudder. An 18-inch stripe was painted across the tailplane. PR657 had these markings in September, 1945, as well as another feature now common, large black underwing serials painted as on trainer aircraft and introduced spasmodically from July.

A few weeks after the end of the war in Europe, large numbers of aircraft were put aside for scrapping. Amongst them were the Gladiators of No 61 OTU, two of which, K8046 and N2311, I noted at Cambridge on July 15. Both were finished in dark green and dark earth and had Sky under sides. Cowling leading edges were worn bronze in colour and Type C roundels appeared above the wings only. A brown and green Hurricane seen on July 30 had yellow and black target-tug stripes beneath its wings, a feature at this time of some Spitfires. Three Mustangs of 309 Sqn seen the same day were led by a Mk III in 'silver' finish with black codes, but such never became a common sight. A wander around one of the innumerable large scrap heaps at this time revealed Typhoon XM-S:JP397 with AEAF stripes beneath the fuselage only, ZX-4:MN513 (with teardrop canopy, black spinner, three-bladed prop), PA-P:JP578 with squadron letters ahead of both roundels, Type C wing roundels, and black spinner. And, finally, 5V-A:PD451, 18-Y:JR530, ZY-H:MN585 and EL-N:MN775 similarly marked except that these all had a Sky fuselage band.

Figure 17: Later Spitfire markings. *(1) LZ-K, a Mk Vb, in usual 1943 type markings. An interesting feature of this aeroplane is the small white serial on the fin above the rudder stripe. This was unusual, but just how frequently such numbers were carried is unknown—this was not unique. (2) MB840, a Mk XII of No 41 Sqn. (3) A Mk XIV, DW-A:RB150 has its serial repeated ahead of the fin stripe. The XII and Vb have the earlier type of gunsight and mirror not fitted to the XIV. The XII and XIV have IFF aerials beneath the fuselage. All camouflage was of the Smooth type.*

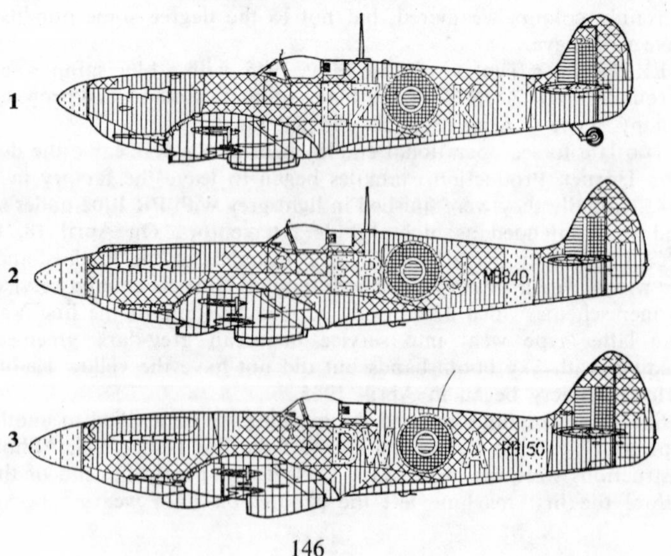

Chapter 16

1945-50: Fighters in peace

DELIVERY OF THE SPITFIRE XXI commenced in September, 1944, but it was March, 1945, before No 91 Squadron, then at Manston, became the first to equip with this type. No 1 Sqn received a few the same month but never became operational with them before the war ended, whereas from April 10, No 91 Sqn used them for reconnaissance and anti-ship/submarine patrols. By the end of the war over 150 sorties had been flown by aircraft including DL-V:LA224 and DL-Y:LA223. These aircraft were marked in the standard specified fashion with ocean grey-dark green-sea grey medium paintwork with Sky trim and yellow wing leading-edge bands. Two Mk XXIs used experimentally at Rotol for propeller research in late August, 1945, were LA214 and LA216. Both had a very glossy finish and under-wing serials, features in evidence on new aircraft at the 1945 White Waltham display for the stand-down of the Air Transport Auxiliary.

The Tempest II was now in service, first with No 183 Sqn, eg, MW747, and soon with No 13 OTU, eg, MW749. By September, 1945, No 247 Sqn was equipping with them. Squadron examples in standard camouflage and white trim included MW755:HF-W, MW759:HF-M of No 54 Sqn, MW768:ZY-Q and MW769:ZY-W of 247 Sqn and MW777:SL-U of No 13 OTU.

Ocean grey-dark green-sea grey medium camouflage with Sky spinner and rear fuselage band, yellow outer wing leading-edge stripe, black serials, Type C1 fuselage roundels, and Type C wing roundels came to be the standard trim in the immediate post-war fighter force with relatively few exceptions. These included the white noses of the Mustangs (wing bands were removed after the war) and Tempest special markings, also removed in due course. Typical markings were to be seen on the Spitfire XXIs of No 91 Sqn at Duxford on March 29, 1946. LA221 (DL forward on the port side, aft on the starboard) coded DL-L was standard in all respects and had a very glossy finish. Night-fighters retained the late war colours with red codes evidenced by Mosquitoes ZK-L:MT487 and NT282:YX-D. A Hornet seen in March, 1946, was PX273 with P M CL B (*sic*) painted in one foot white letters aft of the Type B fuselage roundels which were repeated above the wings and red/blue fin flash. It wore the light grey/PR blue finish, and was a Sector Leader's aircraft.

The first post-war fighter colour scheme was promulgated on April 16,

1946. It stated that fighters would return to the silver finish of long ago—either natural metal or glossy 'silver' (more strictly aluminium) paint work, with black codes and serials. It was many months before this became common and may roughly be said to have come into general use when the Meteor 4 joined Fighter Command. On July 23, 1946, for example, Spitfires of 165 Sqn at Duxford still had the post-war grey-green glossy finish, etc, and included SK-E:MK673 and SK-T:MJ482, both with 'pointed' tails and clipped wings, and SK-R:PT958, a Mk IXe with 'pointed' tail and standard wings.

At the 1946 SBAC Show there was at least some evidence of the newly ordered scheme, if only on the silver prototype 'Attacker' TS409 and Vampire TG285. Hornet PX313 appeared in the light grey/PR blue scheme highly polished, and the Welkin night-fighter Mk II had light grey/yellow trim with prototype markings and Type C wing roundels. Production Welkins mainly appeared in the same trim as the Hornets, but when it was envisaged that these aircraft might serve as high-altitude night-fighters for use in 1944, some were painted in the usual night-fighter camouflage of grey and green. These included DX286 and DX289 of the FIU with red ZQ coding. DX328 wore the scheme when in the hands of RAE in February, 1945.

For the 1946 Battle of Britain Display I took myself to Marham, seeing the unusual Meteor III ZQ-J:EE348, with standard camouflage, Sky codes, yellow wing leading edge stripes and all but matt finish. This machine had A.I. radar in a special nose. More conventional were the grey-green Mustang III UZ-P:FB370 with white nose, Meteor III 4D-S:EE459, and Tempest V RE-M:SN262 from CFE with RP racks. All had codes in the prescribed positions.

In Germany some BAFO squadrons were flying Mosquito VIs with small but interesting variations in markings. HR369 had 'EG' aft in dark blue with 'H' forward. Its finish was the customary grey and green of wartime Mk VIs and night-fighters. Spinners were medium grey, and upper wing roundels of Type C1. No under-wing roundels were carried. PZ953, coded SY-U, had its letters similarly placed and had red spinners, whereas OM-C had blue codes and spinners, all the blues being roundel blue. Similar variations from usual colouring continued for some years.

Although post-war colouring for fighters at Home and Overseas was again confirmed by Official order as silver for day-fighters and grey and green for night-fighters in May, 1947, the wartime colours continued in use for months to come. Post-war camouflage was glossy but it would be erroneous to imagine fighters as shiny in finish as those in the camouflage of recent years. On May 16 the order was given to revert to a variation of Type A roundels on wings and fuselage and to the pre-war type of tail stripe, this time red foremost and painted on the fin. Proportions of the roundels were, however, different, the red centre disc having the same diameter as the width of the blue and white of the roundels. A change was also made to bright shades of red and blue for roundels, but again these were features that took many months to become a general sight in a very cost-conscious post-war atmosphere. The new roundels were designated Type D.

An assortment of fighters seen in December, 1947, gives evidence that the changes were taking long to introduce. Tempest II PR682:EG-A had usual camouflage although the blueish tint in the ocean grey had long since weathered away. It had a red spinner, Sky codes and band and yellow leading edge stripes. EG-S had a dark blue spinner and under the cowling 'T' appeared in black on a small white disc. Nosewheel doors of fighters in recent years have commonly carried such a feature, but it was in use on some squadrons long before the jets came in any number. Tempest V W2-T:EJ896 of No 80 Sqn was painted in usual camouflage, whereas J5-F:NV989, unlike the others, had Type C1 upper wing roundels and a white spinner. Its wing tanks were bright green, for already some squadrons were cautiously introducing their pre-war identity colours, albeit very unofficially. J5-S:NV721 differed from these Mk Vs in that it had no Sky fuselage band. Meteor EE277:FX-H (FX forward on both sides) had the Sky band, yellow leading edge stripes and a silver belly tank. Mosquito VY-B:RK982 had blue spinners and red codes.

Meteors largely took over the Home Defence task in 1948, backed by a fleet of Mosquito NF36s and the Spitfires of the RAuxAF—Mks 16, 21 and 22. Meteor 4s entered squadron service in a very smooth silver finish and wore Type C/C1 roundels and had black codes and serials. Frequently the aircraft's letter was painted on the nosewheel door in black or the Flight colour. Some Mk 4s were camouflaged.

Four home squadrons were equipped with Hornets and in December, 1948, many of these were in smooth silver finish and usually polished at the end of the week's flying. There was special evidence of the return of squadron colours on the Hornets. No 19 Sqn had decorated the spinners and some of the noses of its Mustang IVs in blue and white checks, and at the 1947 Church Fenton Battle of Britain Display the grey and blue Hornet Is on show all had rich blue spinners with a narrow white line painted around them. Black coded, the aircraft included QV-D:PX248 and QV-E:PX278. PX226:QV-A differed in that it had two white lines and was flown by the squadron commander. By December, 1948, the squadron had Hornet IIIs and there was even further evidence of special squadron colours. PX347:QV-D, all silver, had dark blue codes and blue spinners with two narrow white lines. QV-C:PX346 (grey and blue in finish) had black codes and silver spinners, whilst PX298:EB-V of No 41 Sqn, wearing grey/blue finish, had Type B roundels and red/blue fin stripe. But perhaps the most interesting of the Hornets was EB-A:PX366, a silver machine with the crest of No 41 Sqn about six inches high applied to the fin of the squadron commander's aircraft.

There was by this time some liberty available for the painting of aircraft used by high ranking officers. RW393, a Spitfire LFXVIe with Type D roundels, was a glossy white overall and in April, 1949, was seen wearing red serials.

In March, 1949, a new high-gloss silver finish was approved for use on Meteors, an aluminium gloss covered by a special glazed finish which was standard on Meteors for years to come. A Mk 4 which featured it was VW283:KR-K which had a yellow nose tip and K on its nosewheel door.

One more really exciting change came—it simply had to, for the post-war air force was now a reality and not just something left over from the years of fighting. It was the introduction of colourful squadron markings, which have continued to this day. Even in the mid-war years in North Africa attempts had been made to decorate Hurricanes with a squadron flash. Indeed, 85 Sqn had worn its hexagon emblem in France in 1939. In early 1945, No 3 Squadron Tempests wore their squadron crest on their tails, and 616 Squadron's Meteors had their rose emblem boldly placed on their tails. No 21 Squadron's Mosquitoes had various styles of squadron markings and in the late 'forties many other formations decorated their aircraft with special unit motifs. In 1948 it was decided to re-introduce squadron markings.

Initially the markings were designed to appear quite small on the nacelles or noses of Meteors, or fins of the Hornets and Mosquitoes—which they did, flanking a squadron badge. To some units this was a disappointment, and when one very famous squadron placed its pre-war checkerboard markings flanking the fuselage roundels at the suggestion of someone who had better remain nameless, it was hastily told to remove them and replace the black codes.

On April 16, 1950, Meteor VZ429:LJ-Q (LJ aft on both fuselage sides) in silver gloss finish now typified the current style with black codes. Its wings had Type C roundels and the fuselage had Type C1—despite the edict of months ago. On May 30, 1950, UB-K:VT280 and VT194:US-R could be seen similarly marked. But, the first (and only) post-war RAF Display was near—and what better time to bring a note of gaiety which had pervaded those Hendon shows?

So, the visitor to the show was presented with the delightful appearance of No 263 Squadron's Meteors wearing red rectangles flanking the fuselage Type D roundels each bearing two red crosses, VT273, VT328 (ex HE-J), VT336 and VT240 (ex HE-M). And as if this was not enough, No 601 Squadron appeared with red and black triangles flanking the boom roundels of its Vampire 3s which included VT822:C and VT793:G. The squadron's special motif appeared in red on the noses of its aircraft and the individual letter was black on red nosewheel doors. No 604 Squadron's aircraft as yet bore no colours but had large black letters on the sides of the nose as on VT829:B. A Vampire FB5 of 247 Sqn merely satisfied itself with a small replica of its black and red colours flanking a squadron crest on the nose of VZ193:G. The Meteors of Nos 66 and 92 Squadrons appeared with squadron code letters and small squadron markings flanking the nose squadron crests.

By mid-June—three weeks before the RAF Display—56 Sqn Meteor 4s were wearing red and white checks on the fuselages with black fin letters as on VT263:K; and No 63, one of the 'new' fighter squadrons, had adopted yellow and black checks seen on VT346:D. A cruel twist of fate prevented the Hornet squadrons from joining the new scene of brightness—their aircraft had been camouflaged for low attack duties! Squadron codes were retained and whereas all the other squadrons were adopting Type D roundels, the Hornets reverted to Type B, as on PX340:SH-W painted dark sea grey and dark green with PR blue under surfaces. QV-H: PX387, also camouflaged, had blue spinners with one white band and small squadron checks and crest above the fin flash.

With an expanding fighter force, many of the squadrons had no previous colours to revive, and ingenious ideas were submitted in 1948. Nos 1 and

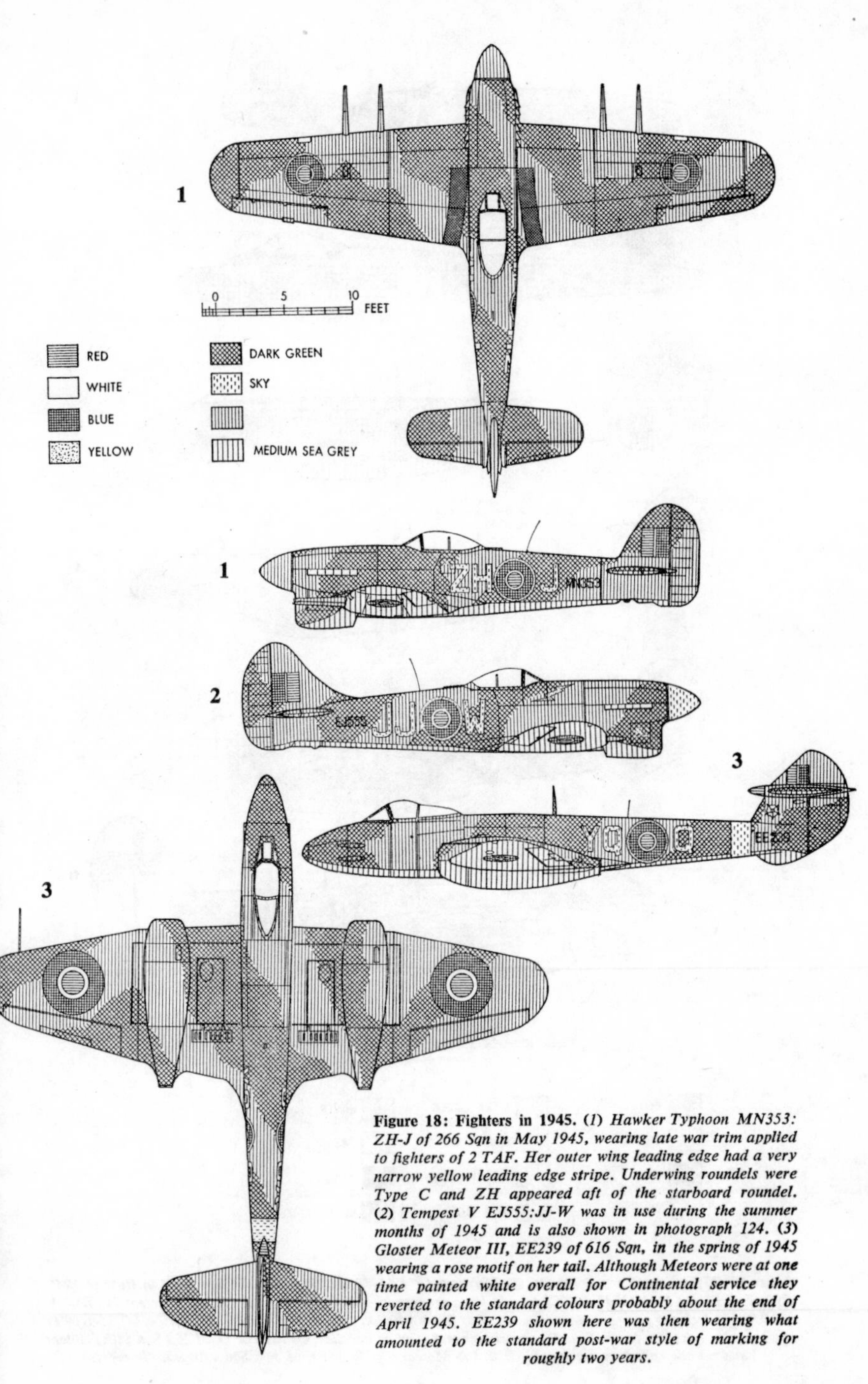

Figure 18: Fighters in 1945. (*1*) *Hawker Typhoon MN353: ZH-J of 266 Sqn in May 1945, wearing late war trim applied to fighters of 2 TAF. Her outer wing leading edge had a very narrow yellow leading edge stripe. Underwing roundels were Type C and ZH appeared aft of the starboard roundel.* (2) *Tempest V EJ555:JJ-W was in use during the summer months of 1945 and is also shown in photograph 124.* (3) *Gloster Meteor III, EE239 of 616 Sqn, in the spring of 1945 wearing a rose motif on her tail. Although Meteors were at one time painted white overall for Continental service they reverted to the standard colours probably about the end of April 1945. EE239 shown here was then wearing what amounted to the standard post-war style of marking for roughly two years.*

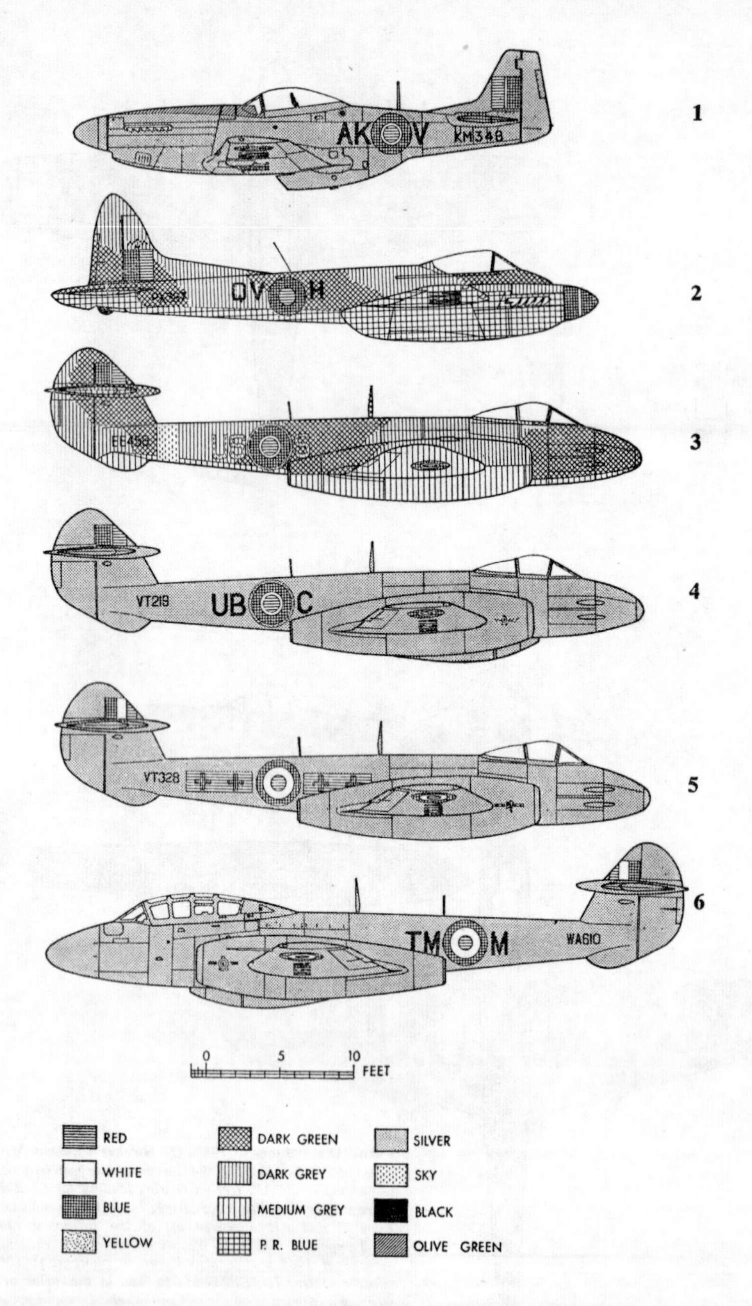

Figure 19: Fighter markings, 1946-50. *(1) Mustang IV KM348:AK-V of No 213 Sqn, used in Italy in 1946. (2) Hornet F3, PX387:QV-H, of 19 Sqn in dark sea grey-green-blue finish as in late 1950. (3) Meteor IV, EE459, of 56 Sqn in dark sea grey-green-medium sea grey finish with sky trim but no leading edge stripe. (4) Meteor IV of 63 Sqn in high gloss finish. Squadron markings and crest on nacelles. (5) Meteor IV of 263 Sqn with fuselage and nacelle squadron markings, 1950. (6) Meteor T7, WA610, of 504 Sqn with nacelle crest.*

41, for instance, vied for the styling of a red band, 41 opting for additional white and red outlining. Scottish Auxiliaries went in for some amazing plaids, whilst others sought to link their colours with past glories or events —or as a last resort based them upon the squadron badge.

Chapter 17

1950-69: Fighters in the Cold War

THROUGHOUT THE WAR YEARS and those immediately following the emphasis was on camouflage, both of aircraft and of unit identity. In the uneasy peace there came relaxation and, to a certain extent, a need to let the unfriendly East learn something of our strength and at the same time foster strong squadron spirit.

An interesting look at the Royal Air Force was provided by the 1950 Display, and the fighters were well in evidence. Amongst the performers were Spitfire LF16es of 17 Sqn. UT-N (UT forward on the port side) was silver, UT-H (UT aft on both sides) had very glossy camouflage, Sky codes, band and a light blue spinner. Spitfires in standard glossy camouflage with Sky trim, etc, included RAQ-B:PK579 and RAT-B:PK574. With the latter, also drawn from 613 Sqn, was Q3-C:PK427, another Mk 22 which featured a return to more conventional squadron letters which Royal Auxiliary Air Force squadrons were now making. A silver Vampire FB5 with black codes flown in the ground attack demonstration was VV461: EG-T. Suggesting that night-fighters of the future would retain grey-green finish was the Meteor NF11 prototype, WA546, with medium grey paintwork and disruptive dark green on its upper surfaces.

During the autumn of 1950, Vampire 5s began appearing in a new scheme of glossy dark sea grey and dark green with PR Blue under surfaces. They were being delivered to 2 TAF. This was a colour scheme that was later to apply to Venom fighter-bombers and Sabres.

Squadron colours return

Throughout the summer of 1950, home-based silver fighters gradually shed their codes in favour of bright squadron colours. By September, Meteor 4 VT263 was 'K' of 56 Sqn with another machine, US-O:VT183, as a silver reminder of the old days at hand. With them was the famous Hurricane LF363 in 'electric' blue with red spinner and red fuselage serials only. Meteor squadrons had now received T7 two-seaters. An interesting feature was that on fighter squadrons these machines for some time did not wear yellow 'T-bands', but were coded or had squadrons colours. The latter, where applicable, consisted of checks about 6 inches square—usually a double row of three each side of the roundel, and directly adjacent to it.

Exceptions were soon, however, plentifully evident, including some of 56 Squadron's aircraft which had six checks aft but only four forward.

The Meteor 8 was introduced in 1951, when, in silver high-gloss finish, it began to replace the Mk 4s. Meteor 8s included WA770:T of 63 Squadron and WA771:P of No 56 Squadron. These had the usual six-a-side checks and black fin letters. WE913 of 64 Sqn had the unit's zig-zags flanking the roundels in two-inch wide striping and a black F on the fin. An interesting innovation of the period was the application of a special Squadron Leader's marking. WA993 of 63 Sqn had the Squadron Leader's pennant on its fin in place of a letter, whereas WA988 of 66 Squadron had the usual blue and white rectangular fuselage marking and Squadron Leader's pennant on the nosewheel door but no fin letter.

Vampires posed a problem for there was not room for a fin letter. WA428 in the summer of 1951 with 72 Squadron's markings had 'H' in black on the sides of the nose. A Vampire 5 of No 54 Sqn now had a blue tailplane, when forming part of an early post-war aerobatic team. The Vampire NF10 was coming into service and this type usually had squadron markings on the booms and an individual letter on the nosewheel door. No 25 Squadron's aircraft had black and white rectangles on the booms, eg, WM669:L and WM672:Q, and two-tone grey-green camouflage with black nosewheel door letters.

There was little change in markings in 1952. Mosquito NF36s, although being replaced, were still around, such as RL264:YP-R (in red). Its spinners, when observed on September 23, 1952, were red and blue. Some NF36s featured squadron markings on the fuselage, eg, RL148 of 85 Sqn with six checks to either side of the fuselage roundels and the squadron hexagon motif on the fin. As an interim measure, RK981:TW-E typified those with a squadron motif on the fin, in this case the snow leopard of 141 Sqn. White spinners had black spirals on them. Silver Mosquito T3s had yellow 'T-bands' and a black code, like RR307:Y of 141 Sqn.

Some Meteor 8s were now in use as target-tug aircraft with a towing hook aft of the belly tank. These did not have the customary black and yellow stripes. One example was WE926:E of 64 Sqn in use in August, 1952.

A new shape now with the night-fighter squadrons was the Meteor NF11 which entered service in 1951 with No 29 Squadron. WD644 was in use with 141 Sqn in September, 1952, with the unit's black and white markings flanking the fuselage roundels and a black W on the fin. Its finish was medium sea grey with disruptive dark green on upper surfaces. A narrow black ring followed by a white one encircled the leading edge of each engine nacelle.

From de Havilland had come their next night-fighter the Venom NF2. WL808 and some more early production examples had the same colouring as the Meteor NF11s, and had heavily framed cockpit canopies. Stability and other troubles initially plagued the Venoms. Some Mk I fighter-bombers including WE255-262 wore a red chord-wise band around each wing over their green-grey-blue camouflage as a warning to limit the speed. Initially a few Venoms flew in silver finish.

The sudden death of His Majesty King George VI early in 1953 was an event of great sorrow, for throughout his life he had shown deep interest in the Royal Air Force. Soon came the turn of the Royal Air Force to salute its new Commander-in-Chief and, led by Jimmy Wallace, Duxford Wing Leader, in Meteor WA893, Fighter Command honoured Her Majesty Queen Elizabeth II on that rainy day when the Coronation took place. There was something particular about the leading aeroplane, for it was representative of the most colourful period in the history of Fighter Command. Duxford's Wing Leader had a red fin, rudder and fairing 'acorn'. It typified a considerable number of Meteors throughout the Command which between 1951 and 1954 were flying with tails of red, blue, green, yellow, black, light blue, red and white and even pink. Wing Leaders, Station Commanders, Squadron Leaders, Flight Leaders, over this period all were flying highly decorated Meteors, some with brightly coloured fins, rudders, tailplanes, acorns and noses too. A wide assortment of coloured trim was seen at the Meteor stations with variations of fin letters, initial letters on fuselages and coloured canopies. In some instances the markings were applied over the fin stripes. In the great fly-past for Odiham's Review which followed the Coronation, many of these machines were momentarily glimpsed and others were shown on the ground. Busy during the build-up for the greatest fly-past the RAF had ever mounted was Richard Atcherley in his high-gloss dark green Meteor 8 WK927:R-A; and some of the Meteors were now flying with long-range tanks on the wing pylons—still a rare sight. WH150:E of 56 Sqn was thus equipped at the time.

Fighters galore

A tour of the static park at Odiham was a joy for any enthusiast and there were fighters galore. Amongst those particularly interesting were four Venom FB1s of No 266 Squadron in grey-green-blue finish with small squadron crests on their nose sides. WE326:A-A wore a red lightning flash on its tip tanks, whereas WE377:A-L had a blue one. Unmarked Vampire 9s in grey-green-blue finish included WR158, WR196 and WR203. The silver Mk 5s of the Auxiliaries were well in evidence and included VZ612:LO-C and WA414:Q3-A. No 614 Sqn sent along WE837 in squadron markings—six and a half triangles flanking the fuselage roundels. A black D was painted on its nosewheel door.

For the last fly-past practice I was at Duxford to see yet another new type, the Sabre 4, now in use with 2 TAF. Again the colours were sombre yet glossy, grey-green-blue. XB737 of 67 Sqn wore a narrow red band across its fin and rudder, flanked by narrow white stripes. The squadron crest was applied on the white stripe of the fin flash. XB600 had a blue fin band flanked white. The former had a white A on the fin, the latter W. Another Sabre here for the review was XB678:L with red fin letter and rich green nose signifying No 3 Squadron. Mixing with these were the station's Mk 8 Meteors, which included WK827:T and WH459:Q of 65 Sqn, both with red rudders. Nevertheless, the all-silver scheme with black fin letter and squadron markings flanking the fuselage roundel was still the most common seen, as for instance on WA763:G of 92 Sqn in September, 1953.

Some of the Meteor night-fighters now had a red fin letter, like WD760 which had a red diamond on its nosewheel door with a white K. Mean-

138 *The old medium sea grey and green scheme dated from the days of Beaufighter and Mosquito night-fighters and continued on Meteors. Here are Meteor NF11s of 29 Sqn in two-tone finish with red and white squadron markings. F:WD725, C:WD603* (Hawker Siddeley).

139 *Vampire 5 of 614 Sqn in July 1953, displaying red/green squadron colours and individual aircraft letter on nose.*

140 *Silver Meteor FR9 WX962 of 208 Sqn in Egypt prior to having camouflage applied (grey/green/blue); note the squadron crest on nacelles*

141/142 *Meteor NF12 WS665 with 25 Sqn in 1956, together with a close-up of the tail to show application of markings. Note the individual aircraft letter in yellow, outlined black.*

143 *Camouflaged Meteor 8 Z:WH484 of 64 Sqn in September 1954. It has a yellow fin letter and squadron crest in the arrowhead marking on the tail.*

144 *Sabres of 234 Sqn in 1954, with red and black nose checks, red letter outlined white on fuselage. D:XB885, E:XB867* (MoD).

145 *Famous marking returns; Sabres of 112 Sqn with their traditional sharks' teeth decor and white codes on fin* (MoD).

146 *Sabre XD727 of 92 Sqn in 1954. D is in yellow outlined black. Green/grey/light grey finish* (MoD).

147 *Swift FR5s of 79 Sqn in grey/green/light blue finish. XD915 is nearest with XD953:F* (MoD).

148 *Three eras of 66 Sqn; Meteor 8 WK656:S, Sabre XD753 with white fin flash and blue and white nose, and Hunter 4 WV409:N with nose markings, pictured in 1957 when all three types were in service* (MoD).

149 *Meteor F8 WK947:W of 245 Sqn, painted with a white tail for Exercise Vigilant in 1958.*

150 *Tail of WH445 of 615 Sqn in blue and white. A selection of colourful tail markings for Meteors is given in the back end papers* (MoD).

151 *Hunter F1s of 43 Sqn in 1955 showing the early Hunter finish with silver undersides* (MoD).

152 *Hunter 4 XE653 of 'The Black Arrows' at the 1959 SBAC Show with nose colours and white outlines to markings. Small serial is in red.*

153 *Javelin XA703:Y of 41 Sqn in May 1959 with white serial and squadron colours on tail.*

154 *XH872, a Javelin 9 of 64 Sqn in 1960. M in white on fin.*

155 *Hunter 9 XG260:B of 54 Sqn in later colours—grey, green and silver with blue and white nose checks and tail fin marking. White serial.*

156 *Lightnings were at their most colourful in 1964-66; this is Lightning F3 XP711 of 111 Sqn.*

157 *In 1966 squadron markings were much reduced. This is a Lightning 3, XP752:O of 23 Sqn landing after the Queen's Birthday flypast in June 1967.*

while, No 64 Sqn had added a horizontal white axe-head to the fins of its aircraft, with the squadron crest in colour. No 65 Sqn had added red ailerons as well as rudders to many aircraft, a practice often frowned upon because it could upset control balance.

In Germany the Meteor FR9 was in service, and many of these were now grey-green-blue like WH542:B-K which had No 2 Squadron's crest on its nacelles in a special form. The underneath of the nose was silver and there was a K on the nosewheel door in black. In the Middle East the Vampire 5s and 9s were still silver, and a Meteor FR9 of 208 Sqn silver with squadron colours was VW361:P.

Camouflage returns

On February 13, 1954, my old sparring partner John Rawlings and I were invited to Biggin Hill to discuss our contributions to the Station history then being written. We were able to see for the first time a new colour scheme brought about by the Cold War. The belligerent attitude of the Communist bloc was only too apparent and so camouflage was re-introduced for the home-based fighters. Those overseas in the Middle East and Far East were to follow suit later. WL111, the Leader's aircraft of 41 Squadron, still had a red and white striping on its fin leading edge without fin flash. Its upper surfaces were now glossy dark green and dark sea grey. Another camouflaged machine we saw was WL106 with a black J on its fin. But the new camouflage took some months to become a general feature and even in September, 1954, there were many silver Meteors.

The black fin letter was not easy to read, therefore some squadrons—56 and 63 were possibly the first—painted a yellow fin letter on camouflaged machines. No 63 Squadron still had yellow and black wing tip checks and of course the Meteors retained squadron colours. Gradually the coloured tails were over-painted in camouflage. Meteor 7s which these squadrons used for training usually remained silver and still had no yellow bands.

The obsolescent Meteors were soon to be replaced and the first of the British supersonic fighters for squadron service, the Supermarine Swift, of which WK209 was an example, touched down at Waterbeach on February 20, 1954. It had a dull silver finish and remarkably bold underwing serials. Soon WK207 was with her, wearing a red swept N on her fin and 56 Squadron's red and white checks.

Throughout 1954 that squadron tried hard to make a success of the new fast aeroplane, but it was dogged by crashes and much unserviceability. By early 1955 there were some camouflaged Swifts amongst the aircraft, including WK245 with H in red outlined white. It had the usual six-a-side checks flanking roundels and wing tip checks too. Aircraft N also now had them. Came the day, though, when 56 had to re-equip fully once more . . . with Meteors. These were now standardised throughout Fighter Command with grey-green-silver finish, yellow fin letters and squadron markings.

Enter the Hunter

With the failure of the Swift as a home defence fighter, hopes centred on the Hawker Hunter, the first examples of which to serve Fighter Command were used by AFDS in July, 1954. That same month camouflaged Mk 1s trickled into No 43 Squadron at Leuchars and a new era for the Command began. WT555, the initial production Hunter 1 in silver finish, had first flown on May 16, 1953. A score were similarly finished. By September, 1954, the camouflaged machines were busy, such as WT575 in high gloss grey-green camouflage with silver undersides, a scheme ultimately applied to the early silver aircraft. At this time the first Hunter F2s with Sapphire engines were flying. A few, including the first, WN888, had silver finish. WN909, flying by September, 1954, had camouflage as applied to the Mk 1s, which also was a feature of all Mk 2s supplied to the first two squadrons equipped at Wattisham, Nos 257 and 263. Their aircraft wore squadron markings flanking the fuselage roundel. Machines of these two squadrons wore yellow fin tip letters and A of 257, WN898 typified its unit's aircraft. This machine also had a green A on a yellow nosewheel door. Production Hunters had black serials.

Attempts continued to develop the Swift as a day-fighter. Production examples of the Mk 4, following the light blue prototype of this mark, wore the same camouflage as production Hunters. For me, 1955 brought more views of the Swifts which were soon to leave 56 Squadron. One machine, WK211 : B in silver finish, had its wing serials both the same way round, reading correctly from astern! Ultimately some of 56's aircraft finished up as scrap and a close appraisal of WK242 : P of 56 Sqn showed its checks to be 6½ inch squares, the base and top line of those adjacent to the roundels being 8½ inches long. The final variant, the FR5, was produced with the grey-green-blue finish of 2 TAF squadrons, but by 1958, WN124 : S of 2 Sqn, and others, had silver under surfaces. This machine had a white S on its fin.

Yellow fuselage serials never became entirely the rule on the Meteor 8s as evidenced in April, 1955, by WA776 : S of 63 Sqn which had yellow fin letter, squadron markings and wing tip checks with black serials and nosewheel door letter. A few Meteor 8s lasted long enough to have white fuselage serials.

New variants of the Meteor night-fighter—NF12 and NF14—were flying by 1954. An interesting feature of the former, which had a fin of increased area and framed canopy, was the finish in medium grey with dark green areas on the upper surfaces. NF14s had dark sea grey and dark green camouflage with medium sea grey under surfaces, a new scheme as applied to the Venom NF3. After modifications to Venom NF2A standard, many of the earlier machines wore three-tone camouflage. One was WR808 of 253 Sqn. As was customary with the Vampire-Venom-Meteor night-fighters, no under-wing serials were carried. Its twin red-white-green triangular squadron colours with silver centre flanked the fuselage roundels. One of similar design decorated each tip tank. Another point of interest colour-wise was that these later aircraft had black or dark brown radomes whereas the NF11s and Venom 2s had theirs painted medium grey.

In July, 1955, RAE held one of its rare open days. Once more Farnborough had much to offer the markings enthusiasts. There was a Meteor FR9 WB116 grey-green-blue with a black G on its fin outlined white, repeated in these colours on the nosewheel door—the usual 2 TAF colours. But more exciting was the first public appearance of the Hunter 4, in use

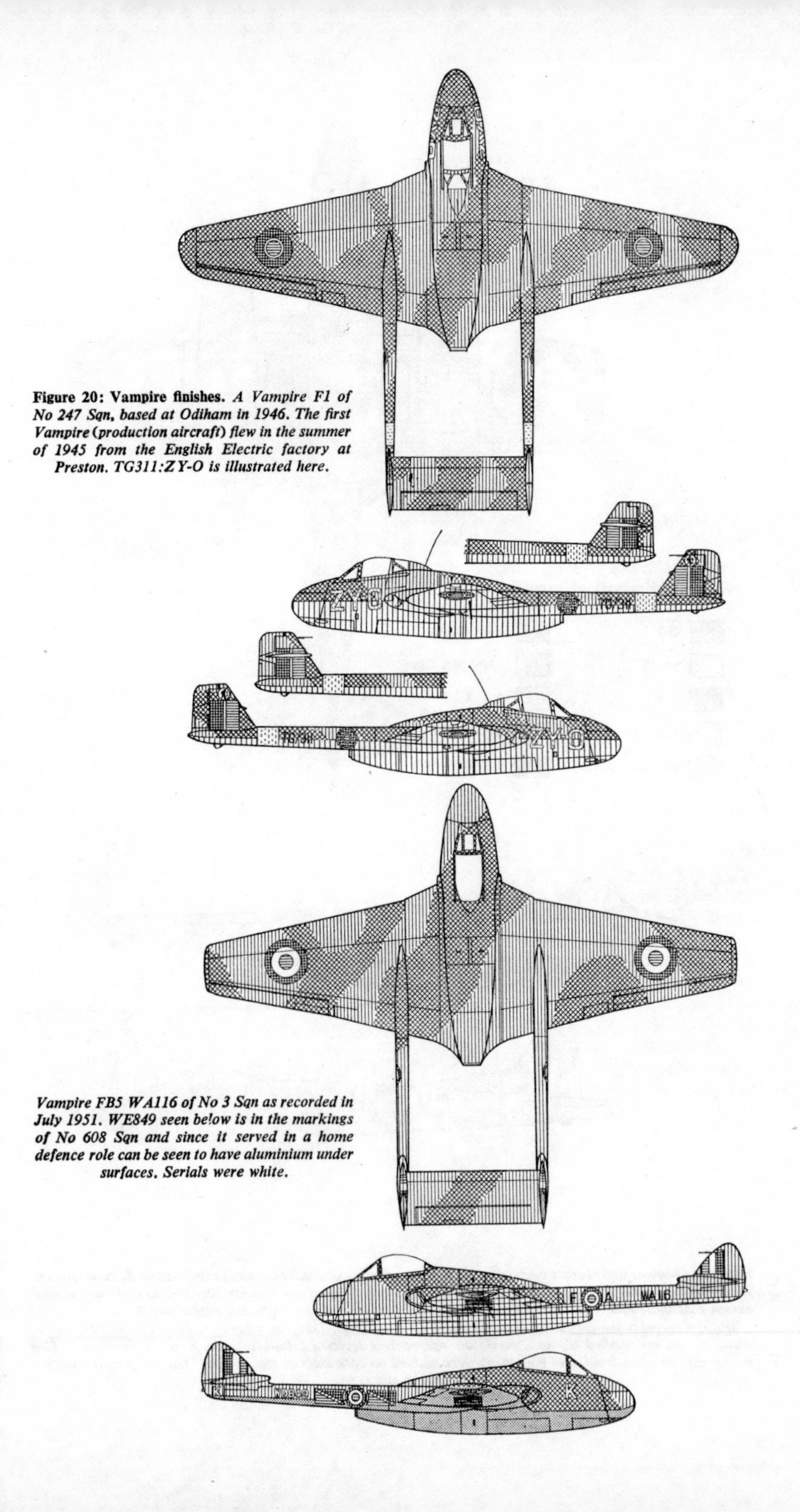

Figure 20: Vampire finishes. *A Vampire F1 of No 247 Sqn, based at Odiham in 1946. The first Vampire (production aircraft) flew in the summer of 1945 from the English Electric factory at Preston. TG311:ZY-O is illustrated here.*

Vampire FB5 WA116 of No 3 Sqn as recorded in July 1951. WE849 seen below is in the markings of No 608 Sqn and since it served in a home defence role can be seen to have aluminium under surfaces. Serials were white.

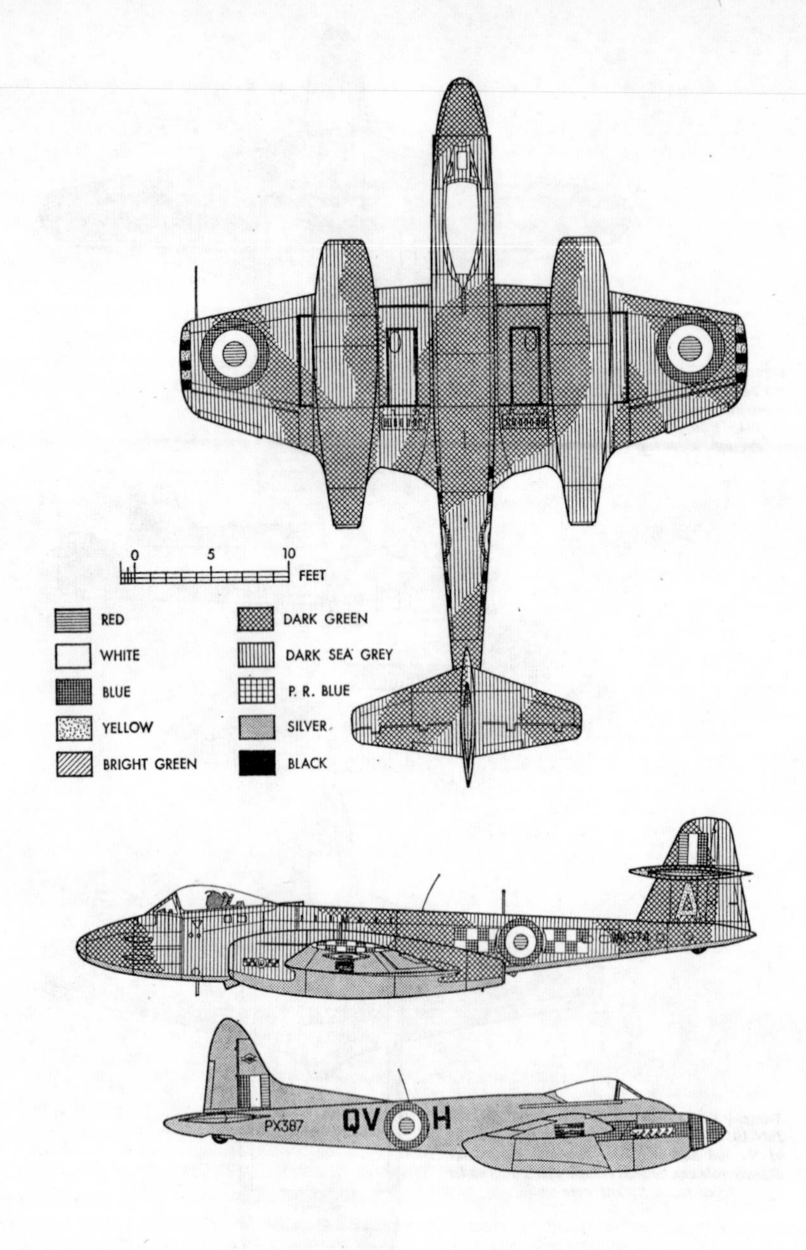

Figure 21: Meteor and Hornet markings, 1950. *Camouflage was usually applied to the Meteor 8s in the pattern shown here certainly applicable to aircraft of 63 Squadron. That of the Meteor 10s, 11s, and 14s was similar except that these had an additional area of green at the rear of the starboard engine nacelle.*

WK974 portrays the typical markings carried by Meteor 8s. This one belongs to No 19 Squadron, one of whose aluminium finished Hornets, previously operated, is depicted below. Spinners were usually roundel blue with a narrow white band, and blue areas were painted on both sides of the nacelles. The fin carried squadron checks and crest.

with Nos 54 and 247 Squadrons. Those of 54 included WT692 wearing the unit's blue and yellow rear fuselage checks, yellow fin letter outlined black and blue wing tips. Other aircraft of the squadron had red tips, eg, WW607:F which had yet to receive squadron colours. 247's machines were similarly marked, WV262:D having a red D on its nosewheel door. A Fighter Command aerobatic team arrived in the form of four Hunter 1s of 43 Squadron. Each had black and white fuselage checks. An unusual feature was that these were set higher on the fuselage than usual. These aircraft had white individual letters at the rear of the fuselage, as on WT594:N. But perhaps the most interesting markings feature appeared on WT682:K of 54 Squadron, which bore squadron checks on its nose flanking the squadron crest. This was a new innovation and one destined to become widespread.

When 56 Squadron re-equipped with Hunter 5s in July, 1955, it, too, wore its red and white checks on the noses of its aircraft, the 3½ rows each side flanking a light blue disc carrying the individual letter. WP109 had a red D repeated, slightly raked, on the fin fillet in red, outlined white. Nose markings for the Hunters came about through damage to the squadron marking from a vent, the efflux from which spread over the rear fuselage. Nose markings were also easier to identify on swept wing aircraft. They did not immediately become universal, however, and 43 Sqn, flying the Avon-engined aircraft, still wore its markings aft for some time. XE266:O with a fighting cock emblem on its nose, had two rows each of 32 checks on its wing tips, and similar but fewer checks were for a long time featured by 43's Hunters.

Assorted colours

At the time of the 1955 Battle of Britain Displays and SBAC Show the fighters could therefore be seen wearing a wide assortment of colours. Venom 2A WR803, in two-tone grey and green of 253 Sqn, had a white Z on its nosewheel door, Meteor 8 of 63 Sqn, WA776:S, had a yellow fuselage serial, WA639 was one of the few camouflaged T7s, two Venom 2s of 23 Sqn, WL822 and '825, had two-tone colours and 23 Sqn checks, Meteor 8 WK713 of 65 Sqn had a white L on its fin. WK970:W of 64 Sqn had a yellow fin letter and a black W on its nosewheel door, and No 41 Squadron's leading Hunter had a large white nose diamond bearing a red lightning flash.

May, 1956, brought the usual Armed Forces Day displays attended by some RAF fighters. Venom 3 WX913 of 125 Sqn showed its three-tone camouflage, black radome, white F on a red nosewheel door and F eight inches tall on either side of the nose in white outlined red. Customary boom markings were carried, as on WX870 of 23 Sqn, whose triple 'squares' to each flank of the roundel were 10 inches deep and 10½ inches long and in roundel colours. V appeared white on a blue nosewheel door. No 33 Squadron's fully modified Venom 2s, colloquially dubbed Mk 2A, had boom stripes, white and blue tips to the wing tanks and individual letters inside the port flap as well as on the nosewheel door.

Meteor 7s of Fighter Command were at last decorated with 'T-bands' as on VZ641:Z of 63 Sqn which had black and yellow squadron markings

For colour key and scale see Figure 24

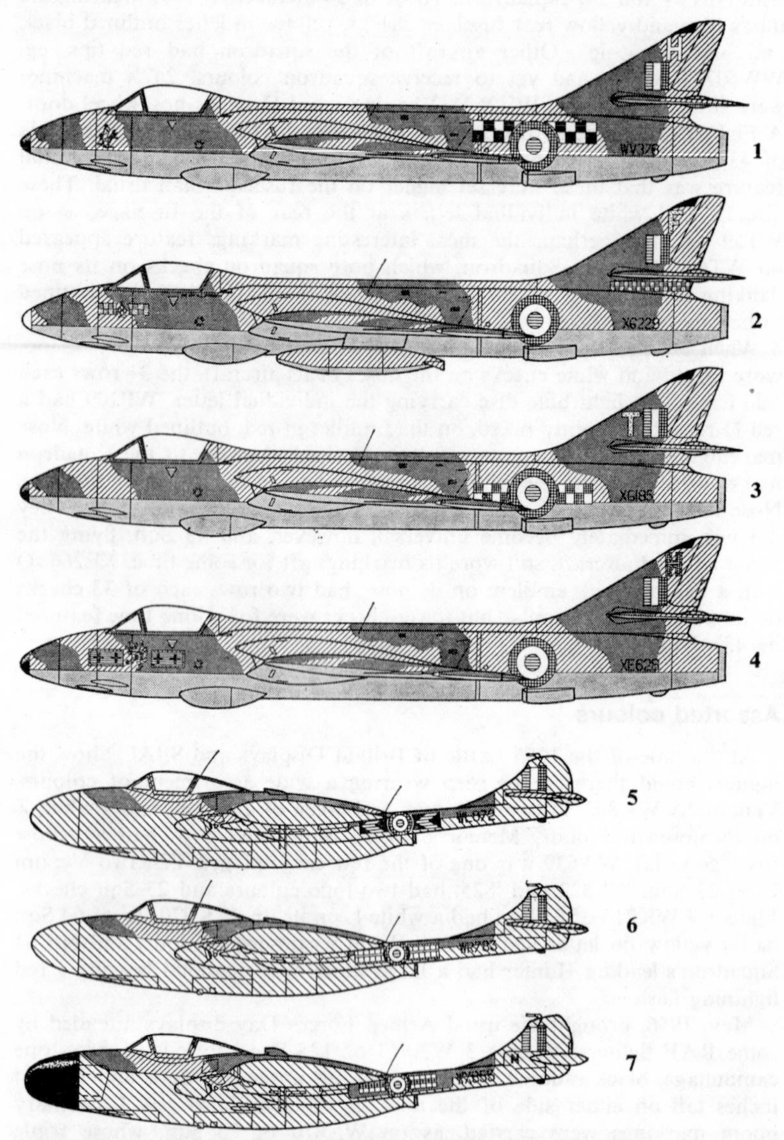

Figure 22: Hunter and Venom markings, 1956-57. ***(1) Hunter F4 WV378:H of 43 Sqn, Leuchars, on August 18, 1957. White fin letter, white letter on red nosewheel door. (2) Hunter F6 XG229:F of 92 Sqn, Middleton-St George, August 18 1957. Yellow fin letter, black on silver nosewheel door. (3) Hunter F6 XG185:T of 19 Sqn, Church Fenton May 18 1957. Yellow fin letter, blue on silver nosewheel door. (4) Hunter F6 XE628:H of 263 Sqn September 1957. Red tail letter outlined yellow.***

Hunter roundels were 3 foot in diameter, and fin code was 18 inches high. (5) Venom NF2 WL872:H of 219 Sqn Driffield, summer 1956. Red letter H on black nosewheel door. (6) Venom NF2 WR783:A of 33 Sqn Driffield, May 18 1957. Dark blue letter A on light blue nosewheel door. (7) Venom NF3 WX855:N of 89 Sqn Stradishall August 18 1957. Red fin letter, and red letter N on light grey nosewheel door. (Venom roundel on boom 18 inches diameter, fin flash was 2 foot square.)

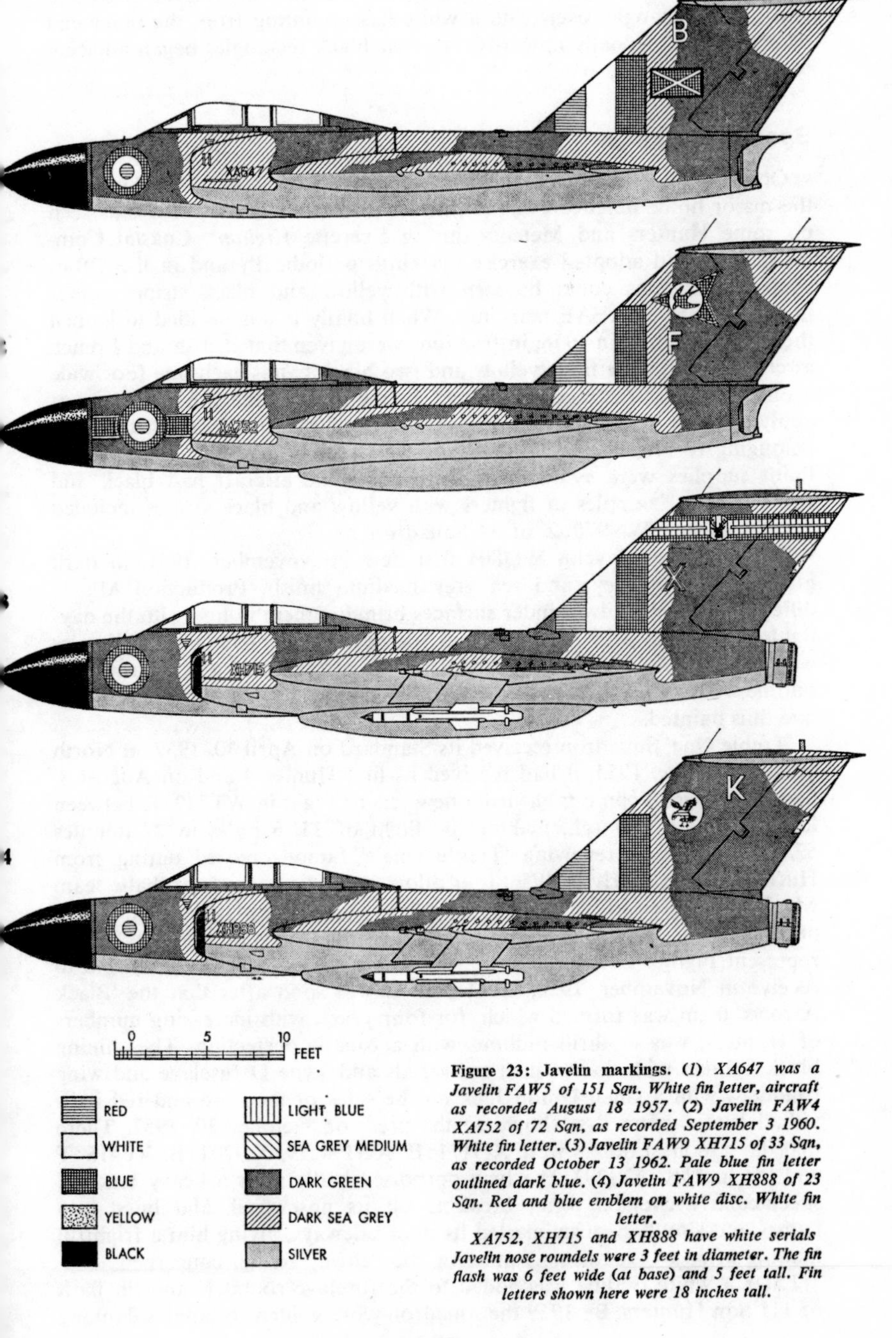

Figure 23: Javelin markings. *(1) XA647 was a Javelin FAW5 of 151 Sqn. White fin letter, aircraft as recorded August 18 1957. (2) Javelin FAW4 XA752 of 72 Sqn, as recorded September 3 1960. White fin letter. (3) Javelin FAW9 XH715 of 33 Sqn, as recorded October 13 1962. Pale blue fin letter outlined dark blue. (4) Javelin FAW9 XH888 of 23 Sqn. Red and blue emblem on white disc. White fin letter.*

XA752, XH715 and XH888 have white serials Javelin nose roundels were 3 feet in diameter. The fin flash was 6 feet wide (at base) and 5 feet tall. Fin letters shown here were 18 inches tall.

and wing tips. Vampire T11s also had yellow bands and WZ611 of 60 Sqn had black rectangles each with a white flash pointing from the outer end of the black diagonally upwards. The rear black rectangles began adjacent to the yellow boom bands.

Special markings

Occasionally, aircraft of Fighter Command wore special markings for the major home defence exercises, as for example white-washed tails seen on some Hunters and Meteors during Exercise *Vigilant*. Coastal Command, too, had adopted exercise markings periodically and in the 'fifties some Shackletons could be seen with yellow and black stripes rather in the manner of AEAF markings. When finally it was decided to launch the Suez operation in 1956, instructions were given that British and French aircraft should wear three yellow and two black bands each one foot wide around the rear fuselage and wings. In the case of the RAF this meant applying such markings to a few Hunter 5s flown out from Britain and belonging to Nos 1 and 34 Squadrons, and some Cyprus-based Venoms. Paint supplies were evidently limited and some aircraft had black and white bands. Examples of fighters with yellow and black stripes included WP136:N and WN970:Z of 34 Squadron.

The prototype Javelin WD804 first flew in November, 1951, in dark green, dark sea grey, and sea grey medium finish. Production Mk 1s differed by having silver under surfaces bringing them in line with the day-fighters, for they were the first real 'all-weather' fighters. First deliveries were made to 46 Sqn in February, 1956. Its aircraft had a red arrowhead outline on a white rectangle placed high on the fin. Javelin XA628 was one thus painted.

'Treble One' Squadron received its Standard on April 30, 1957, at North Weald. In June, 1955, it had received its first Hunter 4 and on August 8, Sqn Ldr Roger Topp established a new record flight in WT739:R between London and Edinburgh, making the flight of 331.6 miles in 27 minutes 52.8 secs, thereby renewing 'Treble One's' famous record dating from Hurricane days. Early in 1956, four pilots formed a special aerobatic team which was chosen to represent 11 Group at various displays, whilst 43 Sqn performed a similar role. In November the squadron were told they would represent Fighter Command in 1957 with a five-man team and to begin to receive in November, 1956, Hunter 6s. It was soon after that the 'Black Arrows' team was formed which, for four years, with increasing numbers of Hunters, was to thrill millions with aerobatic perfection. The shining black fighters with their 4 inch red serials and Type D fuselage and wing roundels, with a small Union Jack on the sides of the nose and red individual letters, were first shown to the press on October 30, 1957. There that day amongst others were XG171:E, XG194:N, XG201:B, XF416:T and the luckless XG203:H which porpoised badly after a heavy landing, spectacularly overshot after breaking off its nosewheel, and burst into flames and simultaneously ejected its pilot sideways, giving him a frightful landing after a hair-raising run along the runway for all concerned.

Later a white outline was added to the fuselage roundels and fin flash of 111 Sqn Hunters. By 1959 the squadron wore golden rectangles flanking a small squadron badge on the nose sides. Red tail and nosewheel door letters were retained.

By now the night-fighter force was flourishing with its Meteor NF12s and NF14s. No 64 Squadron had a mixture in the two-tone colour schemes and three-tone with a white arrowhead carrying the blue squadron motif forward of a yellow fin letter. The Venoms of 253 Sqn, like WL855 (M in white on a blue nosewheel door) had their squadron crest painted aft of the boom markings. Still one saw on day-fighters occasional bright colours as with 63 Squadron's leading Hunter whose entire fin and tail-plane was covered in yellow and black squares. Meteor 8 WK673:Y of 54 Sqn represented the typical colours of the Meteors in the last years with the regular RAF squadrons. On her grey-green-silver finish she had twin rows of 6 inch blue and yellow checks and a yellow Y on her fin in 1½ inch strokes. A target-towing hook was fitted at the end of her belly tank. WS617, an NF12 of 64 Sqn, had the two-tone scheme with a yellow A 2 inches thick and squadron colours in 2 inch wide stripes. She had a blue A on her grey nosewheel door, and had a black radome.

Javelins were now in service in increasing numbers, the Mk 4 joining squadrons at Horsham St Faith in time for Exercise *Vigilant,* although the first example had flown in October, 1955. Initially, 23 Squadron merely had a strip of checks on each engine intake and black serials. Then a red eagle outlined in black was added to the fin. No 141 Squadron settled for its white snow leopard and white and black triangular markings on the fin, with each aircraft's 'last three' above this. All the production machines had dark sea grey, dark green, and silver finish.

Hunters the mainstay

Hunter 6s were the mainstay of the home day fighter force in 1958, typified by XG187:V of 63 Squadron which had a yellow fin letter and a black letter on the nosewheel door outlined in yellow. WS665, a Meteor NF12, L of 25 Squadron, carried a white disc on its fin with a black unit motif. A red L at the rear of the fuselage was outlined black. Aircraft E of the same unit, serial WS686, had in a similar position a dayglo orange E, and the unusual all-grey WS613:J of 153 Sqn had the squadron's bat-like motif on its fin. A red line along the wing leading edge and a red lightning flash on the port side of the nose were other unusual features. Six months later, 25 Squadron had Javelin 7s with two 3 inch black stripes across the fin tip flanking a silver-white 6 inch stripe on either side of a white disc carrying the squadron crest, added in transfer form. One was XH907 with a white E beneath the squadron marking. L:XH956 had silver rims to its engine intakes and, like the others, soon acquired its individual letter in white just aft of the nose roundels. Black radomes were usual on these Javelins.

56 Squadron's Hunter 5s now had their phoenix emblems painted on to the blue disc of the nose. WP106:F of the squadron had nose and wing tip red and white checks and a red nosewheel door letter.

It was in 1958 that white wing tips became a common sight on Hunters, useful for cine assessing work, and carried by XE584:W of 263 Squadron which had a red fin letter outlined yellow and similarly repeated on the nosewheel door.

For their 1958 appearance, 'Treble One' Hunters first displayed the thin white outline to their roundels. A typical '111' machine of the 'Black Arrows' in use in May, 1959, was XG129. Her fuselage serial was still in 4 inch red characters and she bore a red F, 4 inches tall, above the swept tail stripes. The golden nose rectangle markings were ½ inch wide and 4 inches deep from top to bottom and extending outwards over a total of 5¾ inches each side of the crest.

An interesting aspect of 'Treble One's' markings—hitherto unrevealed—is that a number of experimental paint schemes were at one time applied to their aircraft. First came trials with a huge arrow-like cheat line the entire length of the fuselage, initially red then yellow. Another scheme tried was the painting of the wings and tailplane all-yellow, and the trials aeroplane also for a time had the striking yellow arrow decor. The next stage was to paint a Hunter red overall and apply huge white letters RAF on its underside. Another less startling idea was a black Hunter with a white arrow painted on the underside of its fuselage from the tip of the nose to the end of the jet pipe. But, in the end, the more sober black finish prevailed.

Hunters and Javelins now formed the home defence force, and overseas there were fighters wearing the same basic colour schemes. With more rotation of units to the Middle East and even Far East this was the situation that readily came about. Such variations as continued rested upon the placing of unit markings and individual letters. In September, 1959, for instance, Javelins of 64 Squadron had a white fin letter beneath the unit's red and blue motif which was painted on a white stripe at the top of the fin as on XH788:D. No 46 Sqn's red and white arrow design graced its aircrafts' tails along with the yellow code letter, eg, R:XA777. No 85 Squadron had a white hexagon outline with a white letter below as on S:XA832. It was now usual for the Javelins to have white serials—these three did—and some Hunters had them, as they still do.

The Lightning arrives

Late in 1960, No 92 Squadron began to receive additional Hunters. Some came from 111 Squadron as heralds of a new era, when 92 Squadron took on 'Treble One's' role of being Fighter Command's aerobatic team as 'The Blue Diamonds'. XG186:J was the first of its Hunters to be finished in rich royal blue overall, a scheme later applied to others by Marshall (Engineering) at Cambridge. The Squadron's unit markings were retained full size on the noses of the fighters. They had a white cheat line, white outlines to roundels, a white fin code which was soon discarded in favour of a white nosewheel door letter, and 4 inch black fuselage serials as applied to XE532:L. Re-equipment with Lightning 2s in 1963 brought an end at last to the era of the Hunter aerobatic team.

The present era of fighter markings may be considered to have commenced with the arrival at Coltishall on the afternoon of August 2, 1960, of the first natural finish Lightning F1s for No 74 Squadron, whose black and yellow triangular markings soon graced the nose of XM165, the first to adopt them. In a matter of days a tiger head was being painted on the fins of the aircraft, later on a white disc background. For the 1962 SBAC

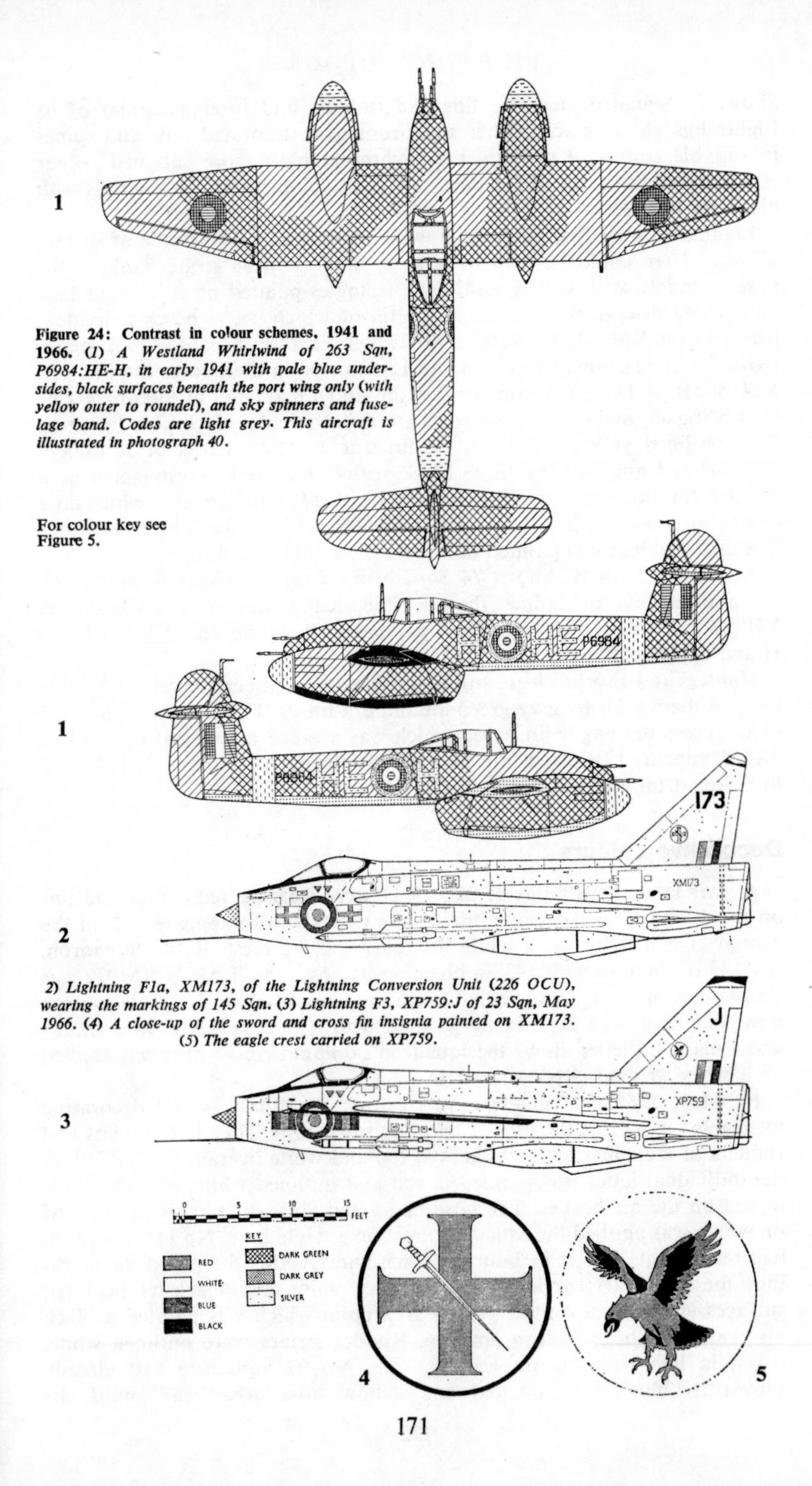

Figure 24: Contrast in colour schemes, 1941 and 1966. *(1) A Westland Whirlwind of 263 Sqn, P6984:HE-H, in early 1941 with pale blue undersides, black surfaces beneath the port wing only (with yellow outer to roundel), and sky spinners and fuselage band. Codes are light grey. This aircraft is illustrated in photograph 40.*

For colour key see Figure 5.

2) Lightning F1a, XM173, of the Lightning Conversion Unit (226 OCU), wearing the markings of 145 Sqn. (3) Lightning F3, XP759:J of 23 Sqn, May 1966. (4) A close-up of the sword and cross fin insignia painted on XM173. (5) The eagle crest carried on XP759.

Show, 74 Squadron had the fins and rudders and fuselage spines of its Lightnings glossy black. Other squadrons also decorated tails and spines in suitable colours. Currently the Lightnings have more subdued colour schemes and have settled for nose squadron colours and black serials with black fin letters.

Lightnings were first publicly shown at Coltishall's 1960 Battle of Britain display. They could be seen to have a one-foot wide stripe flanking the nose roundels, with yellow and black triangles painted on it. A tiger face on a white disc graced the fin, at the tip of which was a black individual letter, D on XM141. By June, 1961, when Exercise *Matador* took place, Nos 56 and 111 Squadrons also had Lightnings, in their cases the Mk 1A. XM186:B of 111 Squadron typified the unit's markings in the process of then being applied to the squadron's aircraft. 'B' had a black nose lightning flash outlined yellow. High on the fin was a yellow Cross of Jerusalem outlined red and bearing three black seaux. Two red swords acted as a ground for the emblem. 56 Squadron's aircraft had red and white nose checks outlined with a half inch wide light blue line. The squadron's 'firebird' emblem was painted on the fin on a pale blue disc.

At the 1962 SBAC Show, 74 Squadron's aircraft appeared with black fins and rudders and spines, the tiger face being painted on a white disc. Yellow individual letters had been painted high on the fins, XM167 being H and XM142:B.

Hunters and Javelins were still in use in some numbers. Javelin 5 XA704 typified them with its grey-green-aluminium finish. This aircraft had a red band across the upper fin, upon which was a green maple leaf on a white disc. J appeared below, white like XA704 the serial number. It belonged to 5 Squadron and was based in Germany.

Decorative colours

A year later, Lightnings of 226 OCU were wearing red spines and fins on to which intruded a white bite. White triangles also appeared aft of the canopy. On the fin was a white disc carrying the crest of 145 Squadron. XM143 of the unit had '143' in black on its nose, and T Mk 4 XM972 was similar except for a yellow band around its rear fuselage. No 19 Squadron now had Lightning 2s sedately painted with blue and white nose checks and a black fin letter above the squadron's dolphin crest which was applied on a white ground. XN780 was H.

By May, 1965, 56 Squadron was getting Lightning 3s and decorating them most gaily like the other Lightning squadrons. They had the fins and rudders of their new aircraft checked red and white overall. On XR719:D the individual letter was painted in red and outlined white, and was positioned on the air brakes. The nose had a red and white arrowhead motif on which was applied the squadron crest on a white base. No 111 Squadron had received its Mk 3s in January, 1965, and E:XR715 typified the markings these aircraft carried, with its black spine and black vertical tail surfaces enclosing a central yellow area upon which was painted a black disc carrying the squadron emblem. Rudder stripes were outlined white, raked in line with the fin leading edge. No 92 Squadron had already shown its blue tails and red and yellow nose arrowhead motif. Its

Lightnings had a small white letter painted at the fin tip, D being XN786. Again the squadron crest was painted on the fin on a white disc. No 23 Squadron chose white tails and spines for its Mk 3s, typified by XP759:J.

Lightning 5s were in service at Coltishall by September, 1965. XS418 had full tail and spine colours as well as a dayglo red band around the rear fuselage. The number '418' appeared on the nose in large black figures. Previously the trainer Lightnings had worn a yellow band as on XM996 a T Mk 4.

Sadly the brilliant colouring of the Lightnings was soon to become a memory. They were but briefly worn, and were possibly the most colourful ever carried by aircraft of Fighter Command except perhaps those of the Wing Leaders in the days of the Meteors.

Gone were the coloured tails and spines by early 1966, removed to meet official orders. No 23 Squadron had to content itself with blue and red checks flanking the roundel, and a blue and red tail motif on a white base. No 226 OCU, whose Lightnings had been so colourful, now settled for 145 Squadron's red and white markings on the nose, and the 'last three' at the fin tip as on XM173. A white fin disc outlined narrowly in blue carried 145's crest. By September, 1966, the T5s were similarly marked, like XS459.

Polyurethane paints arrive

A new feature present by this time was a special shade of Light Grey (BS381-63) applied to the under surfaces of some camouflaged fighters and later common on training and transport aircraft. Hunter FR10 XJ633 of 4 Squadron was now wearing it as well as a red nosewheel door with a white K upon it. This was at the time still an unusual feature, and Hunter FGA9 XE615:G of No 1 Squadron (G on the fin tip in red outlined white) still opted for aluminium under surfaces. Hunter trainers were later to adopt the overall grey finish.

Today's Lightnings have natural metal finish upon which are painted rather sedate markings, consisting of nose squadron identity, fin letter and squadron motif on the tail too. Hunters largely have the grey under surface colouring, camouflage being the same at home and abroad. Harriers are now coming off the production lines wearing dark grey and dark green high gloss finish with grey under surfaces. Polyurethane paint with its lasting properties suggests that the colours of today will long be those of tomorrow.

Study of aircraft markings is a fascinating one, for it inevitably leads to an interest in tactics, operations and history. Surely the mere memory of days long gone brings the richest reward, that of the dainty biplanes, the 'Few' of 1940 and the brave. It is well that we should remember them and the debt that every Britisher owes to Fighter Command.

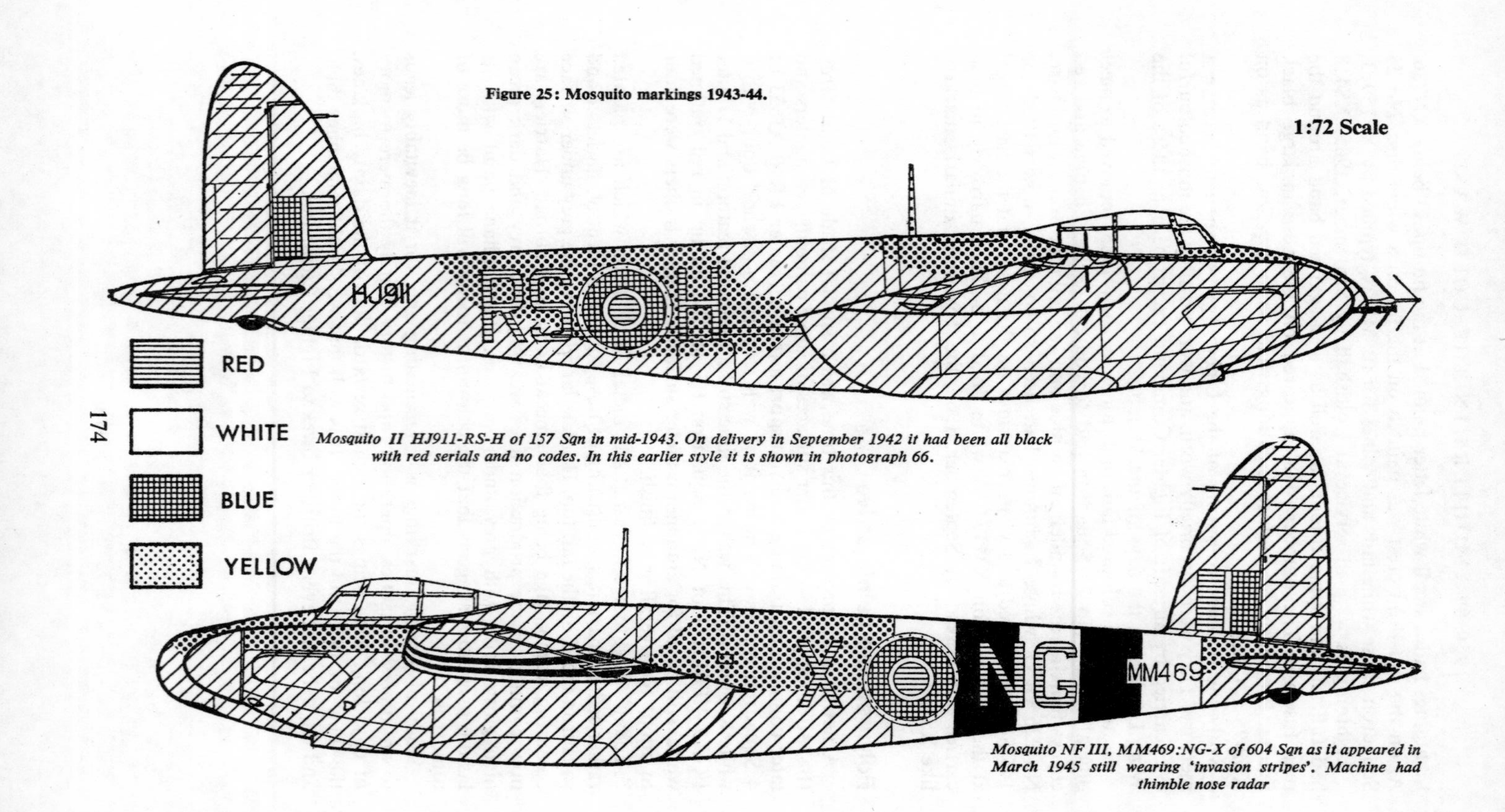

Figure 25: Mosquito markings 1943-44.

Mosquito II HJ911-RS-H of 157 Sqn in mid-1943. On delivery in September 1942 it had been all black with red serials and no codes. In this earlier style it is shown in photograph 66.

Mosquito NF III, MM469:NG-X of 604 Sqn as it appeared in March 1945 still wearing 'invasion stripes'. Machine had thimble nose radar

Figure 26: Mosquito markings post-war.

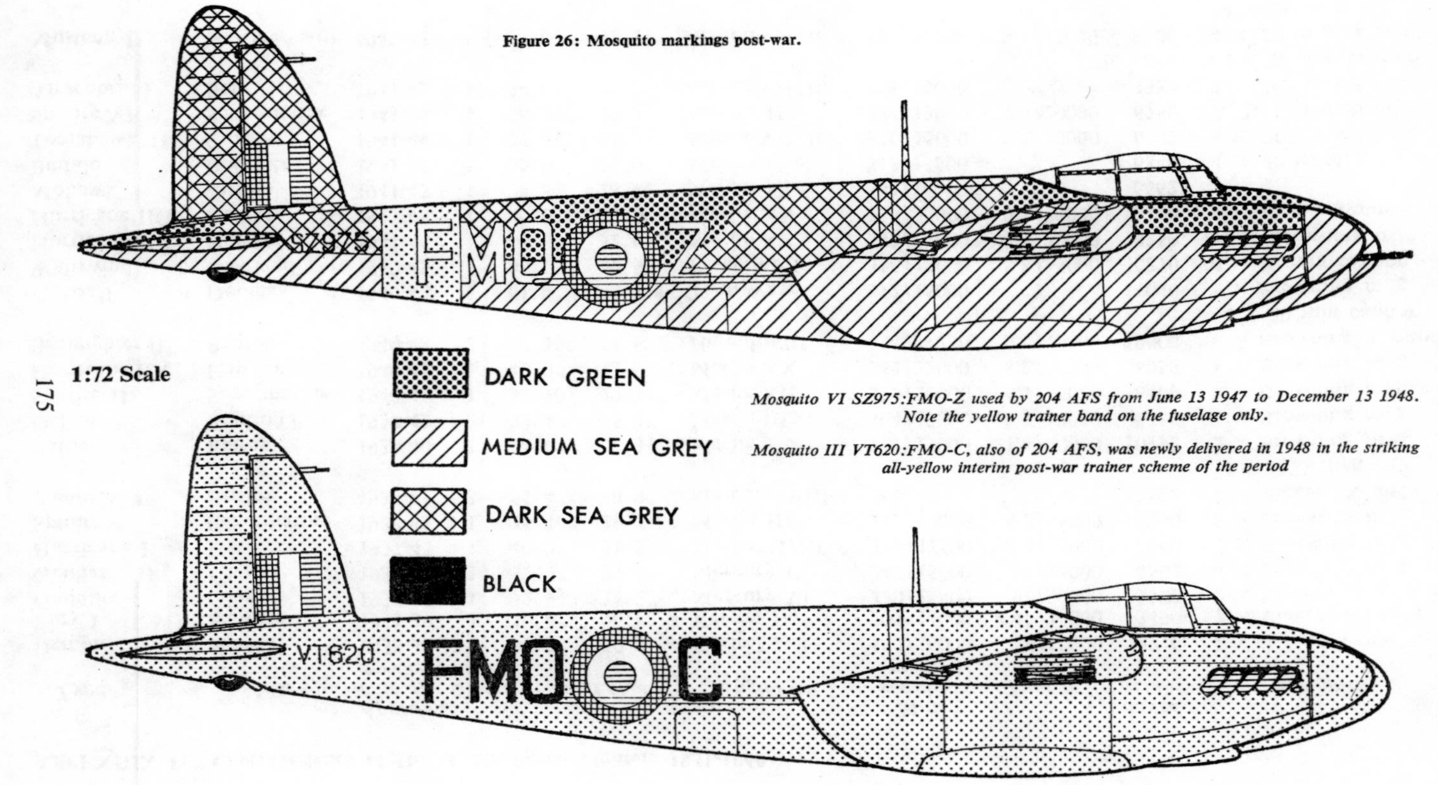

1:72 Scale

Mosquito VI SZ975:FMO-Z used by 204 AFS from June 13 1947 to December 13 1948. Note the yellow trainer band on the fuselage only.

Mosquito III VT620:FMO-C, also of 204 AFS, was newly delivered in 1948 in the striking all-yellow interim post-war trainer scheme of the period

APPENDIX I: Characteristics of Royal Air Force Fighters 1931-1969

Type	*Maker*	*Approx date of service*	*Crew*	*Span*	*Length*	*Engine*	*Max speed/ht (mph/ft)*	*Time to ht (min/ft)*	*Loaded weight (lb)*	*Armament*
Demon	Hawker	1933-39	2	37′ 2″	29′ 7″	Kestrel II	182/16000	7½/10000	4716	2 Vickers, 1 Lewis m/g
Fury I	Hawker	1931-39	1	30′ 0″	26′ 8″	Kestrel IIs	207/14000	4.45/10000	3490	2 × Vickers III m/g
Gauntlet I	Gloster	1935-39	1	32′ 9½″	26′ 2″	Mercury VI	230/15800	9½/20000	3970	2 × Vickers m/g
Gladiator II	Gloster	1937-41	1	32′ 3″	27′ 5″	Mercury IX	245/15000	7/15000	4592	4 × Browning m/g
Hurricane I	Hawker	1937-45	1	40′ 0″	31′ 5″	Merlin II/III	316/17500	6.3/15000	6600	8 × Browning m/g
Spitfire I	Supermarine	1938-45	1	36′ 10″	29′ 11″	Merlin III	355/19000	6.2/15000	6200	8 × Browning m/g
Blenheim IF	Bristol	1938-41	3	56′ 4″	39′ 9″	Mercury VIII	260	?	12500	1 × Vickers K and 5 × .303 m/g
Battle	Fairey	1939-40	2	54′ 0″	52′ 1¾″	Merlin I	241/13000	21.4/20000	10792	2 × Browning m/g
Defiant I	Boulton Paul	1939-42	2	39′ 4″	35′ 4″	Merlin III	304/17000	10.2/18000	8350	4 × Browning m/g
Spitfire II	Supermarine	1940-46	1	36′ 10″	29′ 11″	Merlin XII	370/20000	6.1/15000	6400	8 × Browning m/g
Hurricane IIA	Hawker	1940-45	1	40′ 0″	32′ 0″	Merlin XX	342/22000	8.2/20000	8050	8 × Browning m/g
Beaufighter IF	Bristol	1940-46	2	57′ 10″	41′ 8″	Hercules III	324/11750	9.4/15000	19000	6 × Browning m/g and 4 × 20 mm cannon
Havoc I	Douglas	1940-42	2	61′ 4″	46′ 11¾″	Twin Wasp	312/15000	?	19040	8 × Browning m/g
Whirlwind	Westland	1940-43	1	45′ 0″	32′ 9″	Peregrine 1	356/15000	5.8/15000	10270	4 × 20 mm cannon
Hurricane IIB	Hawker	1941-46	1	40′ 0″	32′ 0″	Merlin XX	342/22000	8.4/20000	8250	12 × Browning m/g
Hurricane IIC	Hawker	1941-46	1	40′ 0″	32′ 0″	Merlin XX	339/22000	9.1/20000	8100	4 × 20 mm cannon
Mohawk	Curtiss	1941-43	1	37′ 3½″	28′ 7¾″	Wright Cycl.	302/14000	?	6662	
Buffalo	Brewster	1941-42	1	35′ 0″	26′ 0″	Wright Cycl.	313/13500	?	6840	4 × .50 in m/g
Tomahawk II	Curtiss	1941-44	1	37′ 3½″	31′ 8½″	Allison V-1710	340/15000	7.8/15000	6789	6 × .303 in m/g
Spitfire VB	Supermarine	1941-46	1	36′ 10″	29′ 11″	Merlin 45	374/13000	7.5/20000	6750	A, B, C armament
Airacobra	Bell	1941-42	1	34′ 0″	34′ 2″	Allison V-1710	358/15000	?	7380	2 × .303 in m/g and 1 × 20 mm cannon
Mustang I	N American	1942-45	1	37′ 0¼″	32′ 2½″	Allison V-1710	390/8000	8.1/15000	8600	4 × .50 in m/g and 4 × .30 in m/g

Typhoon IB	Hawker	1942-45	1	41′ 7″	31′ 10″	Sabre	405/18000	6.2/15000	11200	4 × 20 mm cannon
Spitfire IXB	Supermarine	1942-47	1	36′ 10″	31′ 4½″	Merlin 61	408/25000	6.7/20000	7500	A, B, C, E armament
Beaufighter VIF	Bristol	1942-45	2	57′ 10″	41′ 8″	Hercules VI	333/15600	7.8/15000	21600	4 × 20 mm cannon and 6 × .303 in m/g
Mosquito II	de Havilland	1942-45	2	54′ 2″	41′ 2″	Merlin 21/23	370/14000	7.0/15000	17700	4 × 20 mm cannon
Mosquito XIII	de Havilland	1943-45	2	54′ 2″	41′ 4″	Merlin 21/25	370/14000	6.75/15000	19390	4 × 20 mm cannon
Mosquito XXX	de Havilland	1944-47	2	54′ 2″	41′ 4″	Merlin 72/76	407/28000	7.5/15000	21715	4 × 20 mm cannon
Kittyhawk III	Curtiss	1942-45	1	37′ 4″	31′ 2″	Allison V-1710	346/5000	9/15000	8500	6 × .50 in m/g
Spitfire VIII	Supermarine	1943-46	1	36′ 10″	30′ 4½″	Merlin 61	408/25000	7/20000	7767	B, C armament
Spitfire XII	Supermarine	1943-45	1	32′ 7″	31′ 10″	Griffon III/VI	393/18000	6.7/20000	7280	B armament usual
Spitfire XIV	Supermarine	1944-47	1	36′ 10″	32′ 8″	Griffon 65/66	448/26000	7/20000	8375	C or E armament
Tempest V	Hawker	1944-48	1	41′ 0″	33′ 8″	Sabre II/V	435/19000	7.5/20000	11540	4 × 20 mm cannon
Thunderbolt I	Republic	1944-45	1	40′ 9¼″	36′ 1¾″	Double Wasp	440/29000	11.5/20000	14600	8 × .50 in m/g
Mustang III	N. American	1944-47	1	37′ 0¼″	32′ 3″	Merlin V-1650	442/24500	10/20000	9200	4 × .50 in m/g
Meteor III	Gloster	1945-50	1	43′ 0″	41′ 3″	Derwent 1	476/30000	14/30000		4 × 20 mm cannon
Hornet III	de Havilland	1947-54	1	45′ 0″	36′ 8″	Merlin 130/131	472/22000	4/15000	16100	4 × 20 mm cannon
Vampire I	de Havilland	1945-47	1	40′ 0″	30′ 9″	Goblin	540/20000	4/16000	8578	4 × 20 mm cannon
Meteor 4	Gloster	1948-53	1	37′ 2″	41′ 0″	Derwent 5	480/30000	11.5/40000	15175	4 × 20 mm cannon
Sabre 4	N. American	1953-57	1	37′ 1″	37′ 6″	J-47-GE-13	600/36000	5.2/30000	14500	6 × .50 in m/g
Hunter	Hawker	1954-69	1	33′ 8″	45′ 10½″	Avon	0.94M/36000	12.5/40000	17750	4 × 30 mm cannon
Javelin 8	Gloster	1956-68	2	52′ 0″	56′ 3½″	Sapphire 203/204	628/30000	9.4/50000	38400	2 × 30 mm cannon and 4 × Firestreaks
Lightning 1A	Eng Electric	1960-69	1	34′ 10″	55′ 3″	Avon	1500/36000	2.5/36000	37000	2 × Firestreak Missiles

Notes: Period of service is only approximately given, for some aircraft remained in useful service long after they were withdrawn from front line status. Speeds and climb rates apply to aircraft with useful operational load and are only intended to give an idea of the type's capability which varies much with the load carried. The normal loaded weight is given which generally excludes long range tanks and external weapons load. Speeds and climb rates apply to individual machines on trial at the Aeroplane and Armament Experimental Establishment; different weights and machines would give only similar results. In the case of Spitfires the armament is given in part as possible alternatives: A (eight Brownings), B (two cannon and machine guns), C (four cannon), or E (cannon and 2 × .50 in guns). This notation was added as a suffix to the mark number. Hurricanes were similarly identified.

APPENDIX II: Paint shades used for RAF fighters

For the benefit of aircraft modellers, this listing includes official Air Ministry paint shades and equivalent model paints (numbers only).

Camoutints, 1937-41	*Humbrol*	*Modelcolor*	*Official*	*Airfix*
Dark Green	HB1, 30	RA2	—	M3
Dark Earth	HB2, 29	RA1	—	M5
Duck Egg Green	—	—	—	M16
Sky	HB5, 28	RA5	—	—
Roundel Red	—	—	42	M12
Roundel Blue	—	—	—	—
Night/RDM2	HB10, 33*	RC1	30*	M6*
Smooth paints, 1942-48 (Type S)				
Dark Green	HB1, 30	RA2	—	M3
Dark Earth	HB2, 29	RA1	—	M5
Sky	HB5, 28	RA5	—	—
Roundel Red	—	—	42	M12
Roundel Blue	—	—	—	—
Roundel Yellow	24	RA9	40	M15
Ocean Grey	HB3, 27	RA3	—	M2
Dark Sea Grey	HB7	RA12	—	—
Medium Sea Grey	HB6	RA4	—	—
Middle Stone (Midstone)	HB12	—	—	—
Dark Slate Grey	HB8, 31	—	—	—
Light Slate Grey	—	—	—	—
Deep Sky Blue	—	—	—	—
PRU Blue	—	RA6	—	—
Azure Blue	HB13	—	109	—
Night	HB10, 33	RC1	30	M6
Glossy paints, 1948 et seq †				
Dark Green	HB1, 30	RA2	—	M3
Dark Sea Grey	HB7	RA12	—	—
Aluminium	HB14, 129	—	3	G8
Post Office Red	HM9	RC4*	28*	G1*
Roundel Blue	—	—	—	—
Light Grey	HB6*	RA4*	—	M13*
Signal Red	121	—	—	—
Yellow	24	RA9	40	M15

* close approximation
† matt paints need gloss varnish on models depicting 'as new' aircraft

APPENDIX III:

Royal Air Force Fighter Squadron Identity Letters September, 1939-July, 1950

AD 113
AE 402
AF AFDU
AF 607
AH 332
AK 213
AP 130
AU 421
AV 121
AW 42
AZ 234
BF 54 OTU
BP 457
BQ 600
BR 184
CT 52 OTU
DB 411
DE 61 OTU
DG 155
DL 91
DL 92
DM 248
DN 416
DP 193
DT 257
DU 312
DV 129
DV 237
DW 610
DX 245
DZ 151
EB 41
EE 404
EF 232
EG 16
EH 55 OTU
EH 3 T.E.U.
EL 181
EO 404
EP 84 Grp Flt
EW 307
EX 11
EY 80
FE 56 OTU
FF 132
FG 335
FG 72
FJ 164
FJ 261
FK 219
FL 81
HF 183
HH 175
HI 66
HM 136
HN 93
HO 143
HP 247
HP G.R.U.
HQ 56 OTU
HS 260
HT 154
HT 601
HX 504
HX 61 OTU
HX 226 OCU
IL 195
IO 41 OTU
I8 440
JC 11 Grp Flt
JF 3
JH 317
JJ 274
JU 111
JV 6
JW CFE
JX 1
JZ 57 OTU
KE CAMS
KH 403
KK 333
KL 54
KP 409
KR 61 OTU
KU 457
KW 615
LA 235
LA 607
LD 250
LE 242
LG 13 Grp Flt
LJ 600
LK 87
LN 83 Grp Flt
LO 602
LV 57 OTU
LW 318
LZ 66
MB 236
MD 133
ME 488
MF FLS
OK 450
ON 124
OQ 5
OQ 52 OTU
OQ FLS
OU 485
OI 2
PA 55 OTU
PD 303
PJ 130
PK 316
PL 144
PN 252
PO 46
PQ 2 TEU
PR 609
PS 264
PW 57 OTU
PZ 456
QE CFE
QG 53 OTU
QJ 92
QM 254
QO 3
QV 19
QY 235
RA 410
RD 67
RE CFE
RE 229
RF 303
RG 208
RM 26
RN 72
RO 29
RS 30
RS 157
RU 414
RX 456
RY 313
RZ 241
SA 486
SD 501
SF 137
SH 64
SK 165
SN 152
SO 145
SP 400
ST 54 OTU
SW 253
UU 226 OCU
UW 55 OTU
UX CFE
UZ 306
VA 125
VI 169
VL 167
VY 85
VZ 412
WC 309
WK 135
WM 68
WR 248
WX 302
XB 2 TEU
XC 26
XE 123
XL 226 OCU
XM 182
XO 57 OTU
XP 174
XR 71
XT 603
XV 2
YB 17
YD 255
YO 401
YP 23
YQ 616
YT 65
ZD 222
ZF 308
ZH 266
ZJ 96
ZK 25
ZP 74
ZQ FIU
ZT 258
ZX 145
ZX 55 OTU
5A 329
7A 614
A6 257
4D 74
F3 438
9G 441
I8 440
2I 443
8I APS
9I 326
5J 126

FM 257
FN 331
FT 43
FU 453
FX 234
FY 611
GA 208
GA 112
GE 349
GF 56 OTU
GN 249
GO CFE
GQ 134
GR 64
GW 340
GZ 32
G9 430
HB 239
HE 605
HE 263
HF 54

MN 350
MR 245
MS 273
MT 122
MU 60
NA 146
ND 236
NE 143
NG 604
NI 451
NJ 274
NK 118
NL 341
NM 268
NN 310
NR 605
NS 52 OTU
NV 79
NW 33
OD 56 OTU
OE 268

SY 613
SZ 315
TB 153
TD 126
TH 418
TH 20
TJ 52 OTU
TM 504
TO 61 OTU
TP 73
TP 198
TW 141
UB 455
UB 63
UB 164
UD 452
UF 601
UM 152
UO 266
US 56
UU 61 OTU

J5 3
7L 59 OTU
8L 92
9N 127
2O 84 Grp Flt
P6 489
Q3 613
5R 33
6R 41 OTU
9R 229
S8 328
6T 608
V6 615
V9 502
5V 439
3W 322
8W 612
Y2 442
2Y 345
6Y 171
9Y 132 OTU

APPENDIX IV

Airframe Serial Numbers of Royal Air Force Fighters 1937-1969

Bell Airacobra I: AH570-739 (about 80 in this batch reached the RAF in the UK), DS173-175 for evaluation 1941.

Boulton Paul Defiant I: L6950-7936 (Some converted to TT III), NL535-1582, 1610-1653, 1671-1706, 1725-1773. 1788-1812 (some converted to TT III).
N3306-3340, 3364-3405, 3421-3460, 3477-3520. (Some converted to TT III.)
T3911-3960, T3980-4010, 4036-4076, 4100-4121. (Some converted to TT III.)
V1106-1141, 1170-1183. (Some converted to TT III.)
AA281-330, 350-362. (Some converted to TT III.)

Defiant II: AA363-369, 370-384, 398-447, 469-513, 531-550, 566-595, 614-633, 651-670.

Brewster Buffalo I: W8131-8250, AN168-217, AS410-437, BB450, AX811-820.

Bristol Blenheim IF: All conversions from Blenheim I bomber: K7044, '48, '51, '65, '83, '85, '87, '88, '90, '91, '92, 7104, '17, '18, '20, '22, '23, '24, '25, '26, '30, '32, '33, '35, '36, '39, '40, '43, '56, '59, '60, '65, '69, '72, '75.
L1102, '05, '06, '09, '13, '15, '17, '21, '23, '24, '28, '30, '68, '69, '70, '72, '73, '77, '78, '79, '83, '85, '86, 1200, '07, '12, '22, '26, '29, '32, '33, '35, '36, '37, '40, '48, '51, '53, '57, '61, '65, '69, '72, '77, '78, '79, '81, '84, '85, '86, '89, '90, '91, '92, '95, '96, '97, '99, 1300, '05, '08, '28, '30, '34, '37, '40, '56, '57, 1403, '08, '19, '23, '24, '35, '36, '37, '39, '40, '47, '48, '49, '50-78, 1500-1519, '21-25.
L4904-08, '29-33.
L6595, '97, '99, 6601-05, '07, '08, '11, '12, '13, '14-19, '26, '36-46, '51, '71, '75-86, '88, '89, 6710-12, '19-34, '37, '38-43, '56, '63, '74, '76-82, '87-92, '97-99, 6801, '02-05, '08, '16, 3541, '43.
L8367-73, '77, 8400, '07, '39, '50, '51, '70, 8508, '09, 8613, '14, '16, '17, '55, '56, '57, '58, '59, '60, '65, '69, '72, '75-81, '84-87, '90, 8701, '714-20, '22-31.

Bristol Blenheim IVF: Known conversions from bomber Mk IV:
L4899, 4906.
L8784-86, 8840-42.
L9176, '89, 9252, '59, '61, '62, '99, 9313, '92-97, 9401, '04, '06-09, 9446-57, '80-82.
N3525-31, '33-34, '40, '41-43, '3601-03, '08, '09, '11, '12, N6147, '93, '96, 6233, '39, P4825, '29, '31, '32, '33, '35-37, '44-47, '49-50, 4902, P6950-52, '56-58, R2774, '76-77, '79, '97-99, R3622, '24-27, '3826-27, '39, '78, '86-88, 3909, T1803-12, '69-70, 1941-50, '52-55, 1997-2001, 2078, 2129, '30, '31.
V5392-96, 5429-33, '47-54, '63, 5570, 5645, 5721, 5734-35, 5752, 5764, 5765, 5799, 5801-03, 5816.
Z5723-43, '55, 5750-55, 5800-11, 5952-57, '63, '65-75, 6021-34, '78, '81-82, '84-89, 6102-04, 6144-48, '74-75, '77-78, '81, '84, '87, '90, '92, '93, 6245, '54, '79, 6342, '43.

Bristol Beaufighter IF: R2052-57, R2059-60, R2063-2101, R2120-59, R2180-2209, R2240-2269, V8219-8233, V8246-8289, V8307-8356, V8370-8385, X7540-7541, X7544-7589, X7610-7649, X7670-7719, X7740-7779, X7800-7849, X7870-7879.

Bristol Beaufighter IIF: R2058, R2061-62, R2270-2284, R2300-2349, R2370-2404, R2430-2479, T3009-3055, T3070-3107, T3137-3183, T3210-3227, T3356-3389, T3410-3447, V8131-8170, V8184-8218.

Bristol Beaufighter VIF: V8386-8419, V8433-8472, V8489-8528, V8545-8594, V8608-8657, V8671-8720, V8733-8778, V8799-8848, V8862-8901, X7542-43, X7880-7899, X7920-7924, X7926-7936, X7940-7969, X8000-8029, X8100-8109, 8130-8169, 8190-8229, X8250-8269, BT286-303, EL145-192, EL213-218, KV896-944, KV960-981, KW101-133, KW147-171, KW183-203, MM838-887, MM899-948, ND139-186, ND198-243, ND255-299, ND312-322.

Bristol Beaufighter IC: T3228-3250, T3270-3272, T3290-3333, T3348-3355.

Bristol Beaufighter VIC: X7925, X8030-8039, X8060-8099, EL219-246, EL259-305, EL321-370, EL385-418, EL431-479, EL497-534, JL421-454, JL502-549, JL564-582, JL584-592, JL619-628, JL639-648, JL659, JL704-712, JL723-735, JL756-779, JL812-826, JL836-855, JL869-875.

Bristol Beaufighter VIC (Interim TF): JL583, JL593, JL610-618, JL629-638, JL649-658, JL713-722, JL827-835, JL949-957, JM104.

Bristol Beaufighter TF X: EL393, JM268-291, JM315-356, JM379-417, KW277-298, KW315-355, KW370-416, LX779-827, LX845-887, LX898-914, LX926-959, LX972-999, LZ113-158, LZ172-201, LZ215-247, LZ260-297, LZ314-346, LZ359-384, LZ397-419, LZ432-465, LZ479-495, LZ515-544, NE193-232, NE245-260, NE282-326, NE339-386, NE398-446, NE459-502, NE515-559, NE572-615, NE627-669, NE682-724, NE738-779, NE792-832, RD130-176, RD189-225, RD239-285, RD298-335, RD348-396, RD420-468, RD483-525, RD538-580, RD685-728, RD742-789, RD801-836, RD849-867, SR910-919, NT888-929, NT942-971, NV113-158, NV171-218, NV233-276, NV289-333, NV347-390, NV413-457, NV470-513, NV526-572, NV585-632.

Beaufighter TF XI: JM105-136, JM158-185, JM206-250, JM262-267, LX880.

Curtiss Mohawk Mk I to IV: AR630-694 mixed III/IV, AX880-898 ex-French order, BB918-937, BB974-979, BJ531-550 (Mk IV); BJ574 (IV), BJ575 (IV), BJ577 (IV), BJ581 (IV), BJ582 (IV), BJ587-88 (IV), BK569-588 (III); BK876-879, BL220-223, BS730-738 (IV), BS744-747 (IV), BS784-798 (IV), BT470-472 (IV); LA157, 158, 163-165 all Mk IV.

Curtiss Tomahawk Mk I/II: AH741-880 (I), AH881-990 (IIA), AH991-999 (IIB), AK100-570 (IIB), AM370-519 (IIB), AN218-517 (IIB), BK852-853 (Mk I), AX900 (Mk I for trials). Many diverted to USSR and AVG.

Curtiss Kittyhawk Mk I/IV: AK571-AL230 (I), ET100-999 (IA), EV100-699 (IA), FL219-368 (IIA), FS400-499 (II), FL710-730 (III), FL875-905 (III), FR779-872 (III), FR111-140 (III), FR210-361 (III), FR385-392 (III), FR412-521 (III), FR884-885 (IV), FS270-399 (IV), FT849-954 (IV), FX498-847 (IV).

de Havilland Mosquito NF II: W4052, 4074, 4076, 4078, 4080, 4082, 4083-99; DD600-644, DD659-691, DD712-759, DD777-800, DZ228-272, DZ286-310, DZ653-661, DZ680-727, DZ739-761, HJ642-661, HJ699-715, HJ911-944.

de Havilland Mosquito FB VI: HJ662-682, HJ716-743, HJ755-792, HJ808-833, HP848-888, HP904-942, HP967-989, HR113-162, HR175-220, HR236-262, HR279-312, HR331-375, HR387-415, HR432-465, HR485-527, HR539-580, HR603-649, HX802-835, HX849-869, HX896-922 (less HX902-904 XVIII), HX937-984, LR248-276, LR289-313, LR327-340, LR343-389, LR402-404, MM398-423, MM426-431 (MM424-425 Mk XVIII), NS819-859, NS873-914, NS926-965, NS977-999, NT112-156, NT169-207, NT219-238 (NT220, 224, 225 Mk XVIII), PZ161-203, PZ217-259, PZ273-316, PZ330-358, PZ371-419, PZ435-476 (less PZ251, 252, 300, 301, 346, 467-470 Mk XVIII), RF580-625, RF639-681, RF695-736, RF749-793, RF818-859, RF873-915, RF928-966, RS501-535, RS548-580, RS593-633, RS637-680, RS693-698, SZ958-999, TA113-122, TA369-388, TA469-508, TA523-560, TA575-603, TE587-628, TE640-699, TE683-707, TE708-725, TE738-780, TE793-830, TE848-889, TE905-932, VL726-732.

de Havilland Mosquito NF XII: DD715, DD759, HJ945-946, HK107-141, HK159-204, HK222-235, DZ302, HK369 (also Mk XIII).

de Havilland Mosquito NF XIII: HK363-382, HK396-437, HK453-481, HK499-536 (HK535-536 renumbered SM700/701), MM436-479, MM491-534, MM547-575, MM576-590, MM615-623.

de Havilland Mosquito NF XV: MP469, DZ366, DZ385, DZ409, DZ417.

de Havilland Mosquito NF XVII: HK195, HK236-265, HK278-327, HK344-362.

de Havilland Mosquito NF XIX: MM624-656, MM669-685, TA123-156, TA169-198, TA215-249, TA263-308, TA323-357.

de Havilland Mosquito FB 26: delivered to RAF: KA134-136, 140, 151, 152, 154, 160, 161, 162, 164, 165, 169, 171, 175, 178, 190, 191, 198, 200, 214, 215, 217, 227, 248, 256, 258, 259, 262-264, 266, 273, 277, 282, 284, 286, 294, 304, 308, 309, 310, 322, 324, 325, 329, 333, 337, 338, 341-343, 349, 351, 353, 354, 356, 362, 364, 368, 370, 373, 378, 389, 406, 407, 412, 413, 416, 417.

de Havilland Mosquito T 29: KA117, 119, 120, 138, 139, 158, 280, 288.

de Havilland Mosquito NF 30: MM686-710, MM726-769, MM783-822, MT456-500, MV521-570, NT241-283, NT295-336, NT349-393, NT415-458, NT471-513, NT526-568, NT582-621, RK929-954.

de Havilland Hornet I: PX210-253, PX273-288.

de Havilland Hornet III: PX289-315, PX328-369, PX383-398, WB870-889, WB897-912, WF954-962, WF966-967.

de Havilland Hornet F 4: WF968-979.

de Havilland Vampire F 1: TG274-315, TG328-355, TG370-389, TG419-448, VF265-283, VF300-314.

de Havilland Vampire F 3: VF315-348, VG692-703, VV187-213.

de Havilland Vampire FB 5: VV214-232, VV443-490, VV525-569, VV600-640, VV655-700, VV717-736, VX950-990, VZ105-155, VZ161-197, VZ206-241, VZ251-290, VZ300-359, VZ808-852, VZ860-877, WA101-150, WA159-208, WA215-264, WA271-320, WA329-348, WA355-403, WA411-460, WE830-849, WF578-579, WF584-586, WG793-807, WG826-847.

de Havilland Vampire FB 9: WG848-851, WG865-892, WG922-931, WL493-518, WL547-687, WL602-616, WP990-999, WR102-111, WR114-158, WR171-215, WR230-269.

de Havilland Vampire NF 10: WM659-677, WM703-733, WP232-256, WV689-691.

de Havilland Venom FB 1: WE255-294, WE303-332, WE340-389, WE399-438, WE444-483, WK389-438, WK468-503, WR272-321, WR334-373.

de Havilland Venom NF 2: WL804-833, WL845-874, WP227, WR779-808.

de Havilland Venom NF 3: WX785-810, WX837-886, WX903-949, WZ315-320.

Douglas Boston III (Intruder): W8253, '54, '56, '58, '59, '61, '62-64, '66, '67, '68, '71, '78, '81-83, '84, '90, '92, '98, 8304, '05, '14, '18, '21, '25, '26, '31, '33, '35, '38, '42, '44, '45, '49, '50-51, '56, '58, '59, '61, '65, '74, '80, '85, '90, '95, Z2155, Z2186, Z2241, Z2290, Z2299, AL425, 459, 463, 466-468, 475, 480, 500.

Douglas Boston III (Turbinlite): W8255, '57, '65, '74, '75, '76, '79, '80, '94, '99, 8300, '06, '07, '08, 10, '12-13, '22-24, '39, '43, '46, '53, '57, '62, '67, '79, '97, '98, 8401, Z2185, 2189, 2246, AL458, 470.

Douglas Boston III converted to Havoc II: W8274, W8277, W8317, 8328, 8341, 8352 (Turbinlite), 8366 (Turbinlite), 8369, 8393 (Turbinlite), 8396 (Turbinlite).

Douglas Havoc I/Boston I and II: AE457-472 (AE458-463, AE465-469, AE471 known to have been converted to Havoc I but mainly left with clear nose); AW392-393, AW400-401, AW404, AW406—all Havoc I; AW411, 412 (Havoc I —Turbinlite); AX848 and 851 (Havoc I); AX910-918 (Havoc I); AX921, 923, 924, 930, 936, 974, 975 (Boston I converted to Havoc I), AX923 and 924 fitted with Turbinlite; BB891-895, BB896-904, BB907-909, BB911-912 (converted to Havoc I and 897, 899, 907-909 fitted with Turbinlite); BD110-127 (Havoc I, 110, 111, 120 had Turbinlite); BJ458-477, BJ485-501 (Havoc I, 460, 461, 467, 469, 470 had Turbinlite), BK882 Turbinlite, BK883 Havoc I Intruder and LAM Mk III aircraft, BL227-228 Havoc I, BT460-465 Havoc I, BV203 and DG554-555 Havoc I.

Douglas Boston converted to Havoc II: (T) indicates Turbinlite aircraft. AH431(T), 432(T), 434(T), 436(T), 437, 445-447(T), 450-453(T), 455(T), 458(T), 460(T), 462(T), 470-473(T), 478-479(T), 481(T), 483(T), 484(T), 487, 490, 491(T), 497(T), 500, 502, 503(T), 505, 509-10, 512, 518, 520, 523-24, 525, 528-529.

English Electric/BAC Lightning: Prototypes—XA847, 853, 856; DB—Development Batch aircraft: XG307-313, XG325-337; XM series Mk I/IA aircraft; later fighters in XP, XR and XS ranges.

Gloster Gauntlet I: K4081-4104.

Gloster Gauntlet II: K5264-5367, K7792-7891.

Gloster Gladiator I: K5200, K6129-6151, K7892-8055, L7608-7623, L8005-8032.

Gloster Gladiator II: N2303-2314, N5575-5594, N5620-5649, N5680-5729, N5750-5789, N5810-5859, N5875-5924.

Gloster F9/40 Meteor prototypes: DG202/G to DG209/G.

Gloster Meteor I: EE210-229.

Gloster Meteor III: EE230-253, EE269-318, EE331-369, EE384-429, EE444-493.

Gloster Meteor IV/4: EE517-554, 568-599, RA365-398, RA413-457, RA473-493, VT102-150, VT168-199, VT213-247, VT256-294, VT303-347, VW255-315, VW780-791, VZ386-429, VZ436-437.

Gloster Meteor F 8: VZ438-485, VZ493-532, VZ540-569, WA755-794, WA808-857, WA867-909, WA920-964, WA965-969, WA981-999, WB105-112, WE852-891, WE895-939, WE942-976, WF639-662, WF677-716, WF736-760, WH249-263, WH272-320, WH342-386, WH395-426, WH442-484, WH498-513, WK647-696, WK707-756, WK783-827, WK849-893, WK906-955, WK966-994, WL104-143, WL158-191.

Gloster Meteor FR 9: VZ577-611, WB114-125, WB133-143, WH533-557, WL255-265, WX962-981.

Gloster Meteor NF 11: WA546, 547, WD585-634, WD640-689, WD696-745, WD751-800, WM143-192, WM221-270, WM292-302.

Gloster Meteor NF 12: WS590-639, WS658-700, WS715-721.

Gloster Meteor NF 13: WM308-341, WM362-367.

Gloster Meteor NF 14: WS722-760, WS774-812, WS827-848.

Gloster Javelin 1: XA544-572, 618-628.

Gloster Javelin 2: XA629-640, XA768-781, XA799-814, XD158.

Gloster Javelin 3: XH390-397, XH432-438, XH443-447.

Gloster Javelin 4: XA720-737, XA749-767.

Gloster Javelin 5: XA641-667, XA690-719, XH687-692.

Gloster Javelin 6: XA815-836, XH693-703.

Gloster Javelin 7: XH704-725, XH746-795, XH833-849, XH871-912, XH955-965.

Gloster Javelin 8: XH966-993, XJ113-130. XJ165.

Hawker Fury I: K1926-1946, K2874-2883, K2899-2904, K5663-5682.

Hawker Fury II: K3586, K7263-7285, K8218-8306.

Hawker Demon: K2842-2858, K2905-2908, K3764-3807, K3974-3985, K4496-4544, K5683-5741, K5898-5907, K8181-8217.

Hawker Hurricane I: L1547-2146, N2318-2367, N2380-2409, N2422-2441, N2453-2502, N2520-2559, N2582-2631, N2645-2674, N2700-2729, P2535-2584, P2614-2653, P2672-2701, P2713-2732, P2751-2770, P2792-2836, P2854-2888, P2900-2924, P2946-2995, P3020-3069, P3080-3124, P3140-3179, P3200-3234, P3250-3264, P3265-3279, P3300-3324, P3345-3364, P3380-3429, P3448-3492, P3515-3554, P3574-3623, P3645-3684, P3700-3739, P3755-3789, P3802-3836, P3854-3903, P3920-3944, P3960-3984, P8809-8818, R2680-2689, R4074-4123, R4171-4200, R4213-4232, T9519-9538, V6533-6582, V6600-6649, V6665-6704, V6722-

6761, V6776-6825, V6840-6889, V6913-6962, V6979-7028, V7042-7081, V7099-7138, V7156-7195, V7200-7209, V7221-7235, V7236-7260, V7276-7318, V7337-7386, V7400-7446, V7461-7510, V7533-7572, V7588-7627, V7644-7690, V7705-7737, V7741-7780, V7795-7838, V7851-7862, W6667-6670, W9110-9159, W9170-9209, W9215-9244, W9260-9279, W9290-9329, W9340-9359, Z4022-4071, Z4085-4119, Z4161-4205, Z4223-4272, Z4308-4327, Z4347-4391, Z4415-4434, Z4482-4516, Z4532-4581, Z4603-4652, Z4686-4720, Z4760-4809, Z4832-4876, Z4920-4939, AS987-990.

Hawker Hurricane II (excluding conversions from Mk I): Z2308-2357, Z2382-2426, Z2446-2465, Z2479-2528, Z2560-2594, Z2624-2643, Z2661-2705, Z2741-2775, Z2791-2840, Z2882-2931, Z2959-2993, Z3017-3036, Z3050-3099, Z3143-3187, Z3221-3270, Z3310-3359, Z3385-3404, Z3421-3470, Z3489-3523, Z3554-3598, Z3642-3691, Z3740-3784, Z3826-3845, Z3885-3919, Z3969-4018, Z4940-4969, Z4987-4989, Z4990-5006, Z5038-5087, Z5117-5161, Z5202-5236, Z5252-5271, Z5302-5351, Z5376-5395, Z5434-5483, Z5529-5563, Z5580-5629, Z5649-5693, AP670-714, AP732-781, AP801-825, AP849-898, AP912-936, BD696-745, BD759-793, BD818-837, BD855-899, BD914-963, BD980-986, BE105-117, BE130-174, BE193-242, BE274-308, BE323-372, BE394-428, BE468-517, BE546-590, BE632-651, BE667-716, BG674-723, BG737-771, BG783-832, BG844-888, BG901-920, BG933-977, BG990-999, BH115-154, BH167-201, BH215-264, BH277-296, BH312-361, BM898-936, BM947-996, BN103-142, BN155-189, BN203-242, BN265-298, BN311-337, BN346-389, BN399-435, BN449-497, BN512-547, BN559-603, BN624-654, BN667-705, BN719-759, BN773-802, BN818-846, BN859-882, BN896-940, BN953-992, BP109-141, BP154-200, BP217-245, BP259-302, BP316-362, BP378-416, BP430-479, BP493-526, BP538-566, BP579-614, BP628-675, BP692-711, BP734-772 (DR339-374, DR391-394: Mk I converted to Mk II), HL544-591, HL606-634, HL654-683, HL698-747, HL767-809, HL828-867, HL879-913, HL925-941, HL953-997, HM110-157, HV275-317, HV333-370, HV396-445, HV468-516, HV534-560, HV577-612, HV634-674, HV696-745, HV768-799, HV815-858, HV873-921, HV943-989, HW115-146, HW167-207, HW229-278, HW291-323, HW345-373, HW399-444, HW467-501, HW533-572, HW596-624, HW651-686, HW713-757, HW779-808, HW834-881, KW696-731, KW745-777, KW791, KW793-798, KW801-803, KW805-806, KW811-815, KW818-832, KW846-882, KW893-896, KW898, KW900-907, KW912-913, KW915-917, KW922-936, KW949-982, KX101-141, KX143-146, KX161-164, KX165-177, KX181-187, KX191-197, KX201-202, KX220-261, KX280-307, KX321-369, KX382-404, KX415-425, KX452-491, KX521-535, KX546-564, KX586-621, KX691-696, KX706-736, KX749-784, KX796-799, KX810-819, KX830-838, KX851-861, KX863-866, KX867-875, KX886-892, KX922-967, KZ111-156, KZ169-184, KZ195-201, KZ216-218, KZ229-238, KZ249-250, KZ266-299, KZ327-356, KZ370-373, KZ384-393, KZ405, KZ408-412, KZ424-470, KZ483-526, KZ540-549, KZ560-569, KZ580-582, KZ597-603, KZ614-619, KZ622-632, KZ646-653, KZ664-673, KZ684-689, KZ702-705, KZ716-721, KZ724-725, KZ727-750, KZ766-801, KZ817-862, KZ877-903, KZ917-920, KZ933-949, LA101-144, LB542-575, LB588-624, LB639-642, LB653-681, LB711-742, LB778-801, LB827-848, LB854-862, LB873-913, LB927-973, LB986-992, LD103-131, LD157-159, LD170-185, LD199-215, LD238-266, LD287-289, LD295-315, LD334-351, LD369-416, LD435-441, LD452-464, LD491-508, LD524-539, LD557-562, LD573-580, LD594-604, LD610-632, LD651-695, LD723-749, LD772-787, LD798-809, LD827-861, LD890-905, LD931-968, LD993-999, LE121-131, LE137-146, LE163-183, LE201-214, LE247-268, LE295-309, LE334-368, LE387-392, LE403-405, LE432-449, LE456-484, LE499-504, LE513, LE515-535, LE552-566, LE572-593, LE617-654, LE662-665, LE679-713, LE737-747, LE758-769, LE784-816, LE829-833, LE844-867,

LE885-920, LE938-966, LE979-999, LF101-105, LF116-135, LF153-184, LF197-237, LF256-298, LF313-346, LF359-405, LF418-429, LF475-480, LF511-516, LF529-542, LF597-601, LF620-660, LF674-721, LF737-774, MW335-373, PZ730-778, PZ791-835, PZ848-865.

Hawker Hurricane IV: KW792, KW799-800, KW804, KW807-810, KW816-817, KW897, KW899, KW908-911, KW914, KW918-921, KX142, KX178-180, KX188-190, KX198-200, KX405-414, KX536-545, KX565-567, KX579-585, KX697-705, KX800-809, KX820-829, KX862, KX872-888, KZ185-192, KZ194, KZ219-228, KZ239-248, KZ300-301, KZ319-326, KZ374-383, KZ394-404, KZ406-407, KZ550-559, KZ570-579, KZ604-613, KZ620-621, KZ654-663, KZ674-683, KZ706-715, KZ722-723, KZ726, KZ904-916, LB643-652, LB682-687, LB707-710, LB743-744, LB769-776, LB849-853, LB993-999, LD100-102, LD160-169, LD216-219, LD232-237, LD290-294, LD442-451, LD465-470, LD487-490, LD563-572, LD605-609, LD788-797, LD862-866, LD885-889, LD969-979, LE132-136, LE268-273, LE291-294, LE393-402, LE505-512, LE514, LE567-571, LE653-661, LE748-757, LE834-843, LE921-925, LF106-115, LF430-435, LF451-474, LF481-482, LF495-510, LF592-596.

Hawker Hurricane V: KZ193.

Hawker Hurricane (Canadian Production): P5170-5209 (Mk I became Mk X), T9519-9538 (Mk I), AE958-977 (Mk I became Mk X), AF945-AG344 (Mk I became Mk X), AG665-684 (Mk IIB, 666 and 667 converted to IIC), AM270-369 (Mk X; 228 converted to IIC), AP138-163 (Mk X); BW841 and 880 (Mk X), BW885-999, BX100-134 (both batches Mk XIB but 886, 900 and 921 converted to XIC), JS219-468 (Mk XII less 372 and 373), PJ660-695 (XII), 711-758 (XII), 779-813 (XII), 842-872 (XII).

Hurricane sub series: Any listing of Hurricanes must take account of the sub series, 'A', 'B', 'C', 'D' or 'E'. Often the aircraft were changed in service from one type to another so that a complete listing—complicated and very lengthy—is of questionable value. However, a typical listing of Hurricanes and their sub types as they left the production line between BM898 and BP302 is given as indicative of the complex state of deliveries by sub series.

*BM*898-936 (all IIB), 947-964 (IIB), 965 (IIC), 966-969 (IIB), 970-988 (IIC), 989-996 (IIB), *BN*103-114 (IIB), 115-142 (IIC), 155-159 (IIC), 160-180 (IIB), 181-189 (IIC), 203-207 (IIC), 208-226 (IIB), 227 (IIC), 228 (IIB), 229-237 (IIC), 238-242 (IIB), 265-276 (IIB), 277 (IIC), 278 (IIB), 279-292 (IIC), 293-294 (IIB), 295 (IIC), 296-298 (IIB), 311-329 (IIB), 330-337 (IIC), 346-387 (IIC), 388 (IIB), 389 (IIC), 399-405 (IIC), 406-407 (IIB), 408-415 (IIC), 416-435 (IIB), 449-462 (IIB), 463-484 (IIC), 484-493 (IIB), 494-497 (IIC), 512 (IIC), 513-536 (IIB), 537-547 (IIC), 559-567 (IIC), 568-582 (IIB), 583 (IIC), 584-597 (IIB), 598-599 (IIC), 600-603 (IIB), 624-654 (IIB), 667-670 (IIB), 671-676 (IIC), 677 (IIB), 678-679 (IIC), 680 (IIB), 681 (IIC), 682 (IIB), 683-685 (IIC), 686-691 (IIB), 692-705 (IIC), 719 (IIC), 720-740 (IIB), 741-759 (IIB), 773-779 (IIB), 780-788 (IIC), 789 not delivered, 790-794 (IIB), 795-797 (IID), 798-802 (IIB), 818-839 (IIB), 840-846 (IID), 859-863 (IID), 864-865 (IIC), 866 (IID), 867-882 (IIC), 896-898 (IIC), 899-900 (IIB), 901-902 (IIC), 903-905 (IIB), 906-908 (IIC), 909-940 (IIB), 953-955 (IIB), 958-960 (IIC), 961 (IID), 962 (IIC), 963 (IID), 964 (IIC), 965 (IID), 966 (IIC), 967 (IID), 968 (IIC), 969 (IID), 970 (IIC), 971 (IID), 972 (IIC), 973 (IID), 974 (IIC), 975 (IID), 976 (IIC), 977 (IID), 978 (IIB), 979 (IID), 980-988 (IIB), 989 (IIC), 990-992 (IIB); *BP* 109-111 (IIC), 112-113 (IIB), 114 (IIC), 115-119 (IIB), 120-125 (IIC), 126 (IID), 127-130 (IIC), 131 (IID), 132-135 (IIB), 136 (IID), 137 (IIB), 138-139 (IIC), 140 (IIB), 141 (IID), 154 (IIB), 155 (IIC), 156 (IIB), 157 (IIC), 158 (IID), 159-162 (IIC), 163 (IID), 164-165 (IIC), 166 (IIB), 167 (IIC), 168 (IID), 169 (IIC), 170-171 (IIB), 172 (IIC),

173 (IID), 174-177 (IIC), 178 (IID), 179-182 (IIC), 183 (IID), 184 (IIC), 185 (IIB), 186-187 (IIC), 188 (IID), 189-192 (IIC), 193 (IID), 194-199 (IIC), 200 (IIB), 217-221 (IIC), 222-228 (IIB), 229 (IIC), 230 (IIB), 231-235 (IIC), 236 (IIB), 237 (IIC), 238 (IIB), 239-240 (IIC), 241-245 (IIB), 259-279 (IIB), 280 (IIC), 281-286 (IIB), 287 (IIC), 288-296 (IIB), 297 (IIB), 298 (IIB bomber), 300 (IIB), 301 (IIB bomber), 302 (IIB).

Earlier examples of Mk IIC include: Z2326, Z3050, Z3051, Z3064, Z3068, Z3081, Z3083, Z3088, Z3183, Z3184, Z3224, Z3261, Z3450, Z3454, Z3464, Z3503, Z3561, Z3576, Z3582, Z3591, Z3774, Z3776, Z3778, Z3779, Z3783, Z3831, Z3835, Z3839, Z3840, Z3841, Z3842, Z3843, Z3844, Z3895, Z3899, Z3902, Z3916, Z3919, Z3970, Z4001.

Initially the Hurricane IIB fighter-bomber entered service as the Mk IIE. Basically the aeroplane was unaltered, and the addition of bomb racks was deemed insufficient to change the sub series, so Mk IIB and IIC Hurricanes with bomb racks later were designated FB Mk IIB and FB Mk IIC. The following list gives some examples of aircraft known for a time as Mk IIE: *BE*394, 401, 403, 405, 418-421, 424, 425, 472-479, 483-486, 489, 492, 498, 504-506, 508, 548, 552, 651, 670, 671, 673, 674, 675, 680, 682, 684, 690, 691, *BP*295, 299, 301, 649, 653, 672, 701, 705, 737, 754, 768.

Hawker Typhoon: R7576-7599 (IA), R7613-7655 (IA), R7672-7709 (IA), R7710 (IB), R7711 (IA), R7712-7721, R7738-7775, R7792-7829, R7845-7890 and R7913 7923 all Mk IB. Other Typhoon IBs converted from IA or built finally as IB in the early R series were R7646, 7650, 7673, 7678, 7679, 7680, 7684, 7686, 7687, 7689, 7692, 7693, 7695, 7697, 7702, 7705, 7708. R8198-8200 (IA), R8220-8221 (IA), R8222-8231 (IB), R8630-8663 (IB except 8640 and 8652), R8680-8722 (IB except R8720 and R8709 both IA), R8737-8781 (IB except R8746), R8799-8845 (IB), R8861-8900 (IB), R8923-8947 (IB), R8966-8981 (IB). Mk IB from this point, as follows: DN241-278, DN293-341, DN356-389, DN404-453, DN467-513, DN529-562, DN576-623, EJ900-934, EJ946-995, EK112-154, EK167-197, EK208-252, EK266-301, EK321-348, EK364-413, EK425-456, EK472-512, EK535-543, JP361-408, JP425-447, JP480-516, JP532-552, JP576-614, JP648-689, JP723-756, JP784-802, JP836-861, JP897-941, JP961-976, JR125-152, JR183-223, JR237-266, JR289-338, JR360-392, JR426-449, JR492-535, MM951-995, MN113-156, MN169-213, MN229-269, MN282-325, MN339-381, MN396-436, MN449-496, MN513-556, MN569-608, MN623-667, MN680-720, MN735-779, MN791-823, MN851-896, MN912-956, MN968-999, MP113-158, MP172-203, PD446-480, PD492-536, PD548-577, PD589-623, RB192-235, RB248-289, RB303-347, RB361-408, RB423-459, RB474-512, SW386-428, SW443-478, SW493-537, SW551-596, SW620-668, SW681-716, SW728-772.

Hawker Tempest II: MW375-423, MW435, MW735-778, MW790-835, MW847-856, PR525-567, PR581-623, PR645-689, PR713-758, PR771-815, PR830-876, PR889-921.

Hawker Tempest V: EJ504, EJ518-560, EJ577-611, EJ626-672, EJ685-723, EJ739-788, EJ800-846, EJ859-896, JN729-773, JN792-822, JN854-877, NV639-682, NV695-735, NV749-793, NV917-948, NV960-996, SN102-146, SN159-190, SN205-238, SN253-296, SN310-355.

Hawker Tempest VI: NV997-999, NX113-156, NX169-209, NX223-268, NX281-288.

Hawker Hunter F1: WT555-595, WT611-660, WT679-700, WW599-610, WW632-645.

Hawker Hunter F4: WT702-723, WT734-780, WT795-811, WV253-281, WV314-334, WV363-412, WW646-665, XE657-689, XE709-718, XF289-324, XF357-370, XF932-953, XF967-999, XG341-342.

Hawker Hunter F6: WW592-598, XE526-561, XE579-628, XE643-656, XF373-389, XF414-463, XF495-527, XF833, XG127-137, XG150-168, XG169-172, XG185-211, XG225-239, XG251-274, XG289-298, XJ632-646, XJ673-695, XJ712-718, XK136-156.

Many conversions from Mk 9 to interim Mk 9 or full Mk 9 standard. Sales overseas from RAF orders too.

Hawker Hunter F2: WN888-921, WN943-953.

Hawker Hunter F5: WN954-992, WP101-150, WP179-194.

Hawker Hunter FR10: Some examples—WW595, WW596, XE605, XE625, XJ633, XJ714.

Hawker P1127 Kestrel: XP972, XP976, XP980, XP984, XS688-696.

Hawker Harrier: XV276-281, XV738 et seq.

Lockheed Lightning F1: Examples delivered—AE978, AE979, AF105, AF106, AF108.

North American Mustang 1: AG354-664, AL958-AM257, AP164-263.

North American Mustang IA: FD438-449, FD465, FD470-509.

North American Mustang II: EW998, FR890-939.

North American Mustang III: FB100-399, FR411, FX848-FZ197, HB821-961, KH421-640, SR406-438, SR440.

North American Mustang IV: FR410, KH641-670, KH671-870 (Mk IVA), KM100-743, KN987.

North American Mustang V: FR409.

North American Sabre F2: XB530-532.

North American Sabre F4: XB533-550, XB575-603, XB608-650, XB664-713, XB726-775, XB790-839, XB851-900, XB912-961, XB973-999, XD706-736, XD753-781.

Republic Thunderbolt 1: FL731-850.

Republic Thunderbolt II: KJ128-367, KL168-347, KL838-887.

Supermarine Spitfire I: K9787-9999, L1000-1096, N3023-3072, N3091-3130, N3160-3203, N3221-3250, P9305-9339, P9360-9399, P9420-9469, P9490-9519, P9540-9567, R6595-6644, A6683-6722, R6751-6780, R6799-6818, R6829-6840, R6879-6928, R6957-6996, R7015-7044, R7055-7074, R7114-7163, R7192-7217, R7250-7252, R7257, X4009-4038, X4051-4070, X4101-4110, X4159-4188, X4231-4280, X4317-4356, X4381-4390, X4409-4428, X4471-4505, X4538-4562, X4585-4624, X4641-4685, X4708-4722, X4765-4789, X4815-4859, X4896-4945, X4988-4997, AR212-261.

Within the above listed serial number batches there were many conversions, to Mk IB, Mk V and to various photo-reconnaissance configurations and details of some of these may be found in *British Military Aircraft Serials* (Ian Allan) by Bruce Robertson and in *Spitfire—the Story of a Famous Fighter* (Harleyford) also by Bruce Robertson. Conversions for fighter purposes included the following:

Conversions to Mk IB: R6897, R6904, R6908, R6911, R6912, R6917, R6919, R6923, R6924, R6957, R6960, X4062, X4267, X4272, X4331.

Conversion to Mk III: N3297.

Conversions to Mk V: N3044, N3053, N3059, N3098, N3111, N3124, N3241, N3270, N3281, N3292, R6602, R6620, R6720, R6722, R6759, R6761, R6770, R6776, R6801, R6809, R6817, R6882, R6888, R6889, R6890, R6908, R6911, R6912, R6913, R6917, R6919, R6923, R6924, R6957, R6960, R6992, R7022, R7060, R7127, R7158, R7161, R7192, R7194, R7195, R7196, R7205, R7207, R7208, R7209, R7210, R7213, R7217, R7218, X4062, X4106, X4257, X4258,

X4272, X4280, X4555, X4604, X4605, X4606, X4620, X4621, X4622, X4623, X4624, X4663-4671, X4902, X4922, X4997.

Supermarine Spitfire II: P7280-7329, P7350-7389, P7420-7449, P7490-7509, P7520-7569, P7590-7692, P7661-7669, P7730-7759, P7770-7789, P7810-7859, P7880-7929, P7960-7999, P8010-8049, P8070-8099, P8130-8149, P8160-8209, P8230-8279, P8310-8349, P8360-8399, P8420-8449, P8460-8479, P8500-8549, P8560-8609, P8640-8679, P8690-8698. From this point Mk V aircraft were intermittently completed on the line. P8699-8729, P8740-8759, P8780-8799.

750 Mk IIA were built and 170 Mk IIB. The latter included: P7788, P7895, P7899, P7907, P7965, P7984, P7990, P8042, P8078, P8091, P8135, P8141, P8146, P8149, P8174, P8192, P8232, P8234, P8238, P8244, P8283, P8316, P8320, P8321, P8322, P8329, P8332, P8337, P8343, P8345, P8347, P8383, P8505, P8533, P8575, P8591, P8593, P8644, P8645, P8648, P8649, P8692, P8728.

Laid down as Mk IIA, completed as Mk V: P8532, P8537-8539, P8542, P8560, P8564, P8578, P8581, P8585, P8560, P8600, P8603, P8604, P8606, P8607, P8609, P8640, P8699, P8700, P8703, P8707-8724, P8740-8759, P8780-8799.

Converted from Mk II to Mk V: P7287, P7297, P7299, P7308, P7316, P7324, P7447, P7498, P7532, P7619, P7629, P7672, P7686, P7692, P7789, P7846, P7906, P7910, P7920, P7964, P7965, P7973, P7986, P8017, P8036, P8086, P8095, P8099, P8167, P8195, P8236, P8237, P8239, P8246, P8259, P8262, P8436, P8438, P8459, P8563, P8595.

Supermarine Spitfire V: W3109-3138, W3168-3187, W3207-3216, W3226-3265, W3305-3334, W3364-3383, W3403-3412, W3422-3461, W3501-3530, W3560-3579, W3599-3608, W3618-3657, W3697-3726, W3756-3775, W3795-3804, W3814-3853, W3893-3902, W3931-3970 (all built as Mk VB except for the following Mk VA: W3109-3114, W3118, W3119, W3121, W3123, W3130, W3136, W3138, W3169, W3184, W3185, W3212, W3216, W3379 (W3237 converted to Mk III).

AA833-873 (VB), AA874 (VC), AA875-882 (VB), AA902-946 (VB), AA963 (VC), AA964-967 (VB), AA968 (VC), AA969-975 (VB), AA976-977 (VC), AA978 (VB), AA979 (VC), AA980 (VC), AB124 (VB), AB130 (VA), AB133-152 (VB), AB167-216 (mixed VB and VC less AB176, 200, 211 Mk VI), AB240-247 (VB), AB248 (VC), AB249-284 (probably all VB), AB320-349 (VB), AB363-366 (VB), AB367-368 (VC), AB369-370 (VB), AB371-372 (VC), AB373 (VB), AB374 (VC), AB375-376 (VB), AB377 (VC), AB378-379 (VB), AB380-381 (VC), AB382 (VB), AB401-416 (VB), AB417 (VC), AB418-420 (VB), AB450 (VC), AB451 (VB), AB452-453 (VC), AB454 (VB), AB455 (VC), AB456-460 (built as Mk V converted to Mk IX), AB487 (VB), AB489 (VC), AB490 (VB), AB491-499 (VC), AB500 (VB), AB501 (VC), AB502 (VC), AB503-536 (VC: also see listing under Mk VI). There were in addition some conversions to Mk IX including AA873, AB522 and AB525. AB778-828, AB841-875, AB892-941, AB960-994, AD111-140, AD176-210, AD225-274, AD288-332, AD348-397, AD411-430, AD449-478, AD498-517, AD535-584 all built as Mk VB.

AR274-298 (VB), AR318-347 (VB), AR362-406 (VB), AR422-461 (VB), AB462-471 (VC), AR488-532 (VC), AR546-570 (VC), AR592-621 (VC). BL231-267 (VB), BL285-304 (VB), BL311-356 (VB), BL365-391 (VB), BL403-450 (VB), BL461-500 (VB), BL509-551 (VB), BL562-600 (VB), BL613-647 (VB), BL655-699 (VB), BL707-736 (VB), BL748-789 (VB), BL801-833 (VB), BL846-864 (VB), BL887-909 (VB), BL919-941 (VB), BL956-998 (VB), BM113-162 (VB), BM176-211 (VB), BM227-274 (VB), BM289-329 (VB), BM343-386 (VB), BM402-430 (VB), BM447-493 (VB), BM508-543 (VB), BM556-597 (VB), BM624-653 (VB).

BP844-854 (VB), BP855-878 (VC), BP950-993 (VC), BR106-143 (VC less BR140-143 completed as Mk IX), BR159-205 (VC), BR226-256 (VC), BR282-330 (VC less those built as Mk VI), BR344-393 (VC less 358, 361, 364; BR369-371 built as Mk IX), BR459-499 (VC), BR515-549 (VC), BR562-605 (VC; less those built as Mk VI and BR594, 596, 600-605 built as Mk IX).

BS157-202, BS218-255, BS271-319, BS335-367, BS383-411, BS427-474, BS489-515, BS530-559 (produced as Mks V, VI, VII, IX—see Mks VI, VII, IX).

EE600-644 (VC), EE657-690 (VC), EE713-753 (VC), EE766-811 (VC), EE834-867 (VC).

EF526-570, EF584-616, EF629-656, EF671-710, EF715-753, all VC; EN763-800 (VB), EN821-867 (VB), EN887-932 (VB), EN944-981 (VB), EP107-152, EP164-213, EP226-260 (VB), EP275-316 (VB), EP327-366 (VB), EP380-417 (VB), EP431-473 (VB), EP485-523 (VB), EP536-579 (VB), EP594-624 (VB), EP636-669 (VB), EP682-729 (VB), EP747-795 (VB), EP812-847 (VB), EP869-915 (VB), EP951-990 (VB), ER114-146 (VB), ER159-200 (VB).

ER206-229, ER245-283, ER299-345, ER461-510, ER524-571, ER583-626, ER634-679, ER695-744, ER758-791, ER804-834, ER846-894, ER913-948, ER960-998, ES105-154, ES168-214, ES227-264, ES276-318, ES335-369 all Mk VB except the following: Mk VC as follows: ER265, 280-281, 337, 339, 496, 614, 654-655, 666, 733, 739-740, 760, 762, 765, 777, 781, 782, 787, 804-806, 892, 894, 913-914, 917-921, 924, 927-928, 931-937, 939, 947-948, 990, 993. ES108-112, 114-121, 124, 129, 131, 134, 136, 138-143, 145, 146, 148-150, 152, 168, 171, 174, 178, 182-183, 188, 195-200, 202, 204-214, 229, 231-233, 236-238, 241-243, 245, 249-251, 253-254, 257-260, 263, 277-282, 284-285, 287-290, 292 et seq all VC except ES301 Mk VB. ER126 Mk IX, ES107 Mk IX, ES185 Mk IX, ES291 Mk IX.

JG713-721, JG723-738, JG740-752, JG769-810, JG835-852, JG864-899, JG912-960, JK101-145, JK159-195, JK214-236, JK249-285, JK303-346, JK359-408, JK425-428, JK430-472, JK506-551, JK600-610, JK612-620, JK637-640, JK642-658, JK660-667, JK669-678, JK705-742, JK756-761, JK763-768, JK771-794, JK803-842, JK861-879, JK885-892, JK922-949, JK967-978, JK981-992, JL104-105, JL112-140, JL160-162, JL164-171, JL173-176, JL181-188, JL208-256, JL301-338, JL346, JL348, JL350, JL352, JL355, JL357, JL358, JL360, JL362, JL363, JL365, JL367, JL368, JL371, JL374-384, JL386-394, all built as Mk VC.

LZ807-830 (VC, 816 converted to Mk IX), LZ834-835 (VC), LZ844-848 (VC), LZ861-899 (VC), LZ926-956 (VC), LZ969-988 (VC), MA261-266 (VC), MA279-315 (VC), MA328-368 (VC), MA383-397 (VC), MA644-657 (VC, conversions to Mk IX: 645, 646, 648, 651, 655, 657), MA670-704 (VC), MA850-863 (VC, MA860 converted to Mk IX), MA877 (VC), MA880-906 (VC), MH298-311 (VC), MH581-596 (VC), MH570 (VC), MH605 (VC), MH637-647 (VC).

Supermarine Spitfire VI: X4942, AB176, AB200, AB211, AB498, AB503, AB506, AB513, AB516, AB523, AB527, AB528-530, AB533-534, BR159, BR162, BR164, BR167, BR171-172, BR174, BR178, BR181, BR186, BR189, BR191, BR193, BR197, BR200, BR205, BR243, BR247, BR250, BR252, BR255, BR286-287, BR289, BR297-298, BR302, BR305, BR307, BR309, BR310, BR314, BR318-319, BR326, BR329, BR330, BR563, BR567, BR569, BR571, BR575, BR577-579, BR585, BR587, BR588, BR590, BR593, BR595, BR597-598, BR599, BR979, BR983-984, BR987, BS106, BS108, BS111, BS114-115, BS117, BS124, BS133, BS134, BS141, BS146, BS149, BS228, BS245, BS253, BS427, BS436, BS437, BS442, BS448, BS453, BS460, BS465, BS472, EN176, EN186.

Supermarine Spitfire VII: AB450, BS121, BS142, BS226, BS229, EN178, EN192, EN285, EN297, EN310, EN457, EN465, EN470, EN474, EN477, EN494-497, EN499, EN505, EN506, EN509, EN511-512, MB761-769, MB806, MB808, MB820-828, MB883-887, MB912-916, MB929-931, MB932-935, MD100-112, MD114-146, MD159-190.

Supermarine Spitfire VIII: JF274-300, JF322-364, JF392-427, JF443-485, JF501-528, JF557-592, JF613-630, JF658-676, JF692-716, JF740-789, JF805-850. JF869-902, JF926-967, JG104-124, JG157-204, JG239-275, JG312-356, JG371-387, JG404-432, JG465-500, JG527-568, JG603-624, JG646-695, LV643-681, LV726-756, MB959-976, MD214-256, MD269-303, MD315-356, MD369-403, MT502-527, MT539-581, MT593-635, MT648-689, MT703-748, MT761-802, MT815-846, MT872-915, MT925-969, MT981-999, MV112-156, MV169-208, MV231-245, MV321-329, MV342-346, MV398-441, MV456-487, MV500-514, NH614-636.

Supermarine Spitfire IX: See conversion list in Mk V notes for early aircraft. BR138, BR140-143, BR369-371, BR594, BR596, BR600-605, BR621-640, BR977-987.

BS104-152, BS157-202, BS218-255, BS271-319, BS335-367, BS383-411, BS427-474, BS489-515, BS530-559. All Mk IX except for the following: 106 (VI), 108 (VI), 111 (VI), 114-115 (VI), 117 (VI), 121 (VII), 124 (VI), 133-134 (VI), 141 (VI), 142 (VII), 146 (VI), 149 (VI), 153-156 (VC), 158 (VC), 160-166 (VC), 168-169 (VC), 171 (VC), 173 (VC), 174 (VC), 175 (VC), 178 (VII), 181-182 (VC), 184 (VC), 186-188 (VC), 190-191 (VC), 192 (VII), 193 (VC), 197 (VC), 199 (VC), 201 (VC), 218-225 (VC), 226 (VII), 228 (VI), 229 (VII), 230-238 (VC), 245 (VI), 253 (VI), 291 (VC), 293 (VC), 295 (VC), 298 (VC), 300 (VC), 305 (VC), 356-367 (PR Mk IV), 427 (VI), 436 (VI), 437 (VI), 442 (VI), 448 (VI), 453 (VI), 460 (VI), 465 (VI), 472 (VI), 489 (PR IV), 490-496 (PR IV), 497-502 (PR XI), 503-505 (PR IV), 506-510 (PR XI).

EN112-156, EN171-207, EN239-270, EN285-315, EN329-340, EN344-370, EN385-430, EN444-483, EN490-534, EN551-583, EN628-637, JG722, JG739, JK429, JK535, JK611, JK620, JK641, JK659, JK668, JK762, JK769-770, JK795, JK796, JK840, JK860-892, JK922-949, JK967-992, JL104-140, JL159-188, JL208-256, JL301-338, JL346-395, LZ816, LZ831-833, LZ836-843, LZ915-925, MA221-260, MA298, MA329, MA357, MA369, MA398-428, MA443-487, MA501-546, MA559-601, MA615-643, MA645-646, MA648, MA651, MA655, MA657, MA705-713, MA790-819, MA831-849, MA860, MA878-879, MH312-336, MH349-390, MH413-456, MH470-512, MH526-563, MH597-599, MH570-604, MH606-626, MH635-636, MH647-678, MH691-738, MH750-800, MH813-856, MH924-958, MH970-999, MJ114-156, MJ169-203, MJ215-258, MJ271-314, MJ328-369, MJ382-428, MJ441-485, MJ498-536, MJ549-589, MJ602-646, MJ659-698, MJ712-756, MJ769-801, MJ814-858, MJ870-913, MJ926-967, MJ979-999, MK112-158, MK171-213, MK226-268, MK280-326, MK339-379, MK392-428, MK440-486, MK499-534, MK547-590, MK602-646, MK659-699, MK713-756, MK769-812, MK826-868, MK881-926, MK939-967, MK981-999, ML112-156, ML169-216, ML229-277, ML291-323, ML339-381, ML396-428, NH148-158, NH171-218, NH230-276, NH289-326, NH339-381, NH393-438, NH450-496, NH513-558, NH570-611, PK991-998, PL123-169, PL185-227, PL246-288, PL313-356, PL369-408, PL423-466, PL488-499, PT335-380, PT395-436, PT451-498, PT523-567, PT582-627, PT639-683, PT697-738, PT752-795, PT818-859, PT873-915, PT929-970, PT986-999, PV115-160, PV174-215, PV229-270, PV283-327, PV341-359, RK798-819, RK835-868, RK883-926, RR181-213, RR226-232, RR235, RR237-239, RR241, RR244, RR246, RR251-254, RR258-260, RR262, RR264, SL626-635, SL648-665, SM135-150, SM170-177, SM441-446, SM447-462, SM517-548, TA738-780, TA793-840, TA850-888, TA905-948, TA960-999, TB115-129, TB142-150,

TB168-197, TB213-243, TB249-251, TB253, TB413-450, TB464-474, TB477, TB479, TB482-491, TB503, TB516-518, TB523-524, TB527, TB529-548, TB563-571, TB575-577, TB579, TB584, TB586-587, TB591-598, TB638-674, TB676-712, TB717-718, TB736, TB740, TB771-809, TB824-827, TB830, TB837-843, TB844-857, TB901-918, TB920, TB924-925, TB938-959, TB971-988, TB992, TB994, TD155, TD175, TD178-183, TD192-213, TD287, TD290-292, TD294-315, TD352-368, TD370, TD371, TD373-374, TD378-379, TD395-399, TD952-958, TD970-999, TE115, TE117-118, TE121-158, TE197, TE205, TE211-213, TE215, TE230-234, TE238, TE292-315 (less 300, 310, 311, 314), TE329, TE331, TE333, TE336-337, TE343, TE493-535, TE549-579.

Supermarine Spitfire XII: EN221-238, EN601-627, MB829-863, MB875-882.

Supermarine Spitfire XIV: JF312-321, MT847-858, MV246-273, MV286-320, MV347-386, NH637-661, NH685-720, NH741-759, NH775-813, NH831-875, NH892-929, NM814-823, RB140-189, RM615-625, RM648-656, RM670-713, RM726-770, RM783-825, RM839-887, RM901-943, RM957-999, RN113-160, RN173-221, SM812-842, SM876-899, SM913-938, TP236-240, TP256, TX974-998, TZ102-149, TZ152-176, TZ178-199.

Supermarine Spitfire XVI: RR229-230, RR234, RR236, RR240, RR242-243, RR245, RR247-250, RR255-257, RR261, RR263, RR265, RW344-359, RW373-396, SL541-571, SL573-579, SL594-624, SL666, SL668-676, SL678-681, SL685, SL713, SL715, SL717-721, SL724-725, SL727-728, SL733, SL745, SM178-213, SM226-258, SM273-316, SM329-369, SM383-427, SM463-488, SM503-516, SM563-597, SM610-648, SM663-671, TB130-132, TB136-141, TB244-248, TB252, TB254-256, TB269-308, TB326-349, TB352-396, TB475-476, TB478, TB480-481, TB492-502, TB515, TB519-522, TB525-526, TB528, TB578, TB580-583, TB585, TB588-590, TB613-637, TB675, TB713-716, TB733-735, TB737-739, TB741-759, TB828-829, TB831-836, TB883-900, TB919, TB921-923, TB989-991, TB993, TB995-999, TD113-154, TD156-158, TD176-177, TD184-191, TD229-267, TD280-286, TD288-289, TD293, TD316-325, TD338-351, TD369, TD372, TD375-377, TD400-408, TE116, TE119-120, TE174-215 (except TE197, 205, 211-213, 215), TE228-229, TE231-237, TE239-259, TE300, TE310, TE311, TE314, TE328, TE330, TE332, TE334-335, TE338-342, TE344-359, TE375-408, TE434-480 (less 385 and 472).

Supermarine Spitfire XVIII: SM843-845, SM939-956, SM968-997, TP195-235, TP257-296, TP313-350, TP363-408, TP423-456, TZ200-205, TZ210-240.

Supermarine Spitfire 21: LA187-236, LA249-284, LA299-322.

Supermarine Spitfire 22: PK312-356, PK369-412, PK426-435, PK481-525, PK539-582, PK594-635, PK648-677.

Supermarine Spitfire 24: PK678-689, PK712-726, VN301-334, VN477-496, Last Spitfire delivered February 20, 1948.

Supermarine Swift 1: WK194-213.

Supermarine Swift 2: WK214-221, WK239-246.

Supermarine Swift 3: WK247-271.

Supermarine Swift 4: WK272-281.

Supermarine Swift 5: WK287-315 (also converted to Mk 5: WK274, 276, 277, 278, 280, 281); WN124-127, XD903-930, XD948-977.

Westland Whirlwind I: P6966-7015, P7035-7064, P7089-7122.